武汉实验外国语学校校本课程

丛书主编／李　茵　丛书副主编／王永汉

U1018193

LISTEN TO US

外语学校初中英语听力等级教程

（二级）

外语类总主编　徐　涛　蔡文静

本 册 主 编　钱晶晶

本 册 编 者　陈　娅　梁　静

钱晶晶　向　阳　赵　军

WUHAN UNIVERSITY PRESS

武汉大学出版社

武汉实验外国语学校校本课程

（外语类）

序

如果说，一所一流的大学关注学术研究、创造精神，那么，一所一流的中学应该关注什么？

或许，98 年前的教育家蔡元培先生签署的第一部《中学校令》就能给我们以启迪："中学以完足普通教育、造成健全国民为宗旨。"看似普通的一句话，其中却蕴含着这样的真知灼见：教育的落脚点，最后，必须落脚在学生的能力素养及健康成长上。（"完足普通教育"、"健全国民"本身就包含有个体学习能力素养、终身学习意识等多种涵义。）这与 1996 年国际 21 世纪教育委员会向联合国教科文组织提交的报告《教育——财富蕴藏其中》中所包含的最核心的观点"教育要使学习者学会掌握'学习的四大支柱'"（"学会认知"、"学会做事"、"学会共同生活"和"学会生存"）有内在的关联。也与当下盛行的 PISA（Programme for Internaltional Student Assessment，国际学生评估项目，它是经济合作与发展组织的成员共同开发的项目，其目的是测试十五岁学生是否掌握了参与未来知识社会所必需的基础知识和基本技能，从而建立一套学生评价方面的教育指标）所要求的三大基本方面——阅读能力、数学能力、科学能力，以及其他诸如学习态度、学生如何管理他们的学习等方面的要求，有异曲同工之妙。他们的共同点都在于：教育的核心在于"育人"、"立人"，她必须关注"人"的能力的增强、素质的提升、道德的健全等。

如此说来，在教育的价值取向多元化的今天，一些成年人难逃教育的浮躁和功利化，重温蔡先生的这句话，对于今天的我们而言，是否会有着更多的意味？

对于一所好的学校而言，除了应有较好的物质条件，但更重要的是，应该具有自己的博大胸襟和精神气质。

需要说明的是，这种精神气质和博大胸襟突出表现为：培养走向未来、具有国际视野的人才和有责任感、敢于担当的人，其教育的视野要涵盖现实，更要超越现实。关切的目光绝非只停留在作为"表层"的分数及当下，更要穿越前者，抵达"深层"的价值取向、文化积淀和更为纵深、辽阔的未来！而最能折射这种气质及视野的，我以为，体现在这所学校的方方面面，包括教学安排、课堂氛围、师生关系、社团活动、社会实践、校园环境、学校管理模式、作业布置方式及特色等。其中，学校校本课程的设置及落实，也是众多校园文化、气质承载及体现方式之一。

校本课程的设置与否，也是判断一所学校是否真的将学生的成长放在首位的参考条件之一。丰富多彩的校本课程，植根于对"新课程标准"理念的真切理解，更植根于学生群体的个体差异性和强烈求知欲的现实语境，植根于当下乃至未来的知识社会对学生能力的长远要求，更植根于学生个体的终身学习的需要。它直观地展现出一所学校的精神气质和文化内涵！

作为一所具有基础性、实验性和开放性的现代化学校，我校已在多年的摸索和发展中，培养出众多活跃在外交、文化及社会各个领域的优秀人才，并逐渐形成自己特有的校园文化："一个载体"——以外语教学为载体，"三个特色"——外语特色、开放特色、素质教育特色，五个"学生培养目标内涵"——自主精神、公民意识、科学态度、人文情怀、领袖气质。正是在这样的校园文化的指引下，武汉实验外国语学校形成了"重视学生个性发展，一切为了孩子，为了孩子的一切"的办学特色，在社会上享有较高的声誉。

作为我校特色学科的外语，自然是走在校本课程的最前列。本套"武汉实验外国语学校外语校本课程"丛书，共分为四类课程：一是阅读类，二是听力类，三是社团活动类，四是教学研讨类。

具体来说，阅读类课程选择的是我校在长期外语教学实践中，已经证实为"经典"的阅读文本，与教材呼应，同时又适度提高，是我们武汉实外的学生必须要读的好读物；听力类课程是作为"武汉实外初中听力等级教程"的一部分，其中的内容既包括英语歌曲、英文演讲，也包括精彩英语对话等，内容生动，时代性突出，也贴近学生们的心灵及生活；社团活动类课程主要展现了我校的社团活动及duty show（作者注："值日报告比赛"——一种在课前5分钟，由单人或多人以小组方式展示的包含有表演、电影配音、专题探研诸如"好莱坞电影中的美国生活方式"等成果的教学活动）的精华，学生们的开阔视野和风采都让教师们感受到他们这代人的希望和茁壮成长，其中的"活动现场"、"学生感悟"、"教师点评"的栏目文字能最大限度再现活动的魅力，并带给人思考的愉悦；最后一类是"教学研讨"类课程，它是我校外语老师一直坚持进行的"共同成长"教研活动过程及成果的展现，我校所有外语教师都积极参与其中，并以包括听力课、口语课、概念课、活动课等在内的多种课型，展现出了她们不同风格但却同样精彩的教学活动。

综上所述，这套校本课程是武汉实验外国语师生们精神面貌的生动再现与历史的见证。她记录并见证了一位位外语教师的辛勤善思，记录并见证一个个实外学生的可喜成长，也记录和见证了一个个外语课堂的诗意瞬间，同时，她更体现出这所学校所蕴藏的一种精神气质，一种奔跑的姿态，预示着学校更美好的发展前景。

希望这套"武汉实验外国语学校校本课程"丛书，能给予每一位读者一些触动和思考，也祝福武汉实验外国语学校的发展前景更加辉煌灿烂！

是为序。

全国人大代表
武汉市政府参事 李茵
武汉实验外国语学校校长

2011-1-17

前　言

据美国保罗·兰金(Paul Rankin)教授统计，“听”占人们日常语言活动的45%，“说”占30%，“读”占16%，“写”仅占9%。由此可见，“听”在语言交流中占有重要地位。美国著名成功学大师布莱恩·崔西(Brian Tracy)在其经典著作*21 Secrets of Self-made Millionaire*中提到，通过有声材料学习是21世纪学习方式的革命，“听”于人类获取信息的意义之大可见一斑。听力是获取口语素材，解决“哑巴英语”问题的关键，更是获得英语考试高分的重要保障之一。

听力是英语教学中的四项基本技能之一，也是外语学校学生英语学习的重要组成部分。突破听力难关不仅有助于其他单项技能的训练，同时也为培养学生的英语交际能力奠定了一个良好的基础。在教育部颁布的《初中英语新课程标准》对于七、八、九年级学生在听力方面应达到的标准都做出了详细的规定。如九年级学生应能听懂有关熟悉话题的谈话，并能从中提取信息和观点；能听懂接近正常语速的故事和记叙文，理解故事中的因果关系；能针对所听语段的内容记录简单信息。而外国语学校的英语学习对学生要求更高，通过系统的长期坚持不懈的听力训练，学生要能识别语段中的重要信息并进行简单推断；能听懂故事中对人和物的描写、情节的发展及结果；能听懂国内外一般的英语新闻广播及天气预报；能从原版电影片段中人物的言谈中判断对方的态度、喜恶、立场；能听懂委婉的建议、劝告，理解一般的幽默；能在听的过程中克服一般性的口音干扰。

*LISTEN TO US*就是按照新课程标准的要求，根据外语学校的教学特点而编写的一套听力教程。本教程是武汉实验外国语学校的校本课程听力教材。第二级适用于初中一年级学生和二年级学生。参加本书编写工作的均是武汉实验外国语学校的一线英语教师，他们了解学生在实际学习中的需要和问题，熟悉升学考试的命题方式，使得本书不仅适合初一学生课堂学习，同时也为小学高年级学生准备升学考试提供了丰富的听力练习材料。

在编写过程中我们得到了武汉大学出版社的大力支持，在此表示诚挚的感谢。

编　者

2011年年初于武汉实验外国语学校

Contents

Exercises

Tapescripts

Keys

Exercises

Unit 1

Section 1

一、听对话，根据问题选出最佳答案。

( ) 1. Where does the man probably go?

A. Supermarket. B. Cafe. C. Cinema.

( ) 2. Where do the two people probably go?

A. Gym. B. Cafe. C. Post office.

( ) 3. What does the woman usually do when she gets into a bad mood?

A. Call her friends and have a chat.

B. Sit at home alone.

C. Cry.

( ) 4. Why did the man want to read newspaper?

A. He was tired of studying and wanted to get relaxed.

B. He wanted to know about the murder.

C. He wanted to shock himself.

( ) 5. What doesn't the man like?

A. Rabbits. B. Dogs. C. Cats.

( ) 6. What did Jim get the man as a birthday present?

A. A Sweater. B. Books. C. An MP3.

( ) 7. What does the woman want to do after graduation?

A. To become a doctor.

B. To go into management.

C. To become a lawyer.

( ) 8. What does the woman's father want her to do after graduation?

A. To become a doctor.

B. To go into management.

C. To become a lawyer.

( ) 9. Is the man good at making decisions?

A. No. B. Yes. C. We don't know.

( ) 10. Which country hasn't the man been to?

A. America. B. Canada. C. Korea.

二、你将会听到一段关于世界各国人们的睡眠和饮食时间研究结果的新闻，讲述了世界各国的人花在睡眠和用餐上的不同时间。

（一）听说明，做出正确的选择。

( ) 1. When was the study published?

A. Sunday. B. Friday. C. Monday.

( ) 2. Where does more and more French have their lunch these days?

A. At fast-food chains or at their desks.

B. Cafe.

C. Home.

( ) 3. What do the Japanese like doing in their spare time?

A. Watching television or listening to the radio.

B. Entertaining their friends.

C. Playing baseball.

( ) 4. In which country do people spend more than a third of their leisure time staying with their friends?

A. America. B. Italy. C. New Zealand.

( ) 5. In which country do people spend least time having fun?

A. America. B. Mexico. C. Norway.

（二）再听一次研究结果，在图表的1、2、3、4、5处标注相应的国名。

图表一：The time people spend sleeping.

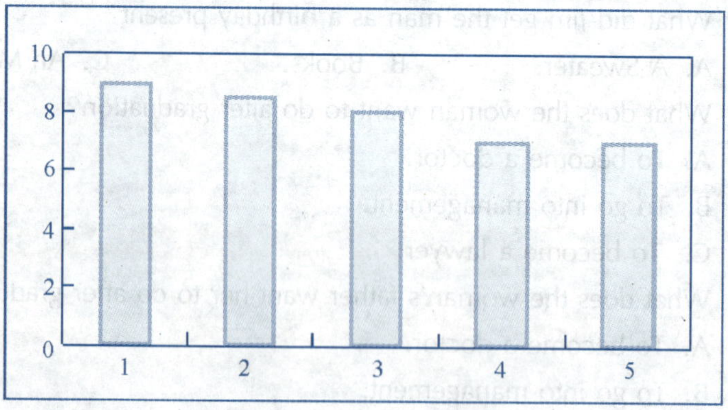

1 = ( ) 2 = ( ) 3 = ( ) 4 = ( ) 5 = ( )

图表二：The time people spend eating.

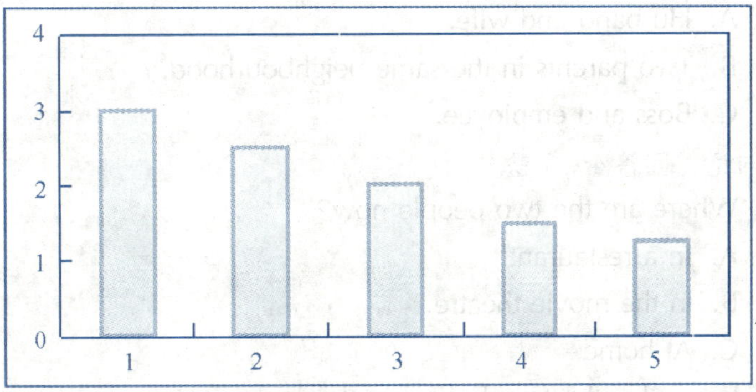

1 = (　　) 2 = (　　) 3 = (　　) 4 = (　　) 5 = (　　)

Section 2

一、听一段关于胡萝卜的科普广播，根据你所听到的内容，在横线上填上所缺的单词。

Carrots are grown on (1) ________ and in family gardens throughout the world. Carrots are easy to raise and easy to (2) ________. They taste good. And they contain a lot of carotene, which the (3) ________ makes into Vitamin A.

When people think of carrots, they usually (4) ________ in their mind a vegetable that is long, (5) ________ and orange in color. But carrots come in many different sizes and (6) ________. And not all carrots are orange.

For example, Paris Market carrots are about (7) ________ centimeters around. Imperator carrots are thin and about (8) ________ centimeters long. And Belgian White carrots are, as their name suggests, (9) ________.

二、听下面三段长对话，每段长对话后都有三至四个小题。从题中所给的 A, B, C 三个选项中选出最佳答案。

听第一段对话，回答 1 ~3 题。

(　　) 1. How long can the man's children watch TV a day?

A. An hour.　　B. Two hours.　　C. Three hours.

(　　) 2. What does the woman want her children to do in their free time?

A. Play football.

B. Go out and play with their friends.

C. Plant potatoes.

(   ) 3. What is the relationship between the two people?

A. Husband and wife.

B. Two parents in the same neighbourhood.

C. Boss and employee.

听第二段对话，回答4 ~6 题。

(   ) 4. Where are the two people now?

A. In a restaurant.

B. In the movie theatre.

C. At home.

(   ) 5. Who play the female lead in the new movie?

A. Lady Gaga. B. Mel Gibson. C. Julia Roberts.

(   ) 6. When should the two people arrive at the theatre?

A. 7 : 55 pm. B. 8 : 30 pm. C. 9 : 30 pm.

听第三段对话，回答7 ~10 题。

(   ) 7. When did Britain win the battle of Trafalgar?

A. In 1805. B. In 1588. C. In 1815.

(   ) 8. Who is NOT buried in Westminster Abbey?

A. Isaac Newton.

B. Winston Churchill.

C. Bill Clinton.

(   ) 9. Where's the statue of Boudicea?

A. On the banks of the Thames.

B. At the Trafalgar Square.

C. Around the Tower of London.

(   ) 10. What did Queen Elizabeth do to fight off the Spanish armada?

A. The Queen built a strong navy.

B. The Queen bought a lot of guns for her soldiers.

C. The Queen built a strong army.

三、你将听到一段关于胡萝卜的科普广播的后半段。根据你听到的内容完成练习。

(一) 听录音，选出最佳答案。

(   ) 1. Which is the best soil for your carrot garden?

A.
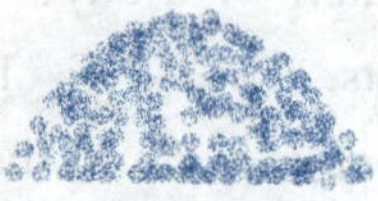
Sandy soil.

B.

Hard soil.

C.
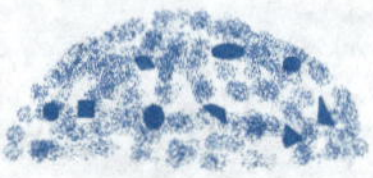
Sandy soil with rocks.

( ) 2. Which is the best weather for growing carrots that taste great?

A.  B.  C. 

( ) 3. Which of the following carrot will taste best?

A. 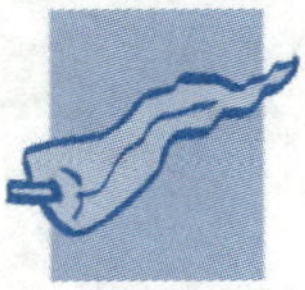 B.  C. 

Small. Medium. Dry and big.

( ) 4. Which carrot is ready to be harvested ?

A. Dark color. B. Pale color. C. Bright color.

( ) 5. Which of the following can be used to prevent your carrot garden from freezing in winter?

A.  B.  C. 

（二）再听一次录音，根据你听到的内容，在横线上填上所缺的词或句子。

1. To prepare your carrot garden, ________, ________, and ________, then, mix in some plant material or animal fertilizer.

2. ________, ________ conditions and ________ will affect the way carrots taste.

3. The best way to judge if a carrot is ready to be harvested is by ________.

4. Most people do not know that carrots can be grown during ________.

5. Carrots are prepared and eaten in many different ways. They are ________ and added to ________. They are cooked by themselves or added to stews. Or, once ________, they are eaten just as they come out of the ground.

Section 3

popcorn kernels 玉米粒

一、听歌曲 *The Climb*，根据你所听到的内容，在横线上填上所缺的单词。

I can almost (1) __________ it
that dream I'm dreaming but
there's a (2) __________ inside my head saying
you'll never reach it
every step I'm taking
every move I make feels
lost with (3) __________ direction
my faith is shaking
but I, I gotta keep trying
gotta keep my (4) __________ held high

there's always gonna be another (5) __________
I'm always gonna wanna make it (6) __________
always gonna be an uphill battle
sometime I'm gonna have to (7) __________
aren't about how (8) __________ I get there
aren't about what's waiting on the other side
it's the climb

二、听下面三段长对话，每段长对话后都有三至四个小题。从题中所给的 A，B，C 三个选项中选出最佳答案。

听第一段对话，回答 1 ~3 题。

( ) 1. What has Carlo been doing these days?
A. Chatting online a lot with friends.
B. Buying a Yahoo Message.
C. Repairing her computer.

( ) 2. What does Carlo use to chat?
A. MSN. B. QQ. C. Yahoo Messager.

( ) 3. Why hasn't Samus chatted online before?
A. His computer is too old.
B. He doesn't have a computer.
C. He doesn't like chatting.

听第二段对话，回答 4 ~6 题。

( ) 4. Where are the two people now?
A. In a café. B. In a supermarket. C. In a computer shop.

( ) 5. What does it mean if a place offers a wireless Internet connection?
A. It means there is no wire connecting with other computers.

B. It means people can get on the net for free while they are there.

C. It means people can get on the net very fast while they are there.

(　　) 6. How many places offer wireless Internet connection in this city?

A. 8 or 10.　　B. 10 or 12.　　C. 12 or 14.

听第三段对话，回答7 ~10 题。

(　　) 7. How come the man doesn't have all of Jay's films on DVD?

A. In some of the DVDs he only played a bit part, so the man doesn't want to buy it.

B. Some of his early films are hard to find nowadays.

C. The DVDs are just too expensive to buy.

(　　) 8. Is the man a member of Jay's fan club now?

A. Yes, he is.

B. No, he isn't.

C. We don't know from the dialogue.

(　　) 9. When did the man get Jay's new posters?

A. Last year.　　B. Last week.　　C. Last month.

(　　) 10. In which magazine can you see the interview with Jay?

A. *City Life.*　　B. *Boss.*　　C. *Cosmopolitan.*

三、你将听到一段关于如何制作 popcorn 的步骤说明。根据你听到的内容，完成练习。

（一）根据你听到的内容，在做 popcorn 所需要材料的图片下打钩。

(　　)　(　　)　(　　)　(　　)　(　　)　(　　)

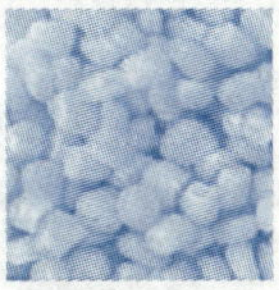

(　　)　(　　)　(　　)　(　　)　(　　)　(　　)

（二）下面你将听到做 popcorn 的具体步骤。请根据所听到的内容，写下每个步骤的名称。每空一词。

When cooking at the stove, have an adult nearby to supervise you.

Step 1: ______ ______

Step 2: ______ ______

Step 3: ______ ______

Step 4: ______ ______

Step 5: ______ ______

Step 6: ______ ______

Step 7: ______ ______

Step 8: ______ ______

Step 9: ______ ______

Step 10: ______ ______

Section 4

一、听寓言，并写下你所听到的故事。

As the north wind was proud of his power, he said, "Ha. Ha. Ha. No one could beat me. I am the strongest."

The sun heard that, he said, "Really? I don't think so."

____

____

____

____

____

____

"I see. I shouldn't have bragged about myself," the north wind felt embarrassed.

二、听下面三段长对话，每段长对话后都有三至四个小题。从题中所给的 A, B, C 三个选项中选出最佳答案。

听第一段对话，回答 1 ~3 题。

(　　) 1. What's the man's problem about learning history?

A. He doesn't like his history teacher.

B. He can't remember all the dates.

C. He just enjoys studying math at school.

(　　) 2. What's the woman's opinion about learning history?

A. Learning the reasons behind events is more important than remembering the dates.

B. History repeats itself.

C. A good teacher is everything.

(　　) 3. What is the meaning of "History repeats itself" according to the woman?

A. The same events never happen twice.

B. People and dates change, but the reasons why things happen stay the same.

C. History happened again and again.

听第二段对话，回答4 ~6 题。

(　　) 4. What is the biography about?

A. A famous American musician.

B. Howard Somerset.

C. Jim Dylan.

(　　) 5. How many chapters hasn't been read by Charlie?

A. 13 chapters.　　B. 3 chapters.　　C. 12 chapters.

(　　) 6. When will the woman have the book?

A. On Thursday.　　B. On Friday.　　C. On Sunday.

听第三段对话，回答7 ~10 题。

sculpture *n.* 雕塑	abstract *adj.* 抽象的

(　　) 7. How often does the man go to an art exhibition in a year?

A. Once or twice.

B. Every month.

C. He never goes there.

(　　) 8. Where will the two people go tomorrow?

A. The City Gallery.

B. The International Gallery.

C. The National Gallery.

(　　) 9. What does the man like?

A. Abstract art.

B. The ancient Rome or Greece sculpture.

C. Modern sculpture.

(　　) 10. When will the two people arrive home after the visiting?

A. After 2:00 pm.　　B. After 3:00 pm.　　C. After 4:00 pm.

三、你将听到一段关于如何制作家庭风味 chips 的录音。

（一）听独白的前半段，选出你所需要的材料。

(　　)　(　　)　(　　)　(　　)　(　　)

(　　)　(　　)　(　　)　(　　)　(　　)

（二）听独白的后半段，完成制作 chips 的步骤。

Step 1

Peel the potatoes and ______________________________.

Step 2

Fill your saucepan ______________________________.

Step 3

______________________________. Slice them about 1/8 of an inch thick.

______________________________ or they'll splatter in the fryer.

Step 4

______________________________.

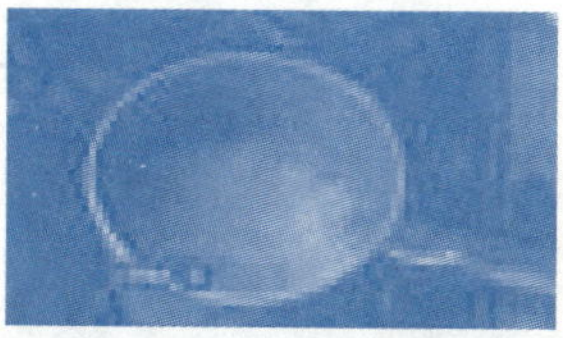

Step 5

____.

Step 6

Remove the cooked chips with a slotted spoon and set them on paper towels to dry the oil.

Step 7

Sprinkle with salt and ______________________________________.

Section 5

一、听歌曲 *Excuse Me*，在歌曲中，表演者连续唱出了 8 个他要找的地方。请根据歌曲依次选择 8 个你所听到地点的图片。

Excuse me, where's the... ?

(　　) 1.

A. Airport.

B. Dry cleaner's.

C. Bank.

(　　) 2.

A. University.

B. Pool.

C. Station.

( ) 3.

A. Station.

B. Dry cleaner's.

C. Post office.

( ) 4.

A. Car park.

B. University.

C. Restaurant.

( ) 5.

A. Gas station.

B. Dry cleaner's.

C. Station.

( ) 6.

A. Airport.

B. Car park.

C. Restaurant.

( ) 7.

A. Cinema.

B. Stadium.

C. Bank.

( ) 8.

A. Zoo.

B. Car park.

C. Museum.

二、听下面三段长对话，每段长对话后都有三至四个小题。从题中所给的A，B，C三个选项中选出最佳答案。

听第一段对话，回答1～3题。

( ) 1. In which country should you never touch someone on the head?

A. China. B. Thailand. C. England.

(　　) 2. Who like chewing with the mouth open?
A. Adults.　　B. Kids.　　C. The men.

(　　) 3. What does the woman do when she is thinking?
A. Scratch her head.　　B. Rub her chin.　　C. Scratch her nose.

听第二段对话，回答4 ~6 题。

(　　) 4. What does the man do when he wants to attract the waiter's attention?
A. He shouts at the waiter.
B. He just tells the waiter to come.
C. He makes eye contact with him and nods his head.

(　　) 5. What's the weather like last night?
A. Warm.　　B. Wet.　　C. Cloudy.

(　　) 6. Why didn't the man chat with Bill?
A. Because they didn't see each other.
B. Because Bill was in a hurry.
C. Because they were on opposite banks of the river.

听第三段对话，回答7 ~10 题。

(　　) 7. How many people are there in Chrisie's family?
A. Three.　　B. Four.　　C. Six.

(　　) 8. What is Elva's nationality?
A. French.　　B. Japanese.　　C. Chinese.

(　　) 9. Do Elva's parents live with her now?
A. Yes, they do.
B. No, they don't.
C. We don't know from the dialogue.

(　　) 10. How long has Chrisie been married?
A. About seven years.
B. About five years.
C. About nine years.

三、你将听到一段短文，将你听到的句子都逐一写下来。

will *n.* 意志力	victory *n.* 胜利	succeed *v.* 成功
failure *n.* 失败者	obvious *a.* 明显	accomplish *v.* 完成

____

____

____

____

____

Unit 2

Section 1

一、听一段新闻，根据你所听到的内容填空。

The best (1) ________ of 2009 is from a light bulb that may be worth (2) ________ million dollars to an electric eye, that (3) ________ for you. The list is out; this is it right here, from *Time* magazine, *Time* website, *Time*. com, which is a partner of CNN. com. They say the best invention of the year is this NASA's Ares Rocket, we have (4) ________ video for you.

"(5) ________! Two! One! Ignition, and lift off of Ares I-X, testing concepts for the (6) ________ of new rocket design."

Time calls this the best and (7) ________ and coolest thing built in 2009, it is designed to usher in the (8) ________ generation of space (9) ________ returning astronauts to the moon, and one day bringing (10) ________ to Mars.

二、听下面十段对话，每段对话后有一个问题，从题中所给的A, B, C三个选项中选出最佳答案。听完每个问题后，你都有五秒钟的时间来作答和阅读下一小题。

( ) 1. A. She will. B. She will not. C. We don't know.

( ) 2. A. Four. B. Five. C. Six.

( ) 3. A. Iris and his mother.
B. Jennies and her mother.
C. Jennies and Iris.

( ) 4. A. A MP4. B. A cell phone. C. A PSP.

( ) 5. A. He is tall. B. He is well built. C. He has blue eyes.

( ) 6. A. She has a toothache.
B. She has a headache.
C. She has a backache.

( ) 7. A. The science-fictional film.
B. The action film.
C. The musicals.

(　　) 8. A. Cheeseburger and fries.
B. Fish and fries.
C. Cheeseburger and cola.

(　　) 9. A. Ariel.　　B. Justin.　　C. Both of them.

(　　) 10. A. In the park.　　B. In a supermarket.　　C. On the beach.

三、听下面一段长对话，根据对话内容填空。

(一) It was Dec. 20 that day, three friends, Racheal, Kate, and Joey were in Oviado Square shopping presents for Christmas. Now, listen to the dialogue and write down all the things they are going to buy.

Shopping list for all:

1. ________________
2. ________________
3. ________________
4. ________________ for brother
5. ________________ for Dad
6. ________________
7. ________________

(二) Listen to the dialogue again and try to connect the present with the people who wants to buy it.

1. Racheal　　2. Kate　　3. Joey

Section 2

一、你将听到一段关于 Gorilla 的新闻，根据你所听到的内容补全所缺的词语，每空一词。

This week, we tell about a discovery of gorillas in the Republic of Congo and the loss of Bengal (1) ________ in Nepal. We also tell about a (2) ________ heart surgeon and what you need to know about your heart.

Deep in the (3) ________ in the northern part of the Republic of Congo, (4) ________ have made a surprising discovery. Researchers discovered more than (5) ________ thousand critically endangered western lowland gorillas.

In the (6) ________, scientists estimated that the total population of western lowland gorillas in Central Africa was fewer than (7) ________ thousand. Since then however, the scientists (8) ________ this number had been reduced by at least (9) ________. They thought the animals were being killed off by (10) ________ and disease, especially the deadly Ebola virus.

二、听录音，完成下列各题。

（一）听一段新闻，并根据问题做出选择。

(　　) 1. The children would usually travel across by ________.

A. 

B. 

C. 

(　　) 2. The flight to neighboring Westray lasts for a few ________.

A. hours　　B. minutes　　C. days

(　　) 3. The kids think that it's a pretty ________ way to get to school.

A. cool　　B. expensive　　C. poor

（二）听一段歌曲，并做出正确选择。

(　　) 1. The singer imagines that there is no ________ below us and above us only sky.

A. heaven　　B. hell　　C. sea

(　　) 2. The singer imagines all the people living for ________.

A. yesterday　　B. today　　C. tomorrow

(　　) 3. People may say the singer is a ________, but he is not the only one.

A. dreamer　　B. sick people　　C. musician

(　　) 4. The name of the song might be ________.

A. *Imagine*　　B. *Me, the Singer*　　C. *Nothing Is True*

三、听对话，并回答下列问题。

（一）Jim 和 Kelly 正在就音乐话题进行讨论，听他们的谈话，选出最佳答案。

(　　) 1. Who is forming his own band?

A. Jim.　　B. Kelly.　　C. Ben.

( ) 2. Ben is good at playing the ________.
A. drum B. piano C. guitar

( ) 3. Jim thinks that Kelly can be a ________ in the future.
A. dancer B. singer C. DJ

( ) 4. How often does Jim go to a disco?
A. Every day. B. Almost every week. C. Once a month.

( ) 5. Research suggests that classical music makes brain more ________.
A. active B. quiet C. slow

（二）重听对话，根据 Jim 和 Kelly 在音乐爱好方面的相同点和不同点补全内容。

Jim	Kelly
He can play the (1) ________.	She can play just a little (5) ________.
He likes listening to music that is (2) ________ and lively, like (3) ________.	She prefers (6) ________, and she often listens to Mozart or Bach in the evening after (7) ________.
He heard that listening to classical music is helpful in (4) ________ stress.	She likes that music partly because students who listen to it while studying perform (8) ________.

Section 3

一、Chloe 和 Presley 正在讨论老师布置的阅读作业，根据你所听到的内容补全对话。

W: I can't believe my English teacher is making me read *Pride and Prejudice*!

M: (1) ________! It's a classic. In fact, it's one of my favorite novels.

W: But it's so old!

M: Don't (2) ________. Do you know what it's about?

W: No, not at all.

M: First of all, it's a romance novel, setting in (3) ________.

W: I didn't realize it was a romance novel. What's the main story about?

M: It's basically about a father who tried to marry off one of his five girls.

W: (4) ________?

M: Since he doesn't have a son, he hopes that one of the girls will marry a wealthy man. That way, all of his daughters will be cared for.

W: Won't they get his inheritance?

M: (5) ________. Though they are rich, (6) ________, his house will go to his nephew. So, When he dies, the girls will have nothing.

W：(7) ________. This sounds interesting! Maybe my teacher isn't so horrible after all.

M：So, are you going to read the novel or watch the movie?

W：There's a movie? (8) ________!

M：That's probably because she wants you to read the book first.

W：(9) ________.

M：How about this? When you finish the book, (10) ________.

W：OK. That sounds like a deal.

二、听歌曲 *What Would You Do*，在歌曲中，表演者连续唱出了 8 件如果他有了 a million dollars 后将会做的事。请根据歌曲，依次做出选择。

( ) 1.

A. I'd party at the hippest night clubs.

B. I'd buy the biggest boat.

C. I'd climb the tallest mountain.

( ) 2.

A. I'd learn to play guitar.

B. I'd eat the nicest food.

C. I'd drive the fastest car.

( ) 3.

A. I'd watch the biggest TV.

B. I'd wear the brightest diamonds.

C. I'd see the greatest movies.

( ) 4.

A. I'd see the greatest movies.

B. I'd speak fluent English.

C. I'd dance with the hottest girls.

(　　) 5.

A. I'd drink the finest wine.　　B. I'd eat the nicest food.　　C. I'd learn to play guitar.

(　　) 6.

A. I'd learn to play guitar.　　B. I'd dance with the hottest girls.　　C. I'd listen to the coolest songs.

(　　) 7.

A. I'd party at the hippest night clubs.　　B. I'd buy the biggest boat.　　C. I'd climb the tallest mountain.

(　　) 8.

A. I'd see the greatest movies.　　B. I'd speak fluent English.　　C. I'd dance with the hottest girls.

三、听一段长对话，完成以下练习。

（一）学校举行的运动会刚刚结束，Rimy，Dorry，Dennis，Kate 的父母 Woods 夫妇正在就他们在运动会中的表现进行讨论。现在根据你听到的内容做出正确的选择。

(　　) 1. Which sport does Rimy prefer?

A. Running.　　B. Jumping.　　C. Football.

(　　) 2. How long does Mr. Wood ask the children to swim?

A. 300 meters each day.

B. 400 meters each day.

C. 500 meters each day.

( ) 3. How do the children do at swimming?

A. They are all very fast.

B. They are not very fast.

C. We do not know.

（二）再听一遍对话，根据对话内容重现他们在运动会上的表现。

	Event	Performance
Rimy	The race of (1) ________ meters.	Finish the race within (2) ________.
	Long jump.	Jump a distance of over (3) ________.
Dorry	(4) ________.	Jump over (5) ________.
Dennis	The (6) ________ meters.	Finish it within (7) ________.
Kate	Diving.	Dive from a height of (8) ________.

Section 4

一、你将会听到一段关于 Christmas 的广播，根据你所听到的内容，补充横线上所缺的动词。

Music (1) ________ the air. Colorful lights (2) ________ brightly in windows. Children and adults (3) ________ gifts from loved ones and friends. These are all Christmas traditions.

Another tradition is snow. Christmas in the northern part of the world (4) ________ a few days after the start of winter. In many places, a blanket of clean white snow (5) ________ the ground on Christmas Day. This is what is meant by a "White Christmas."

Of course, many places do not (6) ________ snow at Christmas. In fact, they may be very warm at this time of year. People who (7) ________ snow, but (8) ________ where it is warm, can only (9) ________ of having a white Christmas.

American songwriter Irving Berlin captured these feelings in his song, *White Christmas*. Hundreds of singers and musicians have (10) ________ *White Christmas*. But the version most people still know best was sung by Bing Crosby.

二、听下面三段长对话，每段长对话后都有三至四个小题。从题中所给的 A，B，C 三个选项中选出最佳答案。

听第一段对话，回答 1 ~3 题。

( ) 1. Where will they most probably go after the chat?

A. To the book store. B. To the airport. C. To the library.

( ) 2. What does the man need for his course?

A. A textbook.

B. Some magazines.

C. Some children's books.

( ) 3. Can the woman fall asleep on the flight?

A. No, she can't. B. Yes, she can. C. We don't know.

听第二段对话，回答 4 ~6 题。

( ) 4. Which country is not mentioned in the dialogue?

A. 

B. 

C. 

( ) 5. Which country is big in Europe but not large at all?

A. 
B. 
C. 

( ) 6. Which country is half the size of France, but is still one of the largest islands in the world?

A. 
B. 
C. 

听第三段对话，回答 7 ~10 题。

( ) 7. What's the distance from there to New York?

A. 180 kilometers. B. 118 kilometers. C. 190 kilometers.

( ) 8. How long will it take them to London if there is a traffic jam?

A. Two hours. B. Three hours. C. Four hours.

( ) 9. What's the length of the man's car?

A. Over 4 meters. B. Over 5 meters. C. Over 6 meters.

( ) 10. What's the highest speed of the man's car?

A. Over 110 kilometers an hour.

B. Over 210 kilometers an hour.

C. Over 310 kilometers an hour.

三、White 夫妇才从国外回来，他们的冰箱已经空了，因此他们准备去超市买一些东西。

（一）听对话的前半部分，完成第一张购物清单。

Shopping List

food	amount（数量）
(1) ________	2 loaves
sugar	(2) ________
(3) ________	2 tins
cooking oil	3 liters
(4) ________	(5) ________
(6) ________	(7) ________
(8) ________ jam	a jar
(9) ________ ketchup	(10) ________

（二）听对话的后半部分，连线完成第二张购物清单。

Shopping List

2 kilos　　a bar of　　half a kilo　　a bunch of　　a bag

half dozen　　three dozens　　a chunk　　some　　a dozen

Section 5

一、听歌曲 *Have You Ever*，在歌曲中，表演者连续用歌唱的方式问了 8 个“*Have You Ever. . .* ？”的经历。请根据歌词，依次做出选择。

Have you ever. . . ?

(　　) 1.

A. been afraid　　B. broken a window　　C. eaten ice cream

(　　) 2.

A. played the piano　　B. written a song　　C. flown a plane

(　　) 3.

A. broken a window　　B. been to Paris　　C. slept on a beach

(　　) 4.

A. been afraid　　B. met a rock star　　C. seen King Kong

(　　) 5.

A. been surfing　　B. met a rock star　　C. slept on a beach

(　　) 6.

A. written a song　　B. been in love　　C. flown a plane

(　　) 7.

A. forgotten a birthday　　B. been in love　　C. played the piano

(　　) 8.

A. forgotten a birthday　　B. broken a window　　C. been in love

二、听下面三段长对话，每段长对话后都有三至四个小题。从题中所给的 A，B，C 三个选项中选出最佳答案。

听第一段对话，回答 1 ~3 题。

(　　) 1. What will not the woman do in summer?
　　A. Have a walk in the countryside.
　　B. Go for bike ride in the countryside.
　　C. Pick some fruits.

(　　) 2. What will not the man do in summer?
　　A. Play tennis.
　　B. Play computer games.
　　C. Sit in the sunshine and read a good book.

(　　) 3. Which season does the man prefer?
　　A. Summer.　　B. Winter.　　C. Autumn.

听第二段对话，回答 4 ~6 题。

(　　) 4. What's the matter with the man?
　　A. He is worrying about his test.
　　B. He is doing some gardening.
　　C. He is preparing for the test.

( ) 5. Can the man find any free time to relax recently?

A. Yes, he can. B. No, he can't. C. We don't know.

( ) 6. What will the woman probably do for the weekend?

A. Gardening. B. Working. C. Shopping.

听第三段对话，回答7 ~10 题。

( ) 7. What does the man think of the physical work on the farm?

A. It will be very tiring.

B. It will make him fit and healthy.

C. It will be so hard.

( ) 8. What's the man's working time now?

A. From 9 to 5. B. From 8 to 5. C. From 9 to 6.

( ) 9. Whom does the man often work with on the farm?

A. His uncle. B. His aunt. C. His friend.

( ) 10. Does the woman want to spend a day working on a farm?

A. Yes, she does.

B. No, she doesn't.

C. She hates it so much.

三、你将听到一段关于冰箱的短文，将你听到的句子逐一写下来。

common *adj.* 常见的	design *n.* 设计	at least 至少

Unit 3

Section 1

一、听歌并补全你所听到的内容。

(1) ________________

you may think you see

who I really am

(2) ________________

every day

it's as if I play a part

now I see

if I wear a mask

(3) ________________

but I cannot fool my heart

(4) ________________

staring straight back at me

when will my reflection show

who I am inside

I am now

in a world where I

have to hide my heart

(5) ________________

but somehow

I will show the world

(6) ________________

and be loved for who I am

who is that girl I see

staring straight back at me

why is my reflection

(7) ________________

二、听句子选出相应的答语。

(　　) 1. A. I don't like you.　　B. Sure, I'd love to.　　C. I agree with you.

(　　) 2. A. I'm looking for my wallet.
B. I did my homework.
C. Terrific!

(　　) 3. A. No, I don't have a hand.
B. Certainly, what can I do for you?
C. I feel so bad.

(　　) 4. A. My pleasure.　　B. That's fine.　　C. It doesn't matter.

(　　) 5. A. You must be late!
B. Good luck!
C. You can take a taxi.

(　　) 6. A. Yes, I bought some medicine at the chemist's.
B. I don't know.
C. No, I went to the doctor.

(　　) 7. A. I just got back from London.
B. I haven't been to New York.
C. I have driven for 2 hours.

(　　) 8. A. It supposed to be late.
B. In 30 minutes.
C. The train leaves on time.

(　　) 9. A. 10 metres.　　B. 25 tons.　　C. 15 dollars.

(　　) 10. A. It was 10 hours.　　B. It is 132 kilometres.　　C. It is not too long.

三、你将听到十段对话和十个问题。请在每小题所给的 A，B，C 三个选项中选出最佳答案。

(　　) 1. A. 　B. 　C. 

(　　) 2. A. 　B. 　C. 

(　　) 3. A.  B.  C. 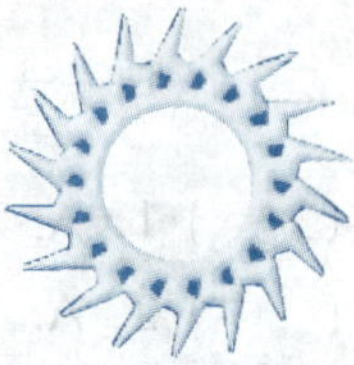

(　　) 4. A.  B.  C. 

(　　) 5. A.  B.  C. 

(　　) 6. A.  B.  C. 

(　　) 7. A.  B.  C. 

(　　) 8. A.  B.  C. 

(　　) 9. A.  B.  C. 

(　　) 10. A.  B.  C. 

Section 2

一、听文章，回答问题。

1. What did the bartender say when he saw a guy walk into a bar with a small dog?

   ________________________________.

2. What did the guy say as a reply to the bartender?

   ________________________________.

3. What did the bartender promise if the dog was able to play the piano?

   ________________________________.

4. Did the bartender and patrons like the music that was played by the dog?

   ________________________________.

5. Did the bigger dog want the small dog to play the piano? Why?

   ________________________________.

二、你将听到十段对话和十个问题，每段对话和每个问题将仅读一遍。请在每小题所给的A，B，C三个选项中选出最佳答案。

(　　) 1. A.

B.

C.

(　　) 2. A.

B.

C.

(　　) 3. A.

B.

C.

( ) 4. A.  B. 

C. 

( ) 5. A.  B.  C. 

( ) 6. A.  B.  C. 

( ) 7. A.  B.  C. 

( ) 8. A.  B.  C. 

( ) 9. A.  B.  C. 

( ) 10. A.  B. 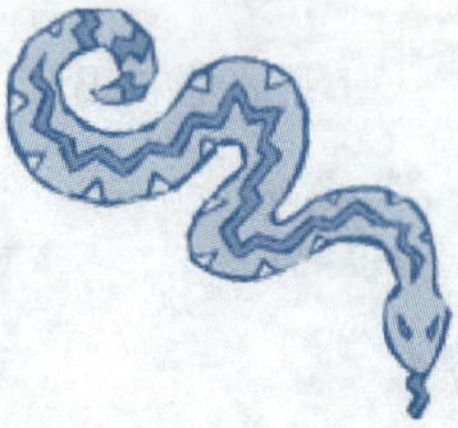 C. 

三、仔细看下面的五张图片，你将会听到五段和图片有关的对话。请依次在序号后写出相应图片下的字母。

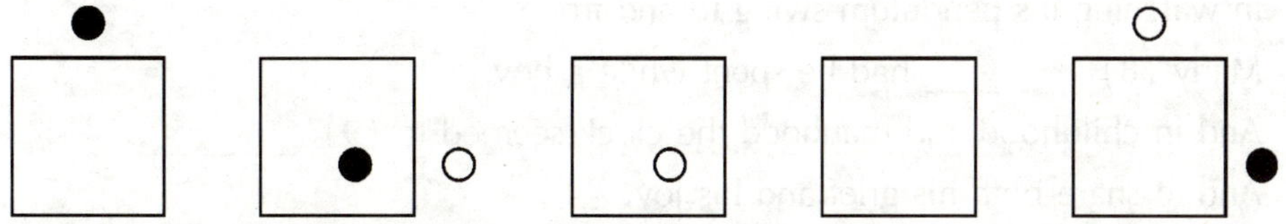

A.　B.　C.　D.　E.

1.（　）　2.（　）　3.（　）　4.（　）　5.（　）

四、看图听句子。图中 Mr. Bean 正在桌边，按照你所听到的内容完成图画。

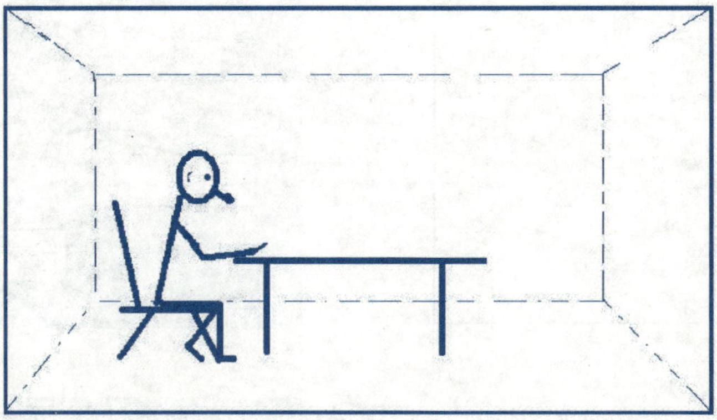

Section 3

一、听歌并补全歌词。

My grandfather's (1) ________ was too large for the shelf.
So it stood ninety years on the floor.
It was taller by half than the old man (2) ________.
Thought it weighed not a penny weight more.
It was bought on the morn of the (3) ________ that he was born.
And was always his treasure and pride.
But it stopped short, never to go (4) ________,
When the (5) ________ man died.

Ninety years (6) ________ slumbering (tick, tock, tick, tock),
His (7) ________ seconds numbering (tick, tock, tick, tock),
It stopped short, never to go again, when the old man died.
In watching it's pendulum swing to and fro,
Many (8) ________ had he spent while a boy.
And in childhood and manhood the clock seemed to (9) ________.
And to share both his grief and his joy.
For it struck (10) ________ when he entered at the door.
With a blooming and beautiful bride.

二、听句子，并按照每题的不同要求完成图画。

1.

2.

3.

4.

5.

三、听下面五个问题，每个问题后有三个答语，从题中所给的A，B，C三个选项中选出最佳答案。听完每个问题后，你都有五秒钟的时间来作答和阅读下一小题。

( ) 1. A. She broke her knee.
B. Sure, she is fine.
C. She has left for school.

( ) 2. A. Watching Television.
B. Go to school.
C. Have breakfast.

( ) 3. A. In the supermarket.
B. Rita.
C. At lunch.

( ) 4. A. In Zhong Shan Park.
B. At eight o'clock.
C. With his dog.

( ) 5. A. I'll go to England someday.
B. Yes, I agree with you.
C. That's all right.

四、听文章，选出正确答案并完成表格。

（一）听文章，根据问题做出正确选择。

( ) 1. What was Jerry doing when his mother asked him to come inside? He was ________.
A. going shopping with his friend
B. playing hide-and-seek with his father
C. playing outside with his friend

( ) 2. What must Jerry learn at school?
A. Math, English, science, and history.
B. Chinese, math, English, and history.
C. Art, math, science, and history.

( ) 3. What kind of programme was on TV last Saturday?
A. Discovery channel. B. Scary movie. C. Cartoon.

( ) 4. It was ________ when I was walking home from school and Tom and Steve bothered me.
A. Friday B. Wednesday C. Monday

( ) 5. For most days of a week, Jerry has to go to bed at ________.
A. 9:00 pm B. 9:30 pm C. 10:00 pm

（二）再听一遍文章，补全句子内容。

Being a kid might look like fun, but sometimes it's not.	
When you are a kid,	When you are an adult,
1. you have to ________ in the morning and go to school. 2. there are many things ________. 3. the ________ sometimes pick on you. 4. you cannot go anywhere by yourself. 5. you have to ________.	1. you do not have to go to school and you never have homework. 2. you can watch anything you want. 3. no one can pick on you. 4. you can ________.

Section 4

一、听写英文诗歌。

Never Give up

Never give up,
(1) ________
Always have faith,
It allows you to cope.
Trying times will pass,
(2) ________.
Just have patience,
(3) ________.
(4) ________.
You'll live through your pain.
(5) ________.
And strength you will gain.

二、听电影原声回答下列问题。

听第一段电影原声，回答1～3题。

( ) 1. A perfect dog was found by ________.
A. Andy and Bruce B. Kate and Kevin C. Erica and Bruce

( ) 2. What do the children need?
A. A home for themselves.
B. A place for the dog to stay.

C. A restaurant.

(　　) 3. What is the name of the movie?

A. Hotel for dogs.　　B. True friendship.　　C. True Love.

听第二段电影原声乐，回答第 4 题。

(　　) 4. The name of the song might be ________.

A. *Running Up That Hill*

B. *The Underdog*

C. *The Spirit of Adventure*

三、听下面五段小对话，听完每段小对话后，你都有十秒钟时间来作答和阅读下一题。

(　　) 1. How did David use to go to school?

A. By bus.　　B. By bike.　　C. On foot.

(　　) 2. What does Monica look like now?

A. Fat.　　B. Tall.　　C. Thin.

(　　) 3. What does the woman mean?

A. She doesn't like the man to smoke here.

B. She asked the man to look at the sign.

C. She says the man can find a sign on the wall.

(　　) 4. Where are they talking?

A. At home.　　B. In the hospital.　　C. At a drugstore.

(　　) 5. What will they do tomorrow?

A. Go to a movie.　　B. Go fishing.　　C. Watch a DVD at home.

四、听两段对话，完成下列各题。

听第一段对话，回答 1 ~3 题。

(　　) 1. Who is Eric?

A. Maggie's friend.　　B. Maggie's dog.　　C. Maggie's child.

(　　) 2. When was Eric hurt?

A. On Friday afternoon.　B. Last night.　　C. Last Friday morning.

(　　) 3. What was Eric doing before he was hurt? He was ________.

A. playing football　　B. going to the park　　C. taking a walk

听第二段对话，回答 4 ~5 题。

(　　) 4. Which school is John studying in?

A. The No. 2 Middle School.

B. The No. 5 Middle School.

C. The No. 3 Middle School.

(　　) 5. How old is John?

A. Forty-three years old. B. Thirty years old. C. Thirteen years old.

五、听文章，选出正确答案并完成表格。

（一）听文章，选出正确答案。

(　　) 1. It is believed that chocolate is made from ________.

A.  B.  C. 

(　　) 2. ________ firstly used the cocoa bean as the main ingredient in a dark, bitter drink that we would call "chocolate".

A. Hernando Cortez B. People in European C. The Mayas

(　　) 3. Cocoa beans were used as a form of ________ that was worth its weight in gold!

A.  B.  C. 

(　　) 4. When Cortez returned to Spain and introduced chocolate to European society, the chocolate was as a ________ mixed with sugar, vanilla, and cinnamon.

A. dessert B. drink C. soup

(　　) 5. ________ are in love with chocolate.

A. The young people

B. The old people

C. People around the world

（二）听文章，完成表格。

The History of Chocolate
1. For centuries, the natives regarded cocoa as a ________ from the gods.
2. Around A. D. ________, the Mayas established the first cocoa plantations.
3. When Hernando Cortez arrived in the New World in ________, he soon established his plantation.
4. In ________, Cortez returned to Spain and introduced chocolate to European society.
5. Today, people found new ways to ________ chocolate.

Section 5

一、听录音，回答下列问题。

听一段电影原音，选出正确答案。

(　　) 1. For over ________ years, the government has trained and deployed animals as espionage agents.

A. 100　　B. 10　　C. 30

(　　) 2. Starting in the Civil War, carrier ________ delivered messages from the frontline.

A. wolves　　B. tigers　　C. pigeons

(　　) 3. Later ________ were trained to detect mines.

A. zebras　　B. mice　　C. dolphins

听一段电影原声乐，选出正确答案。

(　　) 4. The name of the song might be ________.

A. *Reflection*　　B. *Dance in the Wind*　　C. *Fly to Your Heart*

听一段广告，选出正确答案。

(　　) 5. The commercial is about selling ________.

A. a car

B. No. 5 hair shape liquid

C. a kind of TV

二、听句子，选出正确答语。

(　　) 1. A. You can borrow the book from the library.

B. Let me help you.

C. Maybe you're right.

(　　) 2. A. He's tall and fat.

B. He likes all of us.

C. He often plays football with us.

(　　) 3. A. Tell her to turn it down.

B. Tell him to turn it down.

C. Tell her to turn it on.

(　　) 4. A. How I miss you!

B. I'm glad to see you, too.

C. You're welcome.

(　　) 5. A. Good idea!

B. What a beautiful park!

C. How should I know?

三、听两段对话，完成下列各题。

听第一段对话，回答1 ~3 题。

( ) 1. Where is the letter from?

A. China. B. France. C. America.

( ) 2. Who wrote the letter?

A. Kate. B. Kelly. C. Shirley.

( ) 3. What is inside the letter?

A. A leave.

B. Some beautiful paper.

C. A Christmas card.

听第二段对话，回答4 ~5 题。

( ) 4. Why will the woman go to England?

A. For a meeting. B. For a holiday. C. For her pet.

( ) 5. What is Polly?

A. A dog. B. A cat. C. A bird.

四、你将听到一段独白，请把你听到的句子逐一写下来。

language *n.* 语言	expert *n.* 专家	native *adj.* 本土的
spread *v.* 传播	across *prep.* 穿越	

Unit 4

Section 1

一、你将听到几段生活中的小对话，根据你所听到的内容写下对话。

Dialogue 1

W：Hi，Herb.

M：____________________

W：____________________

M：____________________

W：____________________

M：____________________

W：____________________

Dialogue 2

M：Hello，miss. What will you have?

W：____________________

M：____________________

W：____________________

M：____________________

W：____________________

M：Heh，heh. It was just a wild guess. Good luck finding your Internet friend!

二、材料中有五个句子，每个句子听一遍，然后从每小题 A，B，C 三个选项中选出能对每个句子做出适当反应的答语。

(　　) 1. A. Some apples.　　B. Some oranges.　　C. A bottle of water.

(　　) 2. A. She works in a restaurant.
B. She works very easily.
C. She works for six hours a day.

(　　) 3. A. Oh dear! What's wrong?
B. That's all right.
C. It doesn't matter.

(　　) 4. A. That's great.　　B. Wait a moment.　　C. OK. No problem.

(　　) 5. A. Don't go there.　B. That sounds good.　C. It doesn't matter.

三、材料中有五组对话，从每小题 A，B，C 三个选项中选出能回答每个问题的最佳答案。

(　　) 1. What do you know about Byron?

A. He was a famous poet.

B. He was a poet in the 20th century.

C. He only wrote several poems in his life.

(　　) 2. What does the man want to be now?

A. A doctor.　B. An artist.　C. An astronaut.

(　　) 3. How long has Mr. Sheldon taught there?

A. For five years.　B. For two years.　C. For three years.

(　　) 4. What kind of food does the man want to try?

A. Japanese food.　B. Chinese food.　C. Neither.

(　　) 5. What language does the man speak?

A. English.　B. French.　C. Both A and B.

四、听录音，完成下列各题。

(一) 你将听到一段关于西瓜冰淇淋的简易做法的独白。仔细听独白，并根据你所听到的内容，在所需要的材料下打钩。

Sugar
(　　)

Food processor
(　　)

Strawberry
(　　)

Chocolate
(　　)

Watermelon
(　　)

Dessert bowl
(　　)

Ice cream maker
(　　)

Lemon juice
(　　)

(二) 根据你所听到的内容，补全独白。

Imagine, you can make watermelon ice cream on your own. And it's quite simple!

Step 1: Cut watermelon

Cut a watermelon into (1) ________pieces and take away the seeds.

Step 2: Puree

Puree the watermelon in the food processor.

Step 3: Cook with sugar

Cook 1 (2) ________ of the puree with sugar in a pan until the sugar has dissolved. Add the sugar gradually and (3) ________ it to make sure the mixture is (4) ________ enough.

Step 4: Add the lemon juice into it

Mix the rest of the watermelon puree, the lemon juice and watermelon mixture.

Step 5: Cover and cool

Cover the pan and (5) ________ the mixture in the refrigerator until it is (6) ________.

Step 6: Freeze

Freeze the watermelon mixture in the ice cream maker.

Step 7: Enjoy now

Allow the mixture to freeze for at least (7) ________ hours. When it is (8) ________, take it out to the dessert bowls and (9) ________ it!

Section 2

一、听歌曲并补全所缺歌词。

(1) ________________________________

(2) ________________________________

(3) ________________________________

(4) ________________________________

(5) ________________________________

I feel your whisper across the sea

(6) ________________________________

(7) ________________________________

(8) ________________________________

(9) ________________________________

(10) ________________________________

Ooohh ooooh oooh oooh ooh ooh ooh ooh

二、听三段录音，完成下列各题。

请听第一段对话，回答 1 ~3 题。

(　　) 1. What is the man?

A. A policeman.　B. A road cleaner.　C. A repairman.

(　　) 2. When will the woman give the man a phone call?

A. At about five pm.　B. At about five am.　C. At about four pm.

(　　) 3. Where is the woman going this evening?

A. An important meeting.

B. A party.

C. An important city.

请听第二段对话，回答 4 ~7 题。

(　　) 4. Where is the woman from?

A. Korea.　B. China.　C. Australia.

(　　) 5. How long has the woman studied in Brighton University?

A. Six months.　B. One year.　C. One year and a half.

(　　) 6. What does the woman want to be after she goes back to her hometown?

A. A Chinese teacher.　B. An English teacher.　C. A history teacher.

(　　) 7. How long will the woman stay in England in all?

A. Six months.　B. One year.　C. One year and a half.

请听一段独白，回答 8 ~10 题。

(　　) 8. What did the boy have for breakfast?

A. 
B. 
C. 

(　　) 9. What did the boy go back home to get in the morning?

A. 
B. 
C. 

(　　) 10. What did Mom cook for dinner?

A. 
B. 
C. 

三、听一段独白，完成下列各题。

（一）你将听到一段关于如何照出漂亮相片的独白，根据你听到的内容，写下所需要的材料。

Things you will need to look great in photographs.

1. ____.

2. ____.

（二）根据你所听到的内容，写下如何照出漂亮相片的要点。

Step 1: ____.

When choosing your clothes, leave bright colors, crazy patterns, and horizontal stripes in the closet. Neutral colors look best.

Step 2: ____.

Check your face in the mirror. Could your eyes use some drop to clear up redness? Are your eyebrows just fine?

Step 3: ____.

Try to have the pictures taken outside in the above time. The light is soft and flattering at these times, whereas high noon or flash photography can illuminate a little too much.

Step 4: ____.

Make sure the camera lens is at the right level or just slightly higher. Any lower and you'll look like you have a double chin.

Step 5: ____.

To appear more natural when standing for a photo, lean slightly back, with your weight on your rear foot, and angle one hip forward.

Keep your posture erect but not overly posed. Think "Greek Statue", not "William Shatner".

Step 6: ____.

Turn your head two-thirds to one side or the other for a slimming effect on your face. Avoid wide-angle lenses, which will widen the appearance of your face.

Step 7: ____.

Look at the right direction, like a lamp or light, for a few moments. It reduces the possibility of red eyes. However, never look directly at the sun.

Step 8: ____.

Just before the picture is taken, close your eyes and have the photographer count to three. Then open your eyes as he begins shooting. This is the best way to prevent blinking from ruining shots.

Step 9: ____.

The last and most important part of a picture is the smile.

Section 3

一、听写。

Harry saw an ad. in a window. It said: "Wanted the best salesman in the world. Top pay."

"I' m a (1) ________ salesman," Harry told himself. " I can sell anything. I'll go in and ask for that job."

He went into the building and spoke to the (2) ________. "I'm the best salesman in the world," he said, "(3) ________ me the job."

"You must prove you're the best," the manager said.

"I'll pass every (4) ________ you give me," Harry told him.

"Good."

The manager took a box of candy out of his desk.

"Last week, I bought a (5) ________ boxes of this candy. If you can sell them all before the end of the week, you can have the job."

"That's (6) ________," Harry said.

He took the box of candy and left the office.

Every day and night, he went from (7) ________ to shop, trying to sell the candy.

He couldn't sell one. The candy was so bad that he couldn't even give it (8) ________. At the end of the week, he went back to the manager.

"I'm sorry, sir," he said, "I was (9) ________ about myself. I'm not the best salesman in the world, but I know who is."

"Oh," said the manager. "Who?"

"The person who (10) ________ you a thousand boxes of this candy," Harry said.

二、听录音，完成下列各题。

（一）下面你将听到一篇独白，从每小题A，B，C三个选项中选出能回答所提问题的正确答案。

(　　) 1. What was the husband like?

A. He was small and thin.

B. He was large and fat.

C. He was tall and strong.

(　　) 2. How often did the man get his pay?

A. Every month.　B. Every day.　C. Every week.

( ) 3. What was his wife doing when he hurried into the living room?
A. She was listening to the radio and eating apples.
B. She was watching TV and waiting for her husband.
C. She was listening to the radio and cleaning the room.

( ) 4. How did he get the ten thousand dollars?
A. He saved the money little by little.
B. He bought the lottery tickets (彩票).
C. He found the money in his office.

( ) 5. How did his wife feel when she heard the news?
A. She was happy.
B. She was angry.
C. She was happy at first. Then she got angry.

(二) 下面你将听到两则广告，从每小题A，B，C三个选项中选出能回答所提问题的正确答案。

( ) 1. How many bedrooms are there on the second floor of the house?
A. Four. B. Five. C. Six.

( ) 2. Which is NOT true about the house?
A. It has a garden around it.
B. It is by the beach.
C. It is small.

( ) 3. Which is TRUE about the apartment?
A. It is good for a big family.
B. It is in a city.
C. It has a beautiful garden.

( ) 4. If you want to see the house, how could you see inside of it?
A. Call Jim and he will show you.
B. Ask people living there to show you.
C. You can only see pictures.

( ) 5. If you are interested in the apartment, which number will you call?
A. 014-735-8383. B. 014-735-8484. C. 014-753-8484.

三、你将听一段生活小趣味说明，教你如何用小写单词 boy 画出一个男孩。

(一) 根据你听到的内容，写出你所需要的材料。

1. ____________________.
2. ____________________.
3. ____________________.

（二）选出你所听到的图片并排序。

A B C D

E F G H

（ ）→（ ）→（ ）→（ ）→（ ）→（ ）

（三）根据你听到的内容补充横线上所缺的步骤。

Step 1：________________________________.
Use only simple letters. Leave some space between each letter.

Step 2：________________________________.
Put dots inside both the "b" and the "o".

Step 3：________________________________.
Connect the tail of the letter "y" to the left end of the letter "b".

Step 4：________________________________.
Connect the top of the letter "b" to the top right of the letter "y" in an arc.

Step 5：________________________________.
Connect the top left of the "y" to the top of the "b" to form the hairline.

Step 6：________________________________.
Fill in the features like eyebrows, nose, mouth, and ears. This is your chance to be fun. You can make him happy, sad, angry, or surprised—the choice is up to you.

Section 4

一、听写。

One night a hotel caught fire, and the people who were staying in it ran out in their night clothes.

Two men stood outside and looked at the fire.

"(1) ________," said one, "I ran into some of the rooms and found a lot of money. (2) ________. When anyone leaves paper money in a fire, the fire burns it. (3) ________. No one will be poorer because I took them."

"(4) ________," said the other.

"(5) ________."

"(6) ________."

"Oh!" cried the first man. He thought quickly and said, "(7) ________."

"(8) ________," said the policeman.

"(9) ________. (10) ________."

二、下面你将听到三段录音，从每小题A，B，C三个选项中选出能回答所提问题的正确答案。

听第一段对话，完成1～3题。

( ) 1. How is Jerry?

A. He has a bad cold.

B. He has a headache.

C. His leg hurts.

( ) 2. What is Mary going to do this Sunday afternoon?

A. Go to the Children's Centre with the boy.

B. See Mary's nephew.

C. See her father's nephew.

( ) 3. Where is the boy going?

A. To the Children's Palace.

B. To the Children's Centre.

C. To the hospital.

听第二段对话，完成4～5题。

( ) 4. How often does the train start?

A. More than ten minutes.

B. More than 30 minutes.

C. Less than 30 minutes.

(　　) 5. How is the woman going to Shanghai?

A. By plane.　　B. By train.　　C. By bus.

听第三篇独白，完成6 ~10 题。

(　　) 6. How many cities had the Matthews visited before they got to Guangzhou?

A. Four.　　B. Five.　　C. Six.

(　　) 7. How long had they stayed in China then?

A. Two weeks.　　B. Less than two weeks.　C. More than two weeks.

(　　) 8. Mrs. Matthew liked ________.

A. cats only　　B. dogs only　　C. cats and dogs

(　　) 9. What did the waiter think Mrs. Matthew wanted to do?

A. She wanted something to eat.

B. She wanted him to give her dog something to eat.

C. She wanted to eat her dog.

(　　) 10. Which of these sentences is true?

A. The waiter killed the dog because he hated dogs very much.

B. Mrs. Matthew brought her dog to China.

C. Mrs. Matthew thought her dog was eating in the kitchen.

三、听录音，完成下列各题。

(一) Erica 和 Tony 正在讨论他们班上的同学，根据听到的内容，做出正确的回答。

1. What do the boy and the girl think of the people in their class?

____.

2. How does the girl feel about Tom?

____.

3. What kind of music does the girl like?

____.

4. What is Dorry good at?

____.

(二) 仿照例句写下各个同学的特点。

E. g. :　　Mark: Very arrogant.

1. Mike: ________________.

2. Carol: ________________.

3. Tom: ________________.

4. Jane: ________________.

5. Serina: ________________.

6. Dorry: ________________.

Section 5

一、听文章，选出正确答案并完成表格。

（一）听文章，选出正确答案。

(　　) 1. In the UK, most children have their midday meal at ________.

A. school　　B. home　　C. restaurant outside school

(　　) 2. In many schools, ________ can choose what the children eat.

A. the children themselves　　B. parents　　C. teachers

(　　) 3. The junk food includes ________.

A. burgers, pizzas and chips　　B. vegetables　　C. sandwiches

(二) 听文章，完成表格。

Different parents made different lunch decisions for their children:
1. Cathy, a mother of (1) ________ children said, "My children have packed lunches, because they say (2) ________. So I make 3 packed lunches every morning, so we're like (3) ________ in our kitchen in the morning."
2. She said, "My daughter always had school dinners. I think she probably gets better and (4) ________ by having a cooked lunch at school than she would if I made (5) ________."
3. Kaz, a father, wasn't impressed with them, "Very (6) ________ were offered and I think there were a lot of (7) ________."

二、你将听到三段对话或独白，根据你听到的内容回答问题。

听第一段对话，回答 1 ~2 题。

(　　) 1. How long has Aiden worked there?

A. 8 hours.　　B. 12 hours.　　C. 4 hours.

(　　) 2. Why does Aiden feel hungry and tired?

A. Because he ate too much food after work.

B. Because he has had nothing.

C. Because he worked hard.

听第二段对话，回答 3 ~5 题。

(　　) 3. How many post offices does the man talk about?

A. One.　　B. Two.　　C. Three.

(　　) 4. Where are they talking?

A. In the street.　　B. Near a market.　　C. Near a post office.

(　　) 5. What's the time when they are talking?

A. 7:00 pm.　　B. 4:00 am.　　C. 11:00 am.

听第三段独白，回答 6 ~10 题。

(　　) 6. Why did Kayla go to Canada? She went there ________.

A. for business

B. to visit a Canadian family

C. to learn English

(　　) 7. When did she come back from Canada?

A. On December 29.

B. On October 19.

C. On December 19.

(　　) 8. Why did she like staying with the Camerons? Because she could ________.

A. eat western food every day

B. teach them Chinese

C. talk to them in English

(　　) 9. Kayla had time to go to an English class because she ________.

A. had no family there

B. didn't need to cook her meals

C. wanted to be an English teacher

(　　) 10. What did Kayla like best in the Canadian class?

A. The students were friendly.

B. Listening, reading, speaking and writing were all taught.

C. The students were quite free.

三、你将听到一段独白，请将你听到的句子逐一写下来。

special *adj.* 特别的	heart attack 心脏病	thought *n.* 想法

____

____

____

____

____

____

____

____

____

____

Unit 5

Section 1

sign *n.* 标记；符号

一、在横线上写出你所听到的词语。

第一组：

1. ______ 2. ______ 3. ______ 4. ______ 5. ______

6. ______ 7. ______ 8. ______ 9. ______ 10. ______

第二组：

11. ______ 12. ______ 13. ______ 14. ______ 15. ______

16. ______ 17. ______ 18. ______ 19. ______ 20. ______

二、下面你将听到十个句子，请从 A，B，C 三个选项中选出句子中出现的词语。

( ) 1. A. bad B. mine C. my

( ) 2. A. American B. sea C. see

( ) 3. A. walk B. daughter C. doctor

( ) 4. A. their B. bird C. fly

( ) 5. A. who B. newspaper C. whose

( ) 6. A. taxi B. test C. buy

( ) 7. A. write B. right C. light

( ) 8. A. feel B. never C. ever

( ) 9. A. weather B. whether C. letter

( ) 10. A. tall B. strong C. catch

三、你将听到五个句子，根据句子内容选择相应的图片。

A. 

B. 

C. 

D. 

E. 

1	2	3	4	5

四、听下面五段对话，根据对话内容选择相应的图片。

(　　) 1. A. 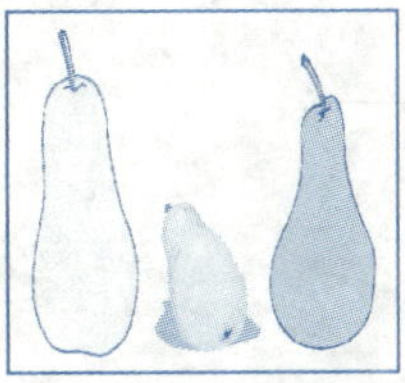 B.  C. 

(　　) 2. A.  B.  C. 

(　　) 3. A.  B.  C. 

(　　) 4. A.  B.  C. 

(　　) 5. A.  B.  C. 

五、听对话，选择合适的答案。

( ) 1. What are the they doing?

A.  B.  C. 

( ) 2. What is the name of the caller?

A. Nick. B. Nate. C. Neil.

( ) 3. According the girl, her father ________.

A. is not home

B. is on another line

C. can't come to the telephone

( ) 4. What is the man's telephone number?

A. 598-7482. B. 587-4728. C. 589-7248.

( ) 5. The man tells the girl ________.

A. that he will call again sometime after 7:00 pm

B. to ask her father to call him later

C. that he will drop by around 8:30 pm

Section 2

freezing *adj.* 严寒的	monster *n.* 怪物	design *n.* 设计

一、请根据要求写出你在句子中所听到的词语。

第一组：写出你所听到的职业名称。

1. ________ 2. ________ 3. ________

4. ________ 5. ________ 6. ________

第二组：写出你所听到的时间或数字。

7. ________ 8. ________ 9. ________

10. ________ 11. ________ 12. ________

二、听下面的句子，并根据句子内容在横线上写出正确的日期或星期。

例如：你将听到 Today is July the 4th.

请写：Today is July 4th.

1．The school begins on ____________.

2．My sister will travel to France on ____________.

3．We'll take the test on ____________.

4．On ____________, the store will have a big sale.

5．Can you send me an email by ____________?

6．My grandparents will come to see me next ____________.

7．Thanksgiving Day falls on the fourth ____________ in ____________.

8．Do you know that next ____________ is my birthday?

9．Will you be free this ____________?

10．Is ____________ or ____________ the first day of a week?

三、听下面五段对话，根据对话内容选择相应的图片，并将代表该答案的字母填在题前的括号内。

(　　) 1．What's the weather like?

A. 
B. 
C. 

(　　) 2．How is the weather?

A. 
B. 
C. 

(　　) 3．What is the temperature?

A. －10℃　　B. 10℃　　C. －1℃

(　　) 4．Which is their family photo?

A. 
B. 
C. 

(　　) 5. Which picture is right?

A. 

B. 

C. 

四、听下面的对话，并根据对话内容选择正确的答案。

(　　) 1. What is the girl shopping for?

A. A present for her mother.

B. A present for a friend.

C. A present for her father.

(　　) 2. How much is the black wallet?

A. $49.95.　　B. $40.95.　　C. $44.95.

(　　) 3. Why doesn't the girl like the brown wallet?

A. There isn't a place to put pictures.

B. It's too big and heavy.

C. She doesn't like the color.

(　　) 4. How much does the girl have to spend?

A. $5.00.　　B. $10.00.　　C. $13.00.

(　　) 5. What does the girl decide to buy?

A. 

B. 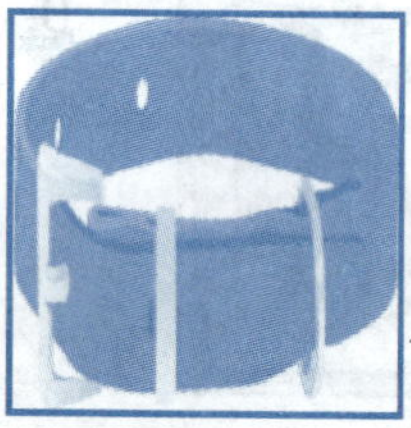

C. 

五、听下面这段文章，选图填空。

(1)

(2)

(3)

(4)

(5)

(6)

顺序：________→________→________→________→________

Section 3

vacation *n.* 假期	bowling alley 保龄球馆
relax *v.*（使）放松，休息	city hall 市政厅

一、听写句子。

1. I ________ eat any ________________.
2. Tom is ________________________ in his class.
3. I didn't ________________________ 10 o'clock last night.
4. Are you ________________________ this box?
5. Mary is ________________________.
6. The ________________________.
7. ________________________ yesterday?
8. How ________________________?
9. It is ________________________.
10. The ________________________.

二、根据你所听到的歌曲内容完成下面的练习。

（一）根据你所听到的歌曲内容给下列交通工具排序。

A. 
B. 
C. 
D. 

排序：________→________→________→________

（二）下面哪一幅图中所描述的是歌曲中没有唱到的。

A. 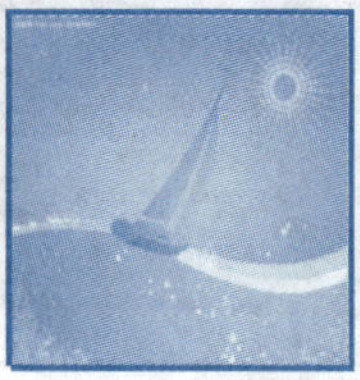
B. 
C. 
D. 

歌曲中没有提到的：________

三、听一段独白，根据下面这幅图判断句子的正误并做出相应的选择。

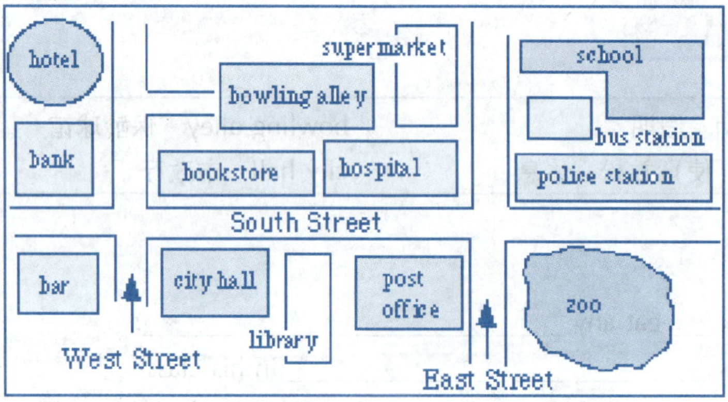

(　　) 1. The hotel is next to the ________.

A. True　　　　B. False

(　　) 2. The zoo is ________ the police station.

A. True　　　　B. False

(　　) 3. The ________ is between the post office and the supermarket.

A. True　　　　B. False

(　　) 4. The bowling alley is on ________ Street.

A. True　　　　B. False

(　　) 5. The ________ corner of ________ Street and ________ Street.

A. True　　　　B. False

四、你将听到两段独白，请根据独白内容完成下面的练习，每空填一个词。

第一段：

The United Kingdom is a small (1) ________. It's in Europe. Germany is in Europe, too. Your Teacher is an English teacher in Germany. She's (2) ________. She's from Derby. Derby is a big city in England. Mr. Smith is an English teacher, too, but he's not English. He's an (3) ________. He's from Washington.

第二段：

Mr. Bean is going to go on (4) ________ this year. What do you think he's going to do? He's not going to (5) ________ and relax. He's going to learn how to swim. He's going to write everyone a (6) ________.

Section 4

inaugurate *v.* 为……举行就职典礼	challenge *n.* 挑战
sharp *adv.* 准时地	typical *adj.* 典型的
chop *v.* 剁；砍；伐	pickled *adj.* 腌制的
ketchup *n.* 番茄酱	bun *n.* 圆形的小面包

一、你将听到几段广播录音片段，请根据内容完成下面的练习。

听第一段录音，完成 1 ~2 题。

(　　) 1. This BBC news is for ________.

A. adults　　B. children　　C. kids

(　　) 2. What is the date today?

A. January 9th.　　B. January 29th.　　C. June 29th.

听第二段录音，完成 3 ~4 题。

(　　) 3. President Barack Obama is the ________ president in ________.

A. first; America

B. forty-fourth; Africa

C. forty-fourth; America

(　　) 4. Barack Obama said: "The challenges we face are real, ________."

A. serious and many

B. easy and difficult

C. serious and different

二、下面你将看到一些同音异形词，请听句子并判断出句子中出现的那个单词。如果表格中的词语是正确的就打"√"，错误的打"×"。

way	allowed	new	flower	weak	right	buy	sun

三、请听句子，并在横线上写出句子中出现的动词词组（写动词的原形）。

例如：你将听到 Look at the picture.

请在横线上写下：look at

1. ________ 2. ________ 3. ________

4. ________ 5. ________ 6. ________

7. ________ 8. ________ 9. ________

10. ________ 11. ________ 12. ________

四、根据你所听到的句子选择合适的图片。

(　　) 1. A. 

B. 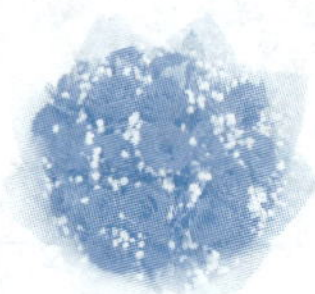
C. 

(　　) 2. A. 
B. 
C. 

(　　) 3. A. 

B. 
C. 

(　　) 4. A. 

B. 
C. 

五、请听五个句子，并完成下面的五个小题。

Bus Schedule

Destination	**Departure Time**	**Arrival Time**	**Fare**
Reno, NV	9:15 am	4:30 pm	$98.00
Fresno, CA	11:00 am	1:45 pm	$62.00
Seattle, WA	8:30 am	5:10 pm	$102.00
Boise, ID	10:40 am	9:35 pm	$95.00

(　　) 1. The bus to Reno, Nevada, ________ at 9:50 am.
A. True　　B. False

(　　) 2. The bus to Boise, Idaho, arrives at ________.
A. True　　B. False

(　　) 3. The bus fare to Seattle, Washington, is ________.
A. True　　B. False

(　　) 4. The bus ________ leaves at ________.
A. True　　B. False

(　　) 5. The bus heading ________.
A. True　　B. False

六、你将听到一篇文章，请根据文章内容完成下面的练习。

(　　) 1. When do the Americans often have a hamburger?
A. At breakfast time.　　B. At lunch time.　　C. At dinner time.

(　　) 2. The hamburger ________.
A. comes from the US
B. is eaten by everybody in the world
C. is an international meal

(　　) 3. A typical hamburger is made of ________.
A. ham　　B. beef　　C. meat

(　　) 4. The name "hamburger" comes from ________.
A. Turkey　　B. Germany　　C. America

(　　) 5. The bun is ________.
A. a kind of bread　　B. a kind of cake　　C. a kind of sandwich

Section 5

suitable *adj.* 合适的	Valentine's Day 情人节
reservation *n.* 保留的座位；预订	website *n.* 网站
balanced *adj.* 平衡的	tough *adj.* 坚强的；困难的
petrol *n.* 石油；汽油	fuel *n.* 燃料；燃油

一、下面你将听到一些电影片段，请根据片段内容完成下面的题目。

听第一段录音，完成1～2题。

(　　) 1. What is the man's name?
A. Franklin Ben.　　B. Forrest Gump.　　C. John Brown.

(　　) 2. His mother always said, "Life was like ______."

A. a box of candy　　B. a bar of chocolate　　C. a box of chocolates

听第二段录音，完成 3 ~4 题。

(　　) 3. Who is going to school for the first day?

A. Nemo.　　B. Nemo's Dad.　　C. Nemo and his Dad.

(　　) 4. How many stripes does his father have?

A. Five.　　B. Four.　　C. Three.

二、听下面的句子，并根据句子内容选择相应的图片。

(　　) 1. A.  B.  C. 

(　　) 2. A.  B.  C. 

(　　) 3. A.  B.  C. 

(　　) 4. A.  B.  C. 

(　　) 5. A.  B.  C. 

三、听下面几段对话，根据题中的问题选择合适的答案。

( ) 1. How is Susan?

A. She is fine. B. She is ill. C. She is tall.

( ) 2. Where are they?

A. In the kitchen. B. In the museum. C. In a restaurant.

( ) 3. What are her uncle and aunt doing?

A. They are watching their car.

B. They are washing their car.

C. They are repairing their car.

( ) 4. What can we learn from this conversation?

A. She didn't see the film.

B. The film was very exciting.

C. The film wasn't as good as she'd expected.

( ) 5. What suggestion does Mike give to the woman?

A. To write an article on geography.

B. To go to the school library.

C. To buy some good books.

四、请听一段对话，并完成下面的练习。

(一) 根据对话内容判断下面句子的正误，正确的写“T”，错误的写“F”。

( ) 1. The two speakers are a couple.

( ) 2. The man lives a very busy life.

( ) 3. The man's wife is a housewife.

( ) 4. The man goes to work by car.

( ) 5. There are three people in the man's family.

(二) 根据对话的内容完成下面的选择题。

( ) 1. What time does the man get up?

A. At 5:00 am. B. At 6:00 am. C. At 7:00 am.

( ) 2. What time does he get to work?

A. At 7:00 am. B. At 8:00 am. C. At 9:00 am.

( ) 3. What does he do with his family at around 6:30 pm?

A. They eat dinner.

B. They play games.

C. They read books together.

( ) 4. What do the man and his wife do after the kids go to bed?

A. They watch TV.

B. They listen to music.

C. They clean the house.

( ) 5. What is one thing the man does NOT say about his wife?

A. She goes shopping for food.

B. She has to take their children to school.

C. She helps the kids with their homework.

五、你将听到一段短文，请将短文内容写在下面的横线上。

____

____

____

____

____

____

____

____

Unit 6

Section 1

disappointed *adj.* 失望的	deliberately *adv.* 故意地
disobey *v.* 不服从，不顺从	scared *adj.* 惊慌的，吓坏的
support *v.* 支撑；维持；供养	oatmeal *n.* 燕麦片
yoga *n.* 瑜伽	garlic *n.* 大蒜

一、写出你所听到的词语，并找出与其他三个不同类的一项，并将代表该选项的字母填在题前的括号内。

例如：你将听到 A. apple B. lemon C. orange D. potato

请写：(D) A. apple B. lemon C. orange D. potato

( ) 1. A. ________ B. ________ C. ________ D. ________

( ) 2. A. ________ B. ________ C. ________ D. ________

( ) 3. A. ________ B. ________ C. ________ D. ________

( ) 4. A. ________ B. ________ C. ________ D. ________

( ) 5. A. ________ B. ________ C. ________ D. ________

二、下面你将听到一些电影或歌曲片段，请根据片段内容完成下面的题目。

听第一段录音，完成1 ~2 题。

( ) 1. This is a conversation between Simba and ________?

A. his brother B. his friend C. his father

( ) 2. We can hear in this conversation that "being brave doesn't mean you ________."

A. go looking for trouble

B. go hunting at any time

C. are not scared of anything

听第二段录音，请填出空格中所缺的英文歌词。

Moon river, (3) ________ than a mile;

I'm crossing you in style some day;

Oh, (4) ________ maker, you (5) ________ breaker;

Wherever you're going, I'm going your (6) ________.

三、你将听到一段对话，请根据对话内容找出下面这段对话中的错误。在错误的地方画上横线，并将正确的内容填在后面的括号内。第一个错误已经给出。

W: I had a terrible evening, John! morning

M: Oh, Rita. What's happened? (1) ________

W: Well, I went to the bus stop at once. (2) ________ I waited for twenty seconds but the bus didn't come. (3) ________

M: So, what did you do?

W: I hurried to the station. I decided to take the eight o'clock train. (4) ________ But I was too unlucky. I missed the train. (5) ________

M: Oh, no!

W: So, I went outside and got into a taxi. But the taxi driver went the wrong way. (6) ________ He got lost! I was late for school again! I got there at nine thirteen! (7) ________

四、听一篇文章，完成下面的练习。

（一）听文章的第一段，按照要求完成下面的练习。

( ) 1. What kind of people is this passage talking about?

A.  B.  C. 

( ) 2. Where are they from?

A. France. B. America. C. England.

( ) 3. They tell their life story in a ________.

A. book B. diary C. newspaper

（二）听文章的第二段，按照要求完成下面的练习。

1. They get up at ________ or ________.
2. They have a good ________.
3. They eat lots of ________.

( ) 4. What do they like to exercise?

A.  B.  C. 

（三）听文章的第三段，判断下面句子的正误。正确的在括号内写“T”，错误的在括号内写“F”。

(　　) 1. A lot of salt and fat are bad for you.

(　　) 2. They didn't get married.

(　　) 3. They always listened to the doctors in their lives.

Section 2

masterpiece	*n.* 杰作，名著		comedy	*n.* 喜剧	
recommend	*v.* 推荐，介绍		cabinet	*n.* 橱柜	
couch	*n.* 长沙发	destination	*n.* 目的地	platform	*n.* 站台，月台

一、请在左边的横线上写出你所听到的国家名称，在右边的横线上写出你所听到的首都名称，然后将对应的国家和首都连线。

1. ______________　　A. ______________

2. ______________　　B. ______________

3. ______________　　C. ______________

4. ______________　　D. ______________

5. ______________　　E. ______________

二、请听一段对话，并根据对话内容填出句子中所缺的词语。

Amy: Hi, Victor. How are you?

Victor: Oh, I'm fine.

Amy: So, are you going to go to class (1) ________?

Victor: (2) ________ . . . But I don't think so.

Amy: Really? What's the (3) ________?

Victor: I don't know. I'm just feeling a (4) ________ (5) ________.

Amy: Listen. Come with me to class, and after class we can go out for (6) ______.

Victor: Now that's a good idea. Thanks a lot, Brian. I'm feeling (7) ________ already.

三、你将听到一些关于英文名著的介绍，请根据介绍将它们与右边的作者连线。

1. *A Tale of Two Cities*　　A. Mark Twain

2. *The Adventures of Tom Sawyer*　　B. Charles Dickens

3. *A Midsummer Night's Dream*　　C. Jules Verne

4. *Pride and Prejudice*　　D. William Shakespeare

5. *Around the World in* 80 *Days* E. Jane Austen

四、请根据你所听到的句子选择合适的图片。

( ) 1. A.  B.  C. 

( ) 2. A.  B.  C. 

( ) 3. A.  B.  C. 

( ) 4. A.  B.  C. 

( ) 5. A.  B.  C. 

五、请听下面关于教室的介绍，根据你所听到的内容选出你所听到的物品。

☐ ☐ ☐ ☐

□ □ □

六、你将听到一段对话，请根据对话内容完成下面的练习。

( ) 1. Where does the man want to go?

A. Tokyo Subway Station.

B. Tokyo Art Museum.

C. Tokyo Tower.

( ) 2. Which of the following is right?

A. He is Japanese.

B. He is a tourist in Japan.

C. He can speak Japanese.

( ) 3. How much is the train fare?

A. 130 yen. B. 140 yen. C. 150 yen.

( ) 4. Where should the man get on the train?

A. Platform number 3.

B. Platform number 4.

C. Platform number 5.

( ) 5. How often do the trains come?

A. About every five minutes.

B. About every six minutes.

C. About every seven minutes.

Section 3

laundry *n.* 洗衣店，洗衣房	rent *v.* 租借	snack *n.* 小吃，点心
donut *n.* 炸面圈	spinach *n.* 菠菜	

一、在横线上写出你所听到的句子。

1. ______________________________?

2. ______________________________?

3. ____.
4. ____?
5. ____.
6. ____?
7. ____.
8. ____.
9. ____.
10. ____!

二、听下面十个句子，根据所听内容选出相应的答语，并将代表该答案的字母填在题前的括号内。

( ) 1. A. Thanks.
B. You must help me.
C. I'm looking for a camera.

( ) 2. A. Who's that?
B. Hello, Anna is speaking.
C. She's Lucy's sister.

( ) 3. A. Thank you. B. What a good idea! C. No, I don't.

( ) 4. A. Thank you. B. Not at all. C. Yes, it is.

( ) 5. A. No, it won't.
B. Yes, it will be rainy.
C. No one likes sunny days.

( ) 6. A. I like to ride a bike. B. By bike. C. It's too far.

( ) 7. A. That's right. B. You're welcome. C. With pleasure.

( ) 8. A. It's a new watch.
B. It doesn't work.
C. My father gave it to me.

( ) 9. A. I am. B. It's mine. C. Certainly.

( ) 10. A. Let me help you. B. What a nice bike! C. I don't know.

三、你将听到几段小对话，请根据对话内容完成下面的练习。

听第一段对话，完成 1 ~3 题。

( ) 1. Who is Jack?
A. A new neighbor. B. A tourist. C. A barber in town.

( ) 2. Where is the grocery store?
A. Near the laundry. B. On Pine Street. C. Near the barber's.

( ) 3. What does Jack look like?

A.  B.  C. 

听第二段对话，完成 4 ~6 题。

(　　) 4. Why is Lisa so excited?

A. Because she will go on a business trip.

B. Because she has two weeks off.

C. Because she can play with Tom.

(　　) 5. What does Tom plan to do at first?

A. Do some shopping.　B. Do some cleaning.　C. Do some reading.

(　　) 6. What kind of place is Lisa going to go?

A.  B.  C. 

听第三段对话，完成 7 ~8 题。

(　　) 7. What is Anna going to do tonight?

A. She is going to finish a test.

B. She is going to work late.

C. She is going to a party.

(　　) 8. Where is Tom going tomorrow?

A. 

B.  C. 

四、你将听到一段对话，请根据对话内容完成下面的练习。

(　　) 1. What time of day does this conversation take place?

A. In the morning.　B. In the afternoon.　C. In the evening.

(　　) 2. Why doesn't the father give his son something to eat?

A. There isn't any food to eat.

B. The boy just ate something.

C. They are going to eat soon.

(　　) 3. What snack does the boy want at the beginning of the conversation?

A. 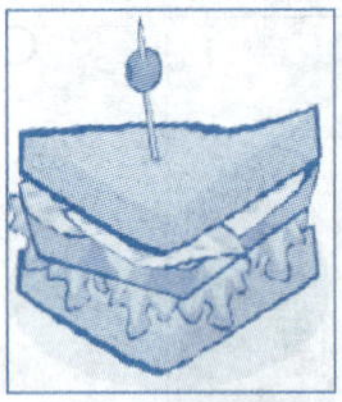 B.  C. 

(　　) 4. Which of the following does the father NOT offer to his son for a snack?

A. 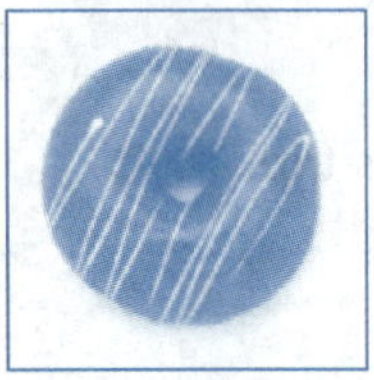 B.  C. 

(　　) 5. What does the father ask the boy to do while he is preparing the snack?

A.  B.  C. 

Section 4

historian *n.* 历史学家	folk *adj.* 民间的	publish *v.* 出版
memory *n.* 记忆力	comfortable *adj.* 舒服的	
driving license 驾驶执照	stuck *adj.* 卡住的	

一、听句子，选出与你所听到的意思相近的句子。

(　　) 1. A. Susan goes to work every day.
B. Susan goes to school on foot every day.
C. Susan drives to school every day.

(　　) 2. A. Lily will leave Paris tomorrow.
B. Lily will go to Paris tomorrow.
C. Lily will stay in Paris tomorrow.

(　　) 3. A. Why don't you see the film tomorrow night?
B. Why not go to see the film tonight?
C. Please come and see the film tomorrow night.

(　　) 4. A. These two dresses are the same price.
B. This dress is not very expensive.

C. This dress is mine.

(　　) 5. A. Who is your father?

B. How is your father?

C. What's your father?

二、你将听到几段广播录音片段，请根据你所听到的内容完成下面的练习。

听第一段录音，完成1～2题。

(　　) 1. What are the names of the two speakers?

A. Sherry Green & Steven Lomax.

B. Shirley Griffith & Steve Ember.

C. Susan Griffith & Sam Lomax.

(　　) 2. They are going to talk about ______.

A. American folk music　B. Voice of America　C. American musicians

听第二段录音，完成3～4题。

(　　) 3. John Avery Lomax was born in ________.

A. 1867　B. 1876　C. 1910

(　　) 4. The book he published was called ________.

A. *Sweet Betsy from Pike*

B. *Home on the Range*

C. *Cowboy Songs and Other Frontier Ballads*

三、请听问句，并标出问句的顺序，然后把问句与相应的答句连线。

☐ What are you doing?

☐ Does Dad enjoy dancing?

☐ What's he doing?

☐ Do you like swimming?

☐ Is Sam's father reading a book?

A. No, he is singing a song.

B. She likes reading story books.

C. Yes, he does.

D. They are running.

E. I am cleaning the room.

F. No, I don't. I like playing football.

G. He is cooking.

四、你将听到几段小对话，请根据对话内容完成下面的练习。

(　　) 1. What does the woman need?

A. 

B. 

C. 

(　　) 2. What is the man looking for?

A.  B. 

C. 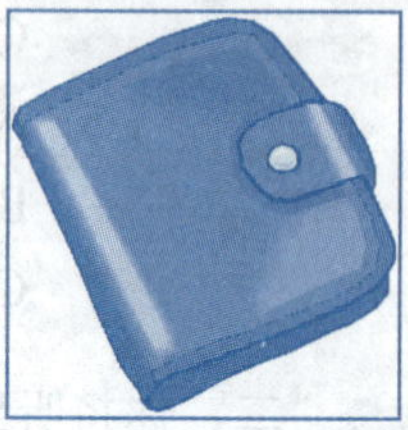

( ) 3. What is his birthday present?

A.  B.  C. 

( ) 4. What do they want to buy?

A.  B.  C. 

五、你将听到两篇短文，请根据文章内容回答下面的问题。

听第一篇短文，回答1～4题。

1. Q：Why didn't my friend go with me together?

A：________________________.

2. Q：Why did I feel lucky?

A：________________________.

3. Q：Did I drive on the wrong side?

A：________________________.

4. Q：On which side should we drive in London?

A：________________________.

听第二篇短文，回答5～8题。

5. Q：How do I go to work every day?

A：________________________.

6. Q：What does "Mrs. Dumpling" mean?

A：________________________.

7. Q：Can the woman get off the bus by herself?

A：________________________.

8. Q：Why wasn't the woman pleased at last?

A：________________________.

Section 5

chilly *adj.* 寒冷的	remote control 遥控装置	salary *n.* 薪水
controller *n.* 控制者，指挥者	stressful *adj.* 有压力的	
towards *prep.* 朝，向	spaceship *n.* 宇宙飞船	

一、你将听到几段广播录音片段，请根据你所听到的内容完成下面的练习。

听第一段录音，完成1～2题。

(　　) 1. This special holiday is on ________.

A. Saturday　　B. Tuesday　　C. Thursday

(　　) 2. What holiday is it?

A. Halloween.　　B. Thanksgiving Day.　　C. Christmas.

听第二段录音，根据歌曲内容在空格处填上合适的词语。

From this valley they say you are going,
I will miss your (3) ________ eyes and sweet (4) ________.
For I know you are taking the (5) ________.
That has lighten my pathway a while.
Come and sit by my (6) ________ if you love me,
Don't hasten to bid me do,
But (7) ________ the Red River Valley,
And the one that has loved you so true.
Just remember the Red River Valley,
And the one who has loved you so true.

二、你将听到一些广告语，根据广告内容选择相应的产品。

(　　) 1. A.  B.  C. 

(　　) 2. A.  B.  C. 

( ) 3. A.  B.  C. 

( ) 4. A.  B. 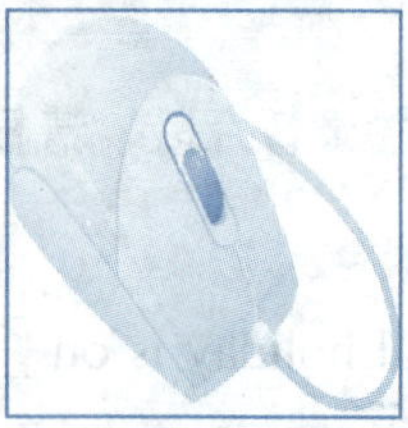 C. 

( ) 5. A. 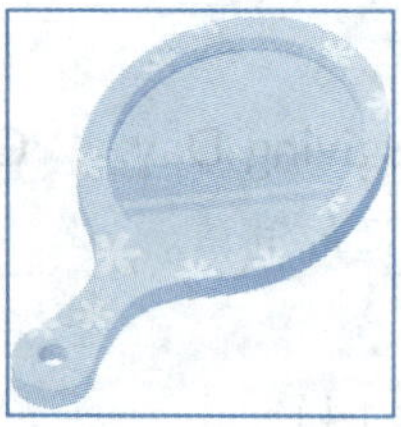 B.  C. 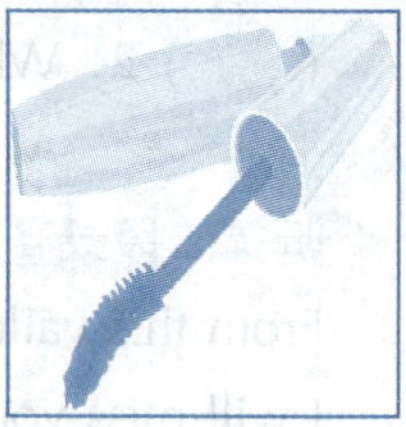

三、你将听到几段小对话，请根据对话内容完成下面的练习。

听第一段对话，完成 1 ~3 题。

( ) 1. How is the weather?

A. It's warm. B. It's hot. C. It's cold.

( ) 2. What didn't the man do for the woman?

A. Turn off the light in the kitchen.

B. Make dinner.

C. Close the window.

( ) 3. What's wrong with the woman?

A. She is very lazy.

B. Her leg is broken.

C. She doesn't know how to do housework.

听第二段对话，完成 4 ~6 题。

( ) 4. Why is the man so surprised at first?

A. Because he meets Diane in the street.

B. Because he doesn't know Diane before.

C. Because Diane has changed a lot.

( ) 5. What isn't the change of Diane?

A. She is thinner. B. Her hair is longer. C. She is taller.

(　　) 6. Which of the saying about Diane is right?

A. She has two kids.

B. She got married two years ago.

C. She works as a teacher.

听第三段对话，完成 7 ~9 题。

(　　) 7. What does the woman do?

A. She is a student.

B. She is a teacher.

C. She is an airhostess.

(　　) 8. Where does the man work?

A. At the airport.

B. At the railway station.

C. At a school.

(　　) 9. What's the man's job like?

A. Boring and stressful.

B. Exciting and stressful.

C. Interesting and relaxing.

四、你将听到一篇短文，请将短文内容写在下面的横线上。

____

____

____

____

____

____

____

____

____

____

____

Unit 7

Section 1

peaceful	*adj.* 安静的	beneath	*prep.* 在……的下方		
program	*n.* 节目	progress	*n.* 进步	block	*n.* 街区

一、请写出你所听到的词语，并在后面的括号内写出它们所属的种类名称。

例如：你将听到 cat dog sheep

请写：___cat___ ___dog___ ___sheep___ (animals)

1. __________ __________ __________ (　　)
2. __________ __________ __________ (　　)
3. __________ __________ __________ (　　)
4. __________ __________ __________ (　　)
5. __________ __________ __________ (　　)

二、听句子，并从选项中选出你所听到的句子。

(　　) 1. A. Mum baked some cakes a little while ago.
B. Mum bought some cakes just now.
C. Mum will bake some cakes in the afternoon.

(　　) 2. A. I would like to smoke.
B. I hope you don't mind my smoking.
C. I hope you would like to smoke.

(　　) 3. A. Africa is four times larger than Europe.
B. Asia is four times as large as Europe.
C. Asia is four times larger than Europe.

(　　) 4. A. He is going to buy a refrigerator this week.
B. He is too weak to carry this refrigerator.
C. He is too weak to work anymore.

(　　) 5. A. What's happening now?
B. What happened in the bank?
C. What's happened in the bank?

三、听下面的歌曲，按要求完成以下练习。

(　　) 1. People sing this song ________.

A. in the morning　　B. in the afternoon　　C. at night

(　　) 2. What can't we hear in this song?

A. 

B. 

C. 

四、你将听到五个句子，根据句子内容选择相应的图片。

A. 

B. 

C. 

D. 

E. 

F. 

G. 

1	2	3	4	5

五、你将听到几段对话，请根据对话内容完成下面的练习。

听第一段对话，完成 1 ~3 题。

(　　) 1. What are they talking about?

A. Changjiang Travel.　　B. TV programs.　　C. An NBA match.

(　　) 2. How does the man know the time for the match?

A. From the woman.　　B. From the paper.　　C. From the TV.

(　　) 3. What do we know from the dialogue?

A. They like basketball.

B. They'll watch an NBA match.

C. They watch TV every evening.

听第二段对话，完成4~6题。

(　　) 4. Which language is the man learning now?

A. French.　　B. English.　　C. Chinese.

(　　) 5. Which language is the man best at?

A. French.　　B. English.　　C. Chinese.

(　　) 6. How does the woman help the man with his language learning?

A. By pair work.

B. By group work.

C. By individual work.

听第三段对话，完成7~8题。

(　　) 7. Where is the woman going?

A. To the City Hall.

B. To the Great Wall.

C. To the Concert Hall.

(　　) 8. Which of the following is wrong?

A. The woman goes the wrong way.

B. It is only two blocks away from here.

C. The woman should turn back and go straight along the street.

Section 2

Portugal *n.* 葡萄牙	Sweden *n.* 瑞典	Egypt *n.* 埃及
plan *v.* 计划	graduate *v.* 毕业	
originally *adv.* 起初，原来	major *n.* 专业，主修课目	

一、在横线上写出你所听到的词组或短语。

1. ________　2. ________　3. ________
4. ________　5. ________　6. ________
7. ________　8. ________　9. ________
10. ________　11. ________　12. ________

二、听下面的句子，并根据句子的内容选择合适的答语。

(　　) 1. A. Juice, please.

B. None of them.

C. I like drinking tea best.

(　　) 2. A. Thank you.

B. I like it very much.
C. I'll go for a walk.

( ) 3. A. Oh! What's wrong?
B. That's all right.
C. It doesn't matter.

( ) 4. A. She likes coffee.
B. She is tall and thin.
C. She doesn't like it at all.

( ) 5. A. Who are you?
B. Jenny is speaking.
C. She's Lucy's sister.

( ) 6. A. Thank you.
B. No, I don't.
C. What a good idea!

( ) 7. A. Yes, I do.
B. Once a month.
C. No, I don't have any pen pals.

( ) 8. A. No, it won't.
B. Yes, it will be sunny.
C. No one likes rainy days.

( ) 9. A. It's a long holiday.
B. Thank you.
C. I'm going to Beijing.

( ) 10. A. No, thank you.
B. It's a red pen.
C. Here you are.

三、你将听到一段歌曲，请根据歌曲内容填上合适的词语。

I'm a policeman (1) ________ in blue, here are some things I (2) ________ to do.

Direct the (3) ________ in your town, help to keep you (4) ________ and (5) ________.

It's my job and I like it fine. No one has a better job than mine.

I'm a policeman dressed in blue, I want to be a (6) ________ to you.

You can (7) ________ me every day, I will (8) ________ my (9) ________ and say.

It's my job and I like it fine. No one has a better job than mine.

四、你将听到一段天气预报，请根据天气预报的内容将下面代表国家的国旗与相应的天气连线。

1 
2 
3 
4 
5 

 A
 B
 C
 D
 E

五、你将听到一篇短文，请根据对话内容将下面的事件按发生的顺序排序。

( ) The rich man knew that he was cheated.
( ) The owner of the shop asked five hundred dollars for the watch.
( ) The rich man spent a hundred dollars buying the watch.
( ) A rich man wanted to buy a nice looking watch.
( ) The young man stole the watch.
( ) The rich man told his friend about the fine watch.
( ) A young man saw the rich man in the shop.

六、请听下面的一段独白，完成下面的表格。

Self-introduction

Name: (1) ________
Place of Birth: (2) ________
Age: (3) ________
Major Subject: (4) ________
Part Time Job: (5) ________
Hobbies: (6) ________, (7) ________ and hanging out with friends.

Section 3

diet *n.* 节食	electric *adj.* 电的
manager *n.* 经理	permit *v.* 允许
intelligent *adj.* 聪颖的	exceptional *adj.* 杰出的
assure *v.* 确保	behave *v.* 举动，表现

一、听下面的句子，并在横线上写出所缺的词语或者完整的句子。

1. That's ________ a lot of people are ________ in the river.
2. It's going to be ________ ________.
3. ________ is here ________ him.
4. ________ of people are ________ ________ in our country.
5. I can see a cat ________ ________ the street.
6. ________________________________
7. ________________________________
8. ________________________________
9. ________________________________
10. ________________________________

二、听下面一段话，补全横线中所缺的词语。

Mr. and Mrs. Brown live in a small (1) ________ in the (2) ________ of England. Mr. Brown is a (3) ________. His wife works in a school. She teaches (4) ________. Mr. and Mrs. Brown go to work (5) ________ by car. Mr. Brown (6) ________ drives. Mrs. Brown never drives. The Browns have a boy and a girl. Peter is fourteen and Ann is (7) ________. Ann doesn't live with her (8) ________. She lives in London and works as a (9) ________ in a (10) ________.

三、听下面的对话，根据对话内容回答相应的问题。

(　　) 1. Where is the man now?
A. In a restaurant.　　B. In a shop.　　C. In a bookstore.

(　　) 2. What time is it now?
A. 1:50.　　B. 2:15.　　C. 1:45.

(　　) 3. What's the number of Jane's sister's room?
A. Room 1004.　　B. Room 1046.　　C. Room 1006.

( ) 4. What are they talking about?

A. Date. B. Time. C. Weather.

( ) 5. What's the man doing?

A. He's telling the way to the woman.

B. He's going to the post office.

C. He's asking the way to the post office.

( ) 6. When does the play start?

A. At 7:00. B. At 7:15. C. At 7:30.

( ) 7. Why hasn't Mike finished reading the book?

A. Because he can't do it.

B. Because he doesn't like it.

C. Because he has been busy.

( ) 8. Where's Jack now?

A. In Australia. B. In Japan. C. At home.

( ) 9. Where does the dialogue take place?

A. In a school. B. At the station. C. At the post office.

( ) 10. What day is it today?

A. It's Monday. B. It's Saturday. C. It's Sunday.

四、你将听到几段对话，请根据对话内容选择合适的图片。

( ) 1. What does the woman need?

A. 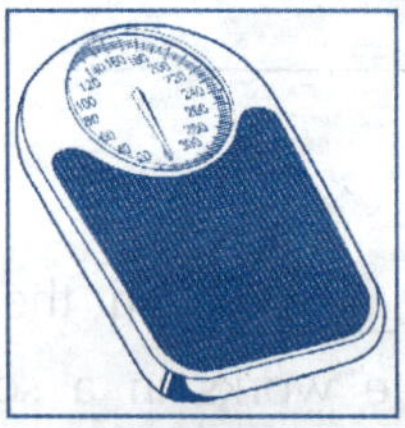 B.  C. 

( ) 2. What does the man need?

A.  B.  C. 

( ) 3. What does the woman need?

A.  B.  C. 

( ) 4. Where should Billy throw away the waste paper?

A.  B.  C. 

( ) 5. What is the man looking for?

A.  B. 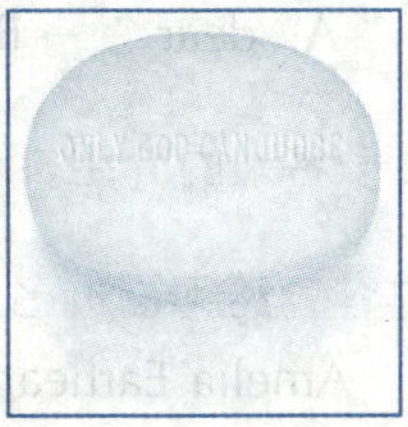 C. 

五、你将听到一段对话，请根据对话内容完成下面的练习。

( ) 1. The story happened in a (an) ________.

A. pet shop B. office C. theater

( ) 2. The woman went with ________.

A. her dog B. her husband C. her sister

( ) 3. How many tickets did the woman buy?

A. Zero. B. One. C. Two.

( ) 4. The manager allowed them to go in because ________.

A. they looked so poor

B. the manager knew the woman

C. the theater was almost empty that night

( ) 5. Which of the saying is true about this story?

A. The manager didn't allow the woman to enter.

B. The dog was very clever.

C. They didn't watch the movie at all.

Section 4

complete *v.* 完成	transatlantic *adj.* 横穿大西洋的
producer *n.* 制片人，制作人	creator *n.* 创造者
astronaut *n.* 宇航员	admission *n.* 承认
resist *v.* 抵抗，反抗	politics *n.* 政治
sneeze *v.* 打喷嚏	cure *n.* 治愈方法

一、请在左边的横线上写出你所听到的词语，并根据你所听到的词语选出它们的反义词。

1. ________ (　　) A. big　B. dirty　C. left
2. ________ (　　) A. dark　B. hot　C. full
3. ________ (　　) A. warm　B. light　C. small
4. ________ (　　) A. dry　B. wide　C. right
5. ________ (　　) A. dear　B. cheap　C. back

二、你将听到一些关于名人的介绍，请根据内容完成下面的练习。

（一）根据你听到的内容，给下面的名人按出现的顺序排序。

Leonardo Da Vinci

____

Amelia Earheart

____

Walt Disney

____

Neil Armstrong

____

（二）根据文章内容完成下面的句子，在横线上写出正确的年份。

1. In ________ this pilot became the first woman to fly across the Atlantic Ocean as a passenger.
2. The woman pilot disappeared over the Pacific in ________.
3. Mickey Mouse's first animated cartoon appeared in ________.
4. This Italian painter lived from ________ to ________.
5. He painted the *Mona Lisa* in about ________.
6. The *Mona Lisa* was stolen in ________.
7. The astronaut stepped onto the moon on July 20, ________.

三、你将听到一些录音片段，请根据所听内容完成下面的练习。

听第一段录音，完成 1 ~3 题。

(　　) 1. This news is a report about ________.
　　A. industry　B. education　C. politics

(　　) 2. March Madness is the name for the busy championship season in American college ________.
　　A. baseball　B. basketball　C. football

(　　) 3. It is talking about the subject of ________.

A. where to live　　B. where to go　　C. what to learn

听第二段录音，完成 4 ~ 5 题。

(　　) 4. These two people are talking about how to impress the ________.

A. barber　　B. butcher　　C. baker

(　　) 5. Where will they meet each other?

A. At the bar.　　B. In the market.　　C. At the hall.

四、下面你将听到一段文章，请根据文章内容分别写出下面各个人物和“我”的关系以及他们的名字。

五、你将听到一段短文，根据短文内容判断下列句子的正误。正确的在括号内写“T”，错误的在括号内写“F”。

(　　) 1. The cold often starts with a headache.

(　　) 2. The cold is not a serious disease, but you can feel quite ill.

( ) 3. You will feel an earache too when you have a cold.

( ) 4. There is no cure for a cold.

( ) 5. You will get well sooner if you take the right medicine.

Section 5

fiction movie 科幻片	rent *v.* 租借
action movie 动作片	violence *n.* 暴力
comedy *n.* 喜剧	horror movie 恐怖片
section *n.* 部分	Statue of Liberty 自由女神像
magnificent *adj.* 壮观的	souvenir *n.* 纪念品

一、根据你所听到的内容，将下面电影票的内容填满。下面已经给出一个例子。

你可能会用到以下电影名称：*Garfield*，*High School Musical*，*Shrek*，*Harry Potter*，*Ica Age*.

(Example) Barnfield Theater
Name: *Cinderella*
Date: February 10th
Ticket Type: adults
Price: £12. 95

(1) ________ Theater
Name: ________
Date: ________
Ticket Type: ________
Price: ________

(2) ________ Theater
Name: ________
Date: ________
Ticket Type: students
Price: ________

(3) Magic Theater
Name: ________
Date: ________
Ticket Type: ________
Price: ________

(4) ________ Theater
Name: ________
Date: ________
Ticket Type: ________
Price: ________

(5) ________ Theater
Name: ________
Date: ________
Ticket Type: ________
Price: ________

二、你将听到几段对话，请根据对话内容选择合适的答案。

( ) 1. A. Mike. B. Lucy. C. Bill.

(　　) 2. A. Amy.
B. His daughter.
C. His daughter's teacher.

(　　) 3. A. Every three minutes.
B. Every seven minutes.
C. We don't know.

(　　) 4. A. Listening to music.
B. Reading a newspaper.
C. Writing a novel.

(　　) 5. A. She's had enough.
B. She's losing weight.
C. She's not feeling well.

三、你将听到两段对话，根据对话内容完成下面的练习。

听第一段对话，完成1 ~5 题。

(　　) 1. Action: A. Like. B. Dislike.

(　　) 2. Comedies: A. Like. B. Dislike.

(　　) 3. Horror: A. Like. B. Dislike.

(　　) 4. Love: A. Like. B. Dislike.

(　　) 5. Foreign: A. Like. B. Dislike.

听第二段对话，完成6 ~10 题。

(　　) 6. What is the father reading at the beginning of the conversation?
A. A novel. B. A magazine. C. A newspaper.

(　　) 7. What kind of book does the girl want to read?
A. A book about animals.
B. A book on dolls.
C. A book about candy and cookies.

(　　) 8. What does the girl's teacher say about reading?
A. The girl can check out books from the library.
B. The girl should read books every day.
C. The girl ought to read at least ten books a night.

(　　) 9. What does the girl want to eat while they are reading?
A. Cookies. B. Ice cream. C. Bananas.

(　　) 10. About what time of day is it in the conversation?
A. The late morning.
B. The early afternoon.
C. In the evening.

四、你将听到一段短文，请将短文内容写在下面这张明信片里面。

Dear Tom,

We're ________________________________

____

____

____

I have bought some souvenirs ____________

____

Hope ________________________________

Love,

Sara

Tom Hanks

Oxford Gardens

London

LN34TW

U. K.

Unit 8

Section 1

additional	*adj.* 额外的，增加的	brand	*n.* 商标，牌子
announcement	*n.* 通知，通告	sweat shirt	运动衫

一、在横线上写出你所听到的词语。

1. ________ 2. ________ 3. ________ 4. ________
5. ________ 6. ________ 7. ________ 8. ________
9. ________ 10. ________ 11. ________ 12. ________
13. ________ 14. ________ 15. ________ 16. ________
17. ________ 18. ________ 19. ________ 20. ________

二、你将听到十个句子，请选出你所听到的词语。

( ) 1. A. live B. believe C. past
( ) 2. A. butter B. break C. best
( ) 3. A. meter B. counter C. corner
( ) 4. A. crowd B. crowded C. loud
( ) 5. A. feel B. fell C. dial
( ) 6. A. a lot B. a lot of C. lots of
( ) 7. A. back B. bed C. bad
( ) 8. A. found B. founded C. richer
( ) 9. A. pear B. shoe C. pair
( ) 10. A. blow B. blouse C. suits

三、请听下面的人物介绍，并为他们的职业选择合适的工具。

A. 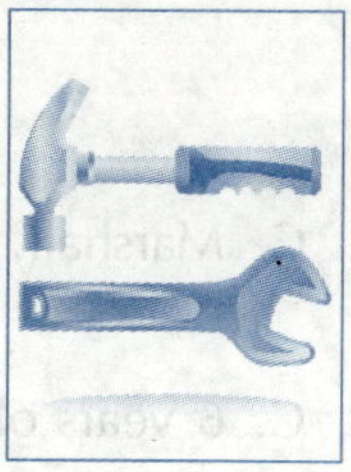

B. 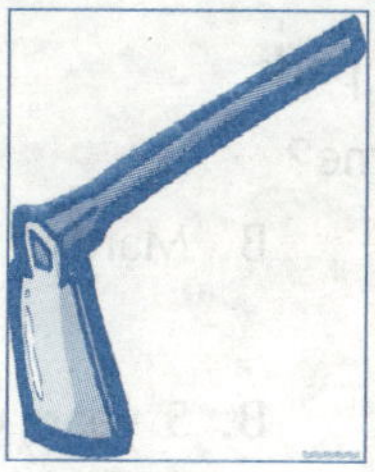

C. 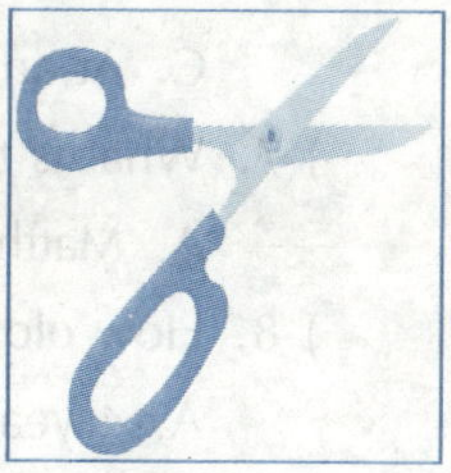

D. 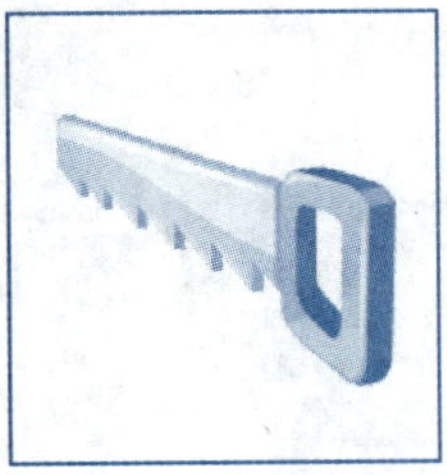 E.  F. 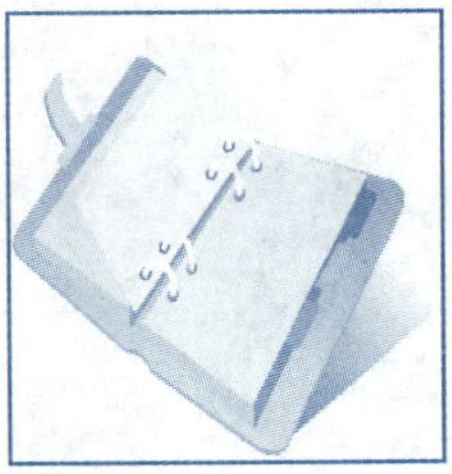

Alice	Mike	Lisa	Roy	John

四、听下面两段独白，根据独白的内容完成下面的练习。

听第一段独白，完成1 ~5 题。

(　　) 1. What does this store sell?

A.  B.  C. 

(　　) 2. What is the name of the store?

A. American Village. B. American Image. C. American Vision.

(　　) 3. What time does the store open on Wednesday?

A. 8 : 00 am. B. 8 : 30 am. C. 9 : 00 am.

(　　) 4. What day is the store closed?

A. Sunday. B. Saturday. C. Friday.

(　　) 5. How much would you pay for this store's main product on Saturday if it cost $100 during the rest of week?

A. $90. B. $80. C. $70.

听第二段独白，完成6 ~10 题。

(　　) 6. Where does the announcement take place?

A. At a department store.

B. In a cinema.

C. At an amusement park.

(　　) 7. What is the boy's name?

A. Matthew. B. Martin. C. Marshall.

(　　) 8. How old is the boy?

A. 4 years old. B. 5 years old. C. 6 years old.

(　　) 9. What is the boy wearing?

A. A blue baseball cap.

B. Black and white pants.

C. A blue and white sweat shirt.

(　　) 10. Where is the boy now?

A. He is at the information desk.

B. He is waiting in the sporting goods section.

C. He is at the cashier where you pay for goods.

Section 2

abroad *adv.* 到国外	set out 出发

一、请根据你所听到的句子写出句子中所缺的部分。

1. This is the ______________.
2. The ______________ is one of Beijing's ______________.
3. It's ______________.
4. I have just ______________.
5. ______________ the students ______________.
6. You'll ______________ Beijing next week, ______________?
7. What is your ______________?
8. There is ______________.
9. I ______________ at 9 last night.
10. She ______________ to go with her.

二、听下面十个句子，选出与你所听到的句子意思相同或最相近的句子。

(　　) 1. A. What a nice picture!

B. How nice the pictures are!

C. What great photos!

(　　) 2. A. I like to live abroad.

B. I hope to go with you together.

C. I hope to go abroad one day.

(　　) 3. A. What is the size of these shoes?

B. What size is this shoe?

C. How big is this shoe?

( ) 4. A. How long is it?
B. How far is it from here to the hospital?
C. How far is the nearest hospital?

( ) 5. A. Did you go to the seaside?
B. Did you enjoy yourself at the seaside?
C. Which seaside did you go?

( ) 6. A. I drink both tea and coffee.
B. I like tea better than coffee.
C. I like coffee better than tea.

( ) 7. A. I don't often go on a business trip.
B. I usually go on a business trip.
C. I never go on a business trip.

( ) 8. A. May I buy you a dictionary?
B. Can I lend you my dictionary?
C. Could you lend me your dictionary?

( ) 9. A. Liz is the cleverest in her class.
B. Liz is very clever.
C. Liz is the cleverest girl in her class.

( ) 10. A. Miss Green left just now.
B. Miss Green has left already.
C. Miss Green has been away for an hour.

三、请看下面这幅地图，根据你所听到的句子判断出以下五个地点，并在横线上填入表示该地点的词语。

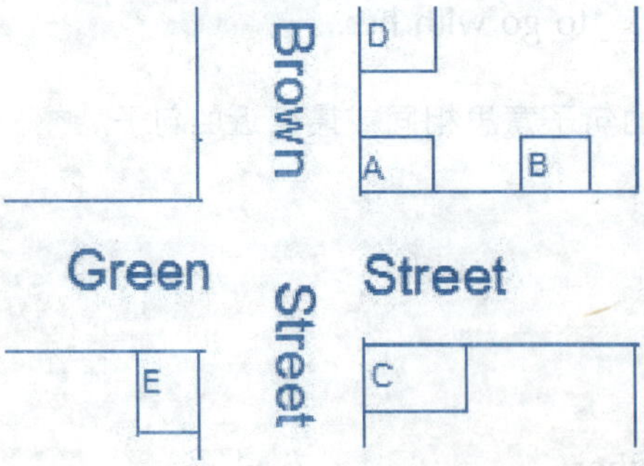

A. ________ shop
B. ________
C. ________
D. ________
E. ________

四、听下面的对话，并根据对话的内容将下面的句子补充完整。

1. There was a new ________ each year when Peter was young.
2. When the ________ child was born, they had to move to another house.

3. Peter's mother often helped her parents to ________ her little brothers or sisters.
4. Peter's mother comes from a ________ family.
5. Peter's family has ________ children.

五、你将听到一篇文章，请根据所听内容判断正误。正确的用“T”表示，错误的用“F”表示。

(　　) 1. The old farmer was going to sell his horse because it was too old.
(　　) 2. The old farmer was too tired to walk on, so he rode on the horse.
(　　) 3. When the boy was riding on the horse, a young lady stopped them.
(　　) 4. The farmer took two old men's advice and rode on the horse with his son.
(　　) 5. The story told us it's impossible to make everyone happy.

Section 3

celebrate *v.* 庆祝	check *v.* 检查

一、听写句子。

1. ________________________________
2. ________________________________
3. ________________________________
4. ________________________________
5. ________________________________
6. ________________________________
7. ________________________________
8. ________________________________
9. ________________________________
10. ________________________________

二、根据你所听到的歌曲内容完成下面的练习。

When you mail a letter, you can (1) ________ it anywhere.
On foot; by (2) ________; by aeroplane. The postman gets it there.
So write a letter to a (3) ________, maybe she'll write you.
No matter what you always know. The mail must go through.
Well, the mail must go through. The mail must go through.
No matter if it rains or snows. The mail must go through.

The mail must go through. The mail must go through.
No matter if it rains or snows. The mail must go through.
Some folks live in a city, some live in a little (4) ________.
Even if you live out on a (5) ________. There's a postman (6) ________ his rounds.
So mail someone a letter, even just a (7) ________ will do.
You know it's (8) ________ when the postman, has a letter in his sack for you.

三、根据你所听到的问句，挑出你所需要的物品。

( ) 1. A.  B.  C. 

( ) 2. A.  B.  C. 

( ) 3. A. 

B. 

C. 

( ) 4. A.  B.  C. 

( ) 5. A.  B.  C. 

四、听下面十个句子，并选择相应的答语。

( ) 1. A. No. I've only seen some of the trailers.

B. Yes. I like it a lot.

C. I really enjoy action movies.

(　　) 2. A. I want to buy it.

B. It's a love story.

C. How about 7 o'clock?

(　　) 3. A. Oh, thanks for reminding me.

B. Thanks. I'd better check my tickets.

C. Yes. I didn't forget to bring my glasses.

(　　) 4. A. It runs about two hours.

B. It ends at 3:00 pm.

C. It starts at noon.

(　　) 5. A. Three people.

B. That'll be all.

C. No. We're not ready yet.

(　　) 6. A. T-bone steak, please.

B. Medium, please.

C. I'd like rice with my steak.

(　　) 7. A. The meal is ready.

B. I'll have another.

C. So far, so good.

(　　) 8. A. Sorry, but books are not included.

B. Yes, you can pay online.

C. Yes, we do. They begin at 7:00 pm.

(　　) 9. A. You can meet many new students in class.

B. The class meets three times a week.

C. Sure. We can meet after the class today.

(　　) 10. A. You can read in the library.

B. The textbook is very cheap.

C. You can get it at the bookstore.

五、你将听到一篇短文，请根据短文内容为下面的事件排序。

(　　) Mr. and Mrs. Smith went to see the movie together.

(　　) Mr. Smith found two movie tickets in his car.

(　　) The policeman said he would try to find Mr. Smith's car.

(　　) Mr. Smith parked his car outside his house as usual.

(　　) Mr. Smith told the police that his car was stolen.

(　　) The thieves stole everything in Mr. Smith's house.

Section 4

nickname *n.* 昵称	identity *n.* 身份
gallery *n.* 画廊	pharmacy *n.* 药店
interview *v.* 采访	environment *n.* 环境
garbage *n.* 垃圾	trashcan *n.* （公共）垃圾桶
littering *n.* 乱扔废弃物的行为	recycle *v.* 回收利用

一、你将听到一段录音片段，请根据所听内容完成下面的练习。

( ) 1. Chapter One is talking about the ________.
A. trouble B. fight C. hometown

( ) 2. What is the weather like?
A. Hot and sunny. B. Cold and dry. C. Cold and rainy.

( ) 3. How many cousins does Jane have?
A. Two. B. Three. C. Four.

二、请根据你所听到的对话，选择最佳的答案。

( ) 1. What would the man order?
A. Wine. B. Tea. C. Nothing.

( ) 2. What fruit does the man want to buy?
A. Apple. B. Orange. C. Banana.

( ) 3. What does the boy want to be?
A. A football player. B. An engineer. C. A nurse.

( ) 4. What does Bob like doing?
A. Fishing. B. Swimming. C. Dancing.

( ) 5. What's the woman going to do this Saturday afternoon?
A. To study at home. B. To see a film. C. To attend a lecture.

( ) 6. How many people will probably attend the meeting?
A. 18. B. 30. C. 35.

( ) 7. When does the library open on Saturdays?
A. 8:00 am. B. 9:00 am. C. 10:00 am.

( ) 8. What does the man think of the movie?
A. It's moving. B. It's interesting. C. He doesn't like it.

(　　) 9. How will the woman go to the Hubei Museum?

A. By underground.　　B. By bus.　　C. By taxi.

(　　) 10. What is Mary?

A. A doctor.　　B. A teacher.　　C. A student.

三、听句子，根据下面这幅图判断句子的正误并做出相应的选择。

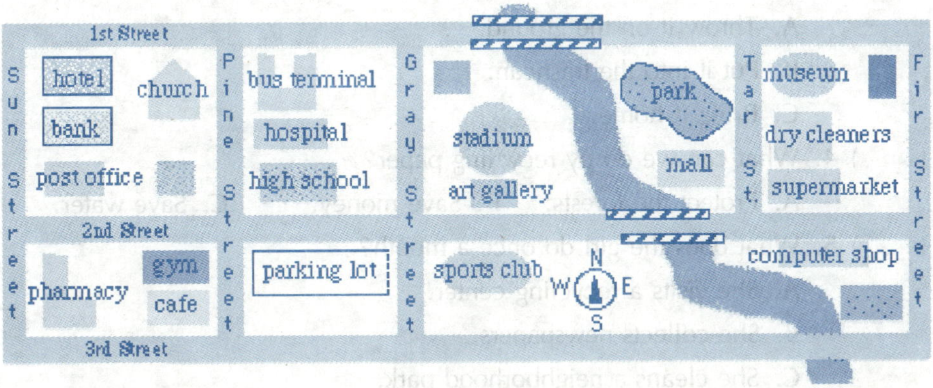

(　　) 1. The ________ is between the museum and the supermarket.

A. True.　　B. False.

(　　) 2. The mall is ________ the supermarket.

A. True.　　B. False.

(　　) 3. The park is ________.

A. True.　　B. False.

(　　) 4. The art gallery ________ the cafe.

A. True.　　B. False.

(　　) 5. The pharmacy is on the corner of ________.

A. True.　　B. False.

四、你将听到一家宾馆对 Tom 电话的回复。请根据所听内容完成下面的表格。

Floor of the 2 rooms	on the (1) ________ floor
Price for each room	(2) ________ per night
Free meal	(3) ________
Things to bring	his (4) ________
Time to arrive	on (5) ________

五、你将听到一段长对话，请根据对话内容完成下面的练习。

(　　) 1. What is the name of the girl?
　A. Emily.　　B. Alice.　　C. Ann.

(　　) 2. When shall we save water according to the girl?
　A. Washing cars.　　B. Watering plants.　　C. Taking a bath.

(　　) 3. What must we do with the garbage?
　A. Throw it on the ground.
　B. Put it into the trashcan.
　C. Bring it home.

(　　) 4. What can we do by recycling paper?
　A. Protect the forests.　　B. Save money.　　C. Save water.

(　　) 5. What does the girl do once a month?
　A. She visits a recycling center.
　B. She collects newspapers.
　C. She cleans a neighborhood park.

Section 5

block *n.* 街区	practice *v.* 练习	survey *v.* 调查
chart *n.* 图表	activity *n.* 活动	place of interests 名胜

一、你将听到一段对话，请根据对话内容找出下面这段对话中的错误。在错误的地方画上横线，并将正确的内容填在后面的横线上。

M: Mary, have I given you my pictures? (1) ________
W: No, you haven't. Are these your pictures of Canada? (2) ________
M: Yes, they are. I took them last week. (3) ________
W: Did you take any pictures of the modern buildings there? (4) ________
M: Yes, I took some. Here they are.
W: You took wonderful pictures! Did you enjoy yourselves in New York? (5) ________
M: Yes, I did. Have you ever been there?
W: No, I haven't. I've never been there! (6) ________
M: Don't you want to go to New York sometime? (7) ________
W: Yes, I do. I'll go there someday.

二、听句子，根据下面这幅图判断句子的正误并做出相应的选择。

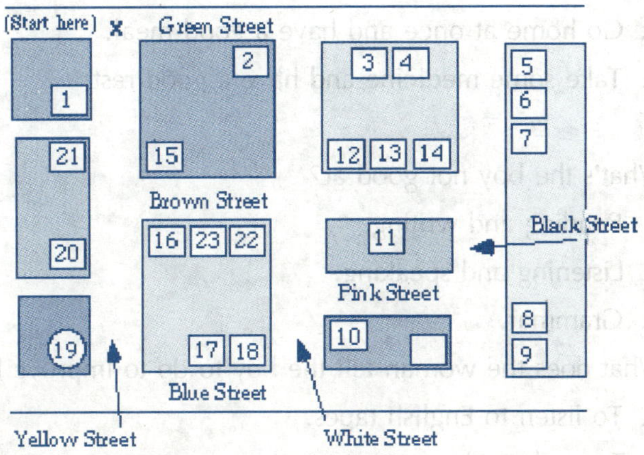

(　　) 1. Where is the bank?

A. 6.　　B. 7.　　C. 14.

(　　) 2. Where is the school?

A. 18.　　B. 19.　　C. 20.

(　　) 3. Where is the library?

A. 22.　　B. 12.　　C. 10.

(　　) 4. Where is the hotel?

A. 23.　　B. 12.　　C. 13.

(　　) 5. Where is the church?

A. 18.　　B. 9.　　C. 10.

三、听下面几段对话，根据题中的问题选择合适的答案。

听第一段对话，回答 1 ~3 题。

(　　) 1. What's the matter with Linda?

A. She has a sore back.

B. She has a headache.

C. She has a fever.

(　　) 2. How will she go to the doctor's?

A. By car.　　B. On foot.　　C. By bike.

(　　) 3. What time must she get there?

A. At 8:45.　　B. At 9:00.　　C. At 9:15.

听第二段对话，回答 4 ~5 题。

(　　) 4. Where are the man and the woman?

A. In a shop.　　B. In the street.　　C. At the doctor's.

(　　) 5. What will the man have to do next?

A. Stay in hospital for some time.

B. Go home at once and have a good meal.

C. Take some medicine and have a good rest.

听第三段对话，回答 6 ~7 题。

(　　) 6. What's the boy not good at?

A. Reading and writing.

B. Listening and speaking.

C. Grammar.

(　　) 7. What does the woman tell the boy to do to improve his speaking?

A. To listen to English tapes.

B. To study with a group.

C. To join an English club.

四、请看下面的图表，根据你所听到的问题选出合适的答案。

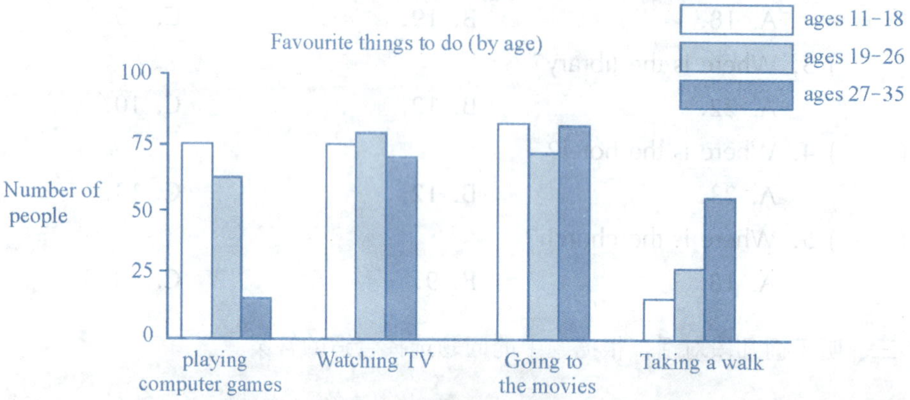

(　　) 1. A. 25.　　B. 50.　　C. 75.

(　　) 2. A. 25.　　B. 50.　　C. 75.

(　　) 3. A. Watching TV.

B. Taking a walk.

C. Going to the movies.

(　　) 4. A. Age 11-18.　　B. Age 19-26.　　C. Age 27-35.

(　　) 5. A. Playing computer games and watching TV.

B. Watching TV and going to the movies.

C. Taking a walk and playing computer games.

五、你将听到一篇短文，请将短文的内容写在下面的横线上。

Unit 9

Section 1

sneaker *n.* 运动鞋	vast *adj.* 广阔的
extend *v.* 延伸；扩大	sleet *n.* 雨夹雪
burn（burnt-burnt） *v.* 燃烧；晒伤	

一、单词听写。

1. ________ 2. ________ 3. ________ 4. ________
5. ________ 6. ________ 7. ________ 8. ________
9. ________ 10. ________ 11. ________ 12. ________
13. ________ 14. ________ 15. ________ 16. ________
17. ________ 18. ________ 19. ________ 20. ________

二、听下面的十个句子，选出与句子内容相关的图片。

(　　) 1. A.  B.  C. 

(　　) 2. A.  B.  C. 

(　　) 3. A.  B.  C. 

(　　) 4. A. 

B. 
C. 

(　　) 5. A. 
B. 
C. 

(　　) 6. A. 
B. 
C. 

(　　) 7. A. 
B. 
C. 

(　　) 8. A. 
B. 
C. 

(　　) 9. A. 
B. 
C. 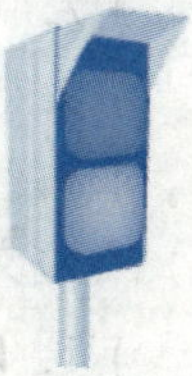

(　　) 10. A. 
B. 
C. 

三、听下面的六段对话，根据对话的内容选出最佳答案。

(　　) 1. How is the weather?

A. It's raining.　　B. It's cloudy.　　C. It's sunny.

(　　) 2. Where did the woman stop?

A. Near the shop.　　B. Near the bus stop.　　C. Near the airport.

(　　) 3. What are they going to do?

A. They are going to stay at home.

B. They are going to the park.

C. They are going to go home.

(　　) 4. What does the man want to borrow?

A. A dictionary.　　B. An English textbook.　　C. A ruler.

(　　) 5. What is the relationship between the speakers?

A. Father and son.

B. Teacher and student.

C. Doctor and patient.

(　　) 6. Who got burnt?

A. Ann did.　　B. The man did.　　C. The woman did.

四、听短文，完成下面两组练习。

（一）听短文，根据所听内容判断哪些事情是 Frank 做的，哪些事情是 Alice 做的，哪些事情是两人一起做的，在括号内标明 F（Frank），A（Alice）或 T（Together）。

(　　) 1. Talking or playing cards.　　(　　) 2. Going shopping.

(　　) 3. Cooking breakfast.　　(　　) 4. Visiting friends.

(　　) 5. Watching TV.　　(　　) 6. Reading the newspaper.

(　　) 7. Cleaning the house.　　(　　) 8. Going to the church.

(　　) 9. Walking the dog.　　(　　) 10. Taking care of the garden.

(　　) 11. Playing baseball.　　(　　) 12. Cooking supper.

（二）听短文，根据所听内容选出最佳答案。

(　　) 1. Frank and Alice are ________.

A. a couple　　B. mother and son　　C. brother and sister

(　　) 2. When do they cook together?

A. On Sunday morning.

B. Every evening.

C. On Sunday evening.

(　　) 3. What is the name of their dog?

A. David.　　B. Alex.　　C. Coddy.

Section 2

handle *n.* 处理；操作	faith *n.* 信仰；忠实	drawer *n.* 抽屉
post *v.* 邮寄	drift *v.* 漂泊；漂流	

一、听一段英文歌，填补所缺的内容。

Hold me like a friend
Kiss me like a friend
Say we'll never (1) ________
Searching for the colors of the rainbow
Melody never (2) ________
I'll be near you
Some people handle love in and never try
I can almost (3) ________ with your wings to set me higher
Some day we'll see the world
And through the grey have faith in our (4) ________
Hold me like a friend
Kiss me like a friend
Say we'll never (5) ________
Searching for the colors of the rainbow
Melody never say goodbye
We'll always be (6) ________

二、听下面的十个句子，选出对应的答语。

( ) 1. A. Certainly. B. Which road, please? C. No, thanks.
( ) 2. A. Yes, he does. B. No, he isn't. C. The same to you.
( ) 3. A. At 10 o'clock. B. It's so hot in summer. C. Beijing.
( ) 4. A. By bike. B. In the water. C. I really enjoy it.
( ) 5. A. Jun. 1st. B. July 1st. C. Sept. 10th.
( ) 6. A. Very quickly. B. Twice every day. C. As you wish.
( ) 7. A. Happy to hear that. B. Help yourselves. C. Quite well.
( ) 8. A. No, not at all. B. Thank you. C. You are the best.
( ) 9. A. It's wonderful. B. 40 yuan each. C. Congratulations.
( ) 10. A. I'm Jennifer. B. Good idea. C. Speaking.

三、听下面的六段对话，选出与对话内容相关的图片。

( ) 1. A. 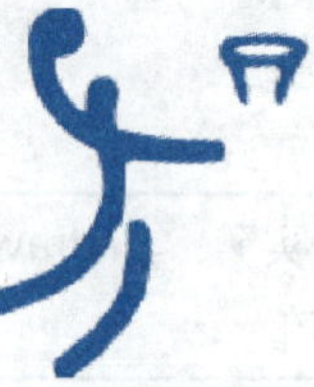 B.  C. 

( ) 2. A.  B.  C. 

( ) 3. A.  B.  C. 

( ) 4. A.  B.  C. 

( ) 5. A. Beijing 2008 B. EXPO 2010 SHANGHAI CHINA C. Unesco FASHION

( ) 6. A.  B.  C. 

四、听短文，按照你所听到的顺序给句子编号。

( ) A bike knocked me down.

( ) I met Mrs. Jenkins in the park.

( ) Mark didn't hear me.

( ) The dog ran away.

(　　) I saw Mark in the street.
(　　) I walked home myself.
(　　) The bike-boy said sorry to me.
(　　) The dog was playing with another dog.

五、听对话，回答问题。

1. Why is Tim so excited?
____
2. How many of the woman's friends are still in touch with her?
____
3. Why is it difficult to keep in touch with old friends?
____

Section 3

backward	*adv.*	相反地；向后地	stain	*n.*	污点；斑点
absurd	*adj.*	荒谬的；可笑的	directory	*n.*	姓名地址录
assistance	*n.*	援助；帮助			

一、听写词组。

1. ________ 2. ________ 3. ________
4. ________ 5. ________ 6. ________
7. ________ 8. ________ 9. ________
10. ________ 11. ________ 12. ________

二、听短文，判断下列句子是否正确，正确用 T（True）表示，错误用 F（False）表示。

(　　) 1. Today is Saturday.
(　　) 2. Sky is going to his grandpa's on Friday evening.
(　　) 3. David is going to his dentist.
(　　) 4. Angela is going to her table tennis class.
(　　) 5. Three girls are going to the beach on Saturday.
(　　) 6. There will be a movie on Saturday afternoon.
(　　) 7. Three boys are going to the park.
(　　) 8. I'm going to Jennifer's party at the weekend.

三、听六段独白，完成连线。

Robin Ester Bill Albert Kyo Bruce

America China Japan Australia France Canada

四、听英文歌，根据歌词内容选择最佳答案。

( ) 1. Where was the man?
A. New York. B. Washington D. C. C. Tennesee.

( ) 2. Where did the old boy sit?
A. Next to the man. B. Before the counter. C. Near the fire.

( ) 3. Why did the man think the boy had been through some hard times?
A. Because he saw it with his eyes.
B. Because the boy told him about it.
C. Because there were tear stains on his shirt.

( ) 4. You can get the following things back except ________.
A. your house B. your best friend C. your old radio

( ) 5. What did they talk about?
A. How to mend the washing machine.
B. How their life would be.
C. How to get their houses and jobs.

( ) 6. That is what you get when you play a ________ song backwards.
A. country B. pop C. rock

五、听对话，填补所缺的内容。

NAME	ADDRESS	TELEPHONE
William Abel	6418 Green St.	(1) ________
Thomas Eakins	(2) ________	(3) ________
(4) ________	279 Woodland Dr.	789-5430
Diana Paxon	(5) ________	(6) ________
James Bingham	5213 Rose Rd.	(7) ________

Section 4

emergency *n.* 紧急状况；突发事件	department *n.* 部门　exist *v.* 存在
care *v.* 关心；在意；喜爱	peace *n.* 宁静；和平
besides *adv.* 而且；此外	relax *v.* 放松；休息；松懈

一、听写单句。

1. ______________________________
2. ______________________________
3. ______________________________
4. ______________________________
5. ______________________________
6. ______________________________
7. ______________________________
8. ______________________________
9. ______________________________
10. ______________________________

二、听下面六段对话，每段对话后有一个问题，仔细听这个问题，并根据对话内容选出最佳答案。

(　　) 1. A. Tea.　B. Milk.　C. I don't know.

(　　) 2. A. A policeman.　B. A singer.　C. A student.

(　　) 3. A. 229 King's Street.　B. 129 Central Street.　C. 329 Maple Street.

(　　) 4. A. Lucy.　B. Lily.　C. Billy.

(　　) 5. A. Schoolwork.　B. Homework.　C. Housework.

(　　) 6. A. On the phone.
B. At the children's hospital.
C. Fire Department.

三、听电影评论，根据你所听到的内容选出最佳答案。

(　　) 1. What is the name of the host?
A. Sid.　B. Marco.　C. Tony.

(　　) 2. Which movie is he talking about?

A. *Ice Age Ⅰ*.　　B. *Ice Age Ⅱ*.　　C. *Ice Age Ⅲ*.

(　　) 3. Which animal still exists today?

A. Mammoth.　　B. Sloth.　　C. Saber-toothed tiger.

(　　) 4. What is the main and favourite character in the movie?

A. The mammoth.　　B. A squirrel.　　C. The tiger.

(　　) 5. Why is the movie different from all the others?

A. It is in 3D format.　B. It is an animated one.　C. Children love it.

四、听独白，完成相应的练习。

（一）根据对话的内容，把相应的人名、图片与地名连线。

Lee　　Sarah　　Jewel

Aspen　　New York　　Acapulco

（二）填补所缺的内容。

1. I'm interested in ________, ________ and the theater.
2. I don't care much for ________; I can't ski and I can't swim. I hate ___________.
3. I enjoy the peace and quiet of the ___________. I love to ski and I want to get away from ___________.
4. I think Acapulco is ___________ and besides I can't speak Spanish.
5. I want to relax, ________, ________ and go to discos in the evening.
6. I think ___________ is dirty, dangerous and expensive.

Section 5

neighbourhood *n.* 街坊；附近一带	energetic *adj.* 精力充沛的；强有力的	
helmet *n.* 头盔	lumberjack *n.* 伐木工人	experience *n.* 经历
apartment *n.* 公寓	continue *v.* 继续	graduate *v.* 毕业
festival *n.* 节日	nursing home 疗养院	

一、听独白，根据所听内容给每个人物写上名字。

__________ __________ __________ __________

__________ __________ __________ __________

二、听四段电影片段，根据你所听到的内容选出最佳答案。

听第一段电影片段，回答1 ~2 题。

(　　) 1. What's wrong with Mrs. Huber?

A. She has a cold.

B. She has a stomachache.

C. She has a toothache.

(　　) 2. Who is going to have a gentleman friend over for dinner?

A. Edie.　　B. Mike.　　C. Susan.

听第二段电影片段，回答3 ~4 题。

(　　) 3. When did the students of William Dawes Elementary imagine what the future might hold?

A. 30 years ago.　　B. 40 years ago.　　C. 50 years ago.

(　　) 4. What is on the paper?

A. A list of names.　　B. A list of dates.　　C. A list of places.

听第三段电影片段，回答5 ~6 题。

(　　) 5. What is the relationship between Serena and Eric?

A. Father and daughter.　　B. Schoolmates.　　C. Brother and sister.

(　　) 6. Where was Eric according to Serena?

A. Rhode Island.　　B. Miami.　　C. Boarding school.

听第四段电影片段，回答 7 ~8 题。

(　　) 7. How many children does Maggie have?

A. Three.　　B. Two.　　C. Four.

(　　) 8. What did Ben do to the girl?

A. Let her get into the house.

B. Leave her standing outside.

C. Get her a seat.

三、听对话，填补所缺的内容。

Event	Wilmette Elementary School			Munich	UCLA		
Year	1960	1968	1972			1979	1982

四、听写。

____

____

____

____

____

____

____

____

____

____

____

Unit 10

Section 1

escalator *n.* 手扶电梯	choice *n.* 选择
frame *n.* 框架	instead of 代替
greet *v.* 问候	common *adj.* 平常的
rude *adj.* 粗鲁的	

一、单词听写。

1. ________ 2. ________ 3. ________ 4. ________
5. ________ 6. ________ 7. ________ 8. ________
9. ________ 10. ________ 11. ________ 12. ________
13. ________ 14. ________ 15. ________ 16. ________
17. ________ 18. ________ 19. ________ 20. ________

二、听下面的十个时间，根据你听到的顺序给表盘排序。

( ) ( ) ( ) ( ) ( )

( ) ( ) ( ) ( ) ( )

三、听下面的六段对话，选出与所提问题相关的最佳图片。

( ) 1. Which place is the woman looking for?

A. 
B. 
C. 

( ) 2. What is the woman going to do?

A. 
B. 
C. 

( ) 3. What are they talking about?

A. 
B. 
C. 

( ) 4. Where does the woman want to visit?

A. 
B. 
C. 

( ) 5. What are they doing now?

A. 
B. 
C. 

( ) 6. Which of the following is not mentioned in the dialogue?

A. 
B. 

C. 

四、听对话，填补所缺内容。

Kelly's Schedule (January, 2010)

	Time	Event	With
Monday			
Tuesday			
Wednesday			
Thursday			
Friday			
Saturday			

五、听短文，完成下面两组练习。

（一）判断下列句子是否正确，正确用 T（True）表示，错误用 F（False）表示。

( ) 1. "How are you" is only a question.

( ) 2. People always say they are fine even if they are not.

( ) 3. People want to hear your own idea when they ask "do you think so?"

( ) 4. Sometimes, people don't say exactly what they are thinking about.

( ) 5. When you say "I have too much homework", you mean the teachers give you too much homework.

（二）根据所听内容选出最佳答案。

( ) 1. "How are you" and "fine" are ________.

A. ways of greeting each other

B. ways to ask and answer questions

C. ways of playing a game of language

( ) 2. If you don't think someone is right, you say "________" to be friendly.

A. no, I think you are wrong

B. I don't agree with you

C. well, I'm not sure about it

( ) 3. Which of the following statements is not mentioned in the passage?

A. Sometimes people don't say directly what they mean.

B. Sometimes people don't mean exactly what they say.

C. Sometimes people don't say exactly what they are thinking about.

( ) 4. You say "________" when you want to end a talk.

A. I have nothing to say now

B. I have too much homework

C. I have to go now

Section 2

service *n.* 服务	microwave oven 微波炉	advise *v.* 建议
speech contest 演讲比赛	prepare *v.* 准备	photography *n.* 摄影

一、听句子，填补所缺的单词。

1. Western people don't like to ________ people their ________.
2. They are very tired and ________ now.
3. Tony is born into a ________ family.
4. He turns ________ the boat and runs ________ the hat.
5. We can't buy anything ________ we don't have enough ________.
6. George Washington was the ________ president of the United States.
7. I ________ for two days and ________ to a village.
8. He is now ________ ________ some sheep at the top of a small hill.
9. Every day he carried ________ from down the hill and cooked for ________.
10. By this time, the bears were ________ ________ ________ back home.

二、听下面的六段对话，选出与所提问题相关的最佳图片。

(　　) 1. A.

B.

C.

(　　) 2. A.

B.

C.

(　　) 3. A.

B.

C.
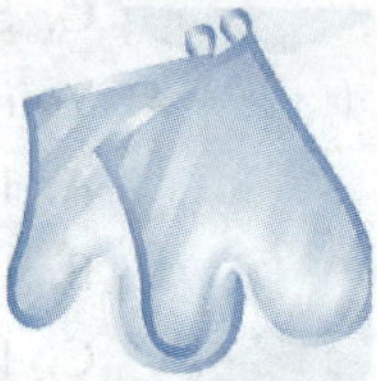

(　　) 4. A.  B. 

C. 

(　　) 5. A.  B.  C. 

(　　) 6. A.  B.  C. 

三、听下面的五段对话，填补所缺的时间。

Place	Post Office	Citibank	Museum of Modern Art	Macy's	Rexall Drugstore
Open					
Close					

四、听下面的五段对话，根据对话内容选出最佳答案。

听第一段对话，回答1～2题。

(　　) 1. What is the girl probably going to do tomorrow evening?

A. Go shopping. B. Wash the car. C. Go to the party.

(　　) 2. When will there be a party?

A. Tomorrow evening.

B. The day after tomorrow.

C. Saturday night.

听第二段对话，回答3～4题。

(　　) 3. How does Susan like the picnic?

A. Very much. B. Not bad. C. Just so so.

(　　) 4. Where does Mike work?

A. IBM. B. B&Q. C. P&G.

听第三段对话，回答5~6题。

( ) 5. Where is Cinema One?

A. 600 meters from here. B. Next to Pine. C. On Macy's.

( ) 6. What kind of building is Cinema One?

A. A department store. B. A movie theater. C. A restaurant.

听第四段对话，回答7~8题。

( ) 7. Which musical instrument can May play well?

A. The piano. B. The guitar. C. The violin.

( ) 8. What does Ricky suggest Ben to do?

A. To learn to take photos of autumn fruit.

B. To have a photographic journey.

C. To take pictures when leaves turn color.

听第五段对话，回答9~10题。

( ) 9. How many pets does Angela have?

A. Two. B. Three. C. Four.

( ) 10. How long has Lizzy been at Larry's house?

A. A month. B. Two months. C. Three months.

五、听短文，完成下面的两组练习。

(一) 根据所听到的内容选择最佳答案。

( ) 1. What is the name of the program?

A. American Stories.

B. Words and Their Stories.

C. This Is America.

( ) 2. Which parts of the body is talked about in today's program?

A. Eyes, ears and nose.

B. Back, shoulders and chest.

C. Heart.

( ) 3. "Behind one's back" means ________.

A. when one is not here

B. when someone has a backache

C. when someone wants to play hide and sick

( ) 4. To "give someone the cold shoulder" means to ________.

A. give someone a sweater because he is cold

B. be unfriendly to someone

C. take away the coat from someone

(　　) 5. The program is read by ________.

A. Jill Moss　　B. Faith Lapidus　　C. Shirley Griffith

（二）填补所缺的内容。

1. When I am facing a lot of pressure at work, my back and neck will start to ________.
2. I have too many things to do because my supervisor is ________ ________ ________ all the time.
3. It is never ________ to unfairly harm or say bad things about other people.
4. This means she will do something for me, if I do something ________ for her in exchange.
5. I will keep silent because talking or repeating ________ will not do any good.

Section 3

caterpillar *n.* 毛毛虫	promise *v.* 承诺
triangle *n.* 三角形	circle *n.* 圆形
rectangle *n.* 长方形	result *n.* 结果

一、听下面的一段英文歌，填补所缺的内容。

Caterpillar in the tree
How you wonder (1) ____________
Can't go far but you can dream
Wish you may and wish you might
(2) ____________, hold on tight
I promise you there will come a day
Butterfly fly away
Butterfly fly away (Butterfly fly away)
Got your wings, now you can't stay
Take those dreams and (3) ____________
Butterfly fly away (Butterfly fly away)
You've been waiting for this day
All along and (4) ____________
Butterfly, butterfly, butterfly
(5) ____________

二、数字游戏。回答你听到的每个问题并将答案写在相应的图形内，然后按照要求计算。

（一）What's my lucky number?

（二）When is the meeting?

三、听下面的几段对话或短文，完成相应的练习。

（一）听一段短文，完成连线。

Monday	Japanese food
Tuesday	French food
Wednesday	Chinese food
Thursday	Indian food
Friday	Mexican food
Saturday	American food
Sunday	Italian food

（二）听下面的几段对话，根据对话和上一篇短文的内容选出最佳答案。

(　　) 1. When does the woman want to go to Jimmy's Restaurant?

A. Friday.　　B. Thursday.　　C. Sunday.

(　　) 2. Why doesn't she go to Jimmy's Restaurant?

A. Because she doesn't like English food.

B. Because the restaurant doesn't cook English food.

C. Because she likes homemade food very much.

(　　) 3. What kind of food does the woman like?

A. Chinese food, Japanese food and Mexican food.

B. Mexican food, Italian food and Chinese food.

C. Italian food, French food and American food.

(　　) 4. What day is it today?

A. Tuesday.　　B. Thursday.　　C. Saturday.

四、听下面的一段短文，回答问题。

1. Mr. Clark will go on ________________.
2. Mrs. Clark will go on ________________.
3. Sandy will go on ________________.
4. Sue will go on ________________.

Section 4

aspirin *n.* 阿司匹林（药物）	iron *v.* 熨烫
form *v.* 形成	balance *n.* 平衡
detox *n.* 排毒	bulk *n.* 容积；大量
protection *n.* 保护	commercial grade appliances 商用电器
satellite navigation 卫星导航	

一、听写单句。

1. ________________________________
2. ________________________________
3. ________________________________
4. ________________________________
5. ________________________________
6. ________________________________
7. ________________________________
8. ________________________________
9. ________________________________
10. ________________________________

二、听下面的几段对话，根据所听到的内容连线。

1. He is looking for — In the medicine cabinet.

On the desk.

2. He is looking for — On the table next to the sofa.

In the woman's purse.

3. He is looking for — On the iron board.

In the drawer on the right.

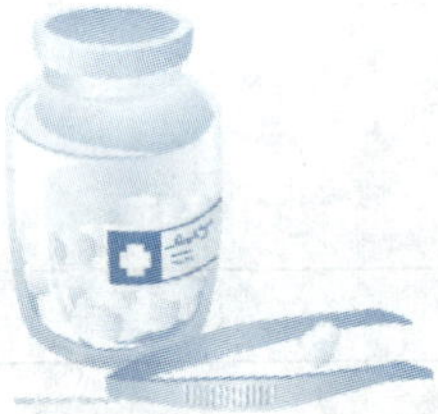

4. He is looking for — On the shelf to the right of the door.

In the file.

5. He is looking for — On the dresser in the bedroom.

On the television.

三、听下面的三段对话，根据对话内容选出最佳答案。

听第一段对话，回答 1 ~3 题。

(　　) 1. What is the weather like?
A. Cloudy.　　B. Windy.　　C. Sunny.

(　　) 2. Which is the woman's favourite sport?
A. Swimming.　　B. Dancing.　　C. Doing yoga.

(　　) 3. How does the woman like doing yoga?
A. Peaceful.　　B. Fun.　　C. Interesting.

听第二段对话，回答 4 ~6 题。

(　　) 4. Who is calling?
A. Steve.　　B. Mike.　　C. Tracy.

(　　) 5. When are they going to meet?
A. At 6 : 30.　　B. At 7 : 00.　　C. At 7 : 30.

(　　) 6. What is the man going to bring?
A. Flowers.　　B. Toys.　　C. Chocolates.

听第三段对话，回答 7 ~9 题。

(　　) 7. How did the man travel before?
A. By air.　　B. By land.　　C. By sea.

(　　) 8. Where is he going this time?
A. Shanghai.　　B. Beijing.　　C. Xi'an.

(　　) 9. Which of the following statements is true?
A. The man is worried before the trip.
B. You must get to the airport an hour before the plane takes off.
C. Going by overnight train is nice.

四、听短文，完成下面两组练习。

(一) 根据所听内容给下面的句子排序。

(　　) Detox
(　　) Big Box Bulk
(　　) Credit Card Protection Plans
(　　) Jeans
(　　) Commercial Grade Appliances
(　　) Gag Gifts
(　　) Kleenex Box Covers
(　　) Air Fresheners
(　　) Satellite Navigation
(　　) Home Exercise Equipment

（二）填补所缺的内容。

1. A penny ________ is a penny ________.
2. ________ are eating out more than ever.
3. The average American woman owns ________ pairs or more. Even at ________ off put them back.
4. If your house stinks, ________ it.
5. If you ________ ________ ________, it's not a bargain. It's a waste.

Section 5

opposite *prep.* 相反；相对	concert *n.* 演唱会；音乐会
experiment *n.* 实验	both *pron.* 两者

一、听五段对话，在地图中按顺序用数字在方框内标明所找的地点。

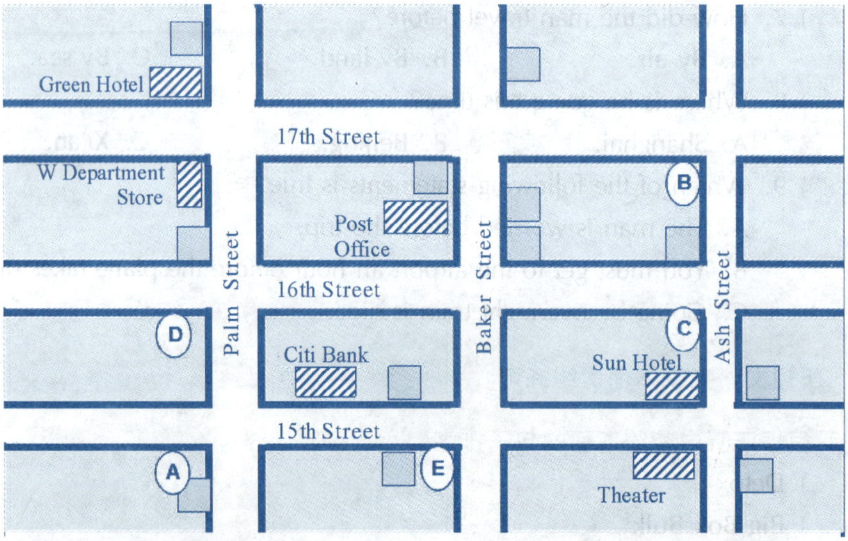

二、听下面的四段电影片段，根据你所听到的内容选出最佳答案。

听第一个电影片段，回答1～2题。

(　　) 1. The woman tells Mia that she is going to be a ________.

A. Queen　　B. Princess　　C. Prince

(　　) 2. Mia is going to learn the following things except ________.

A. languages　　B. art　　C. swimming

听第二个电影片段，回答3 ~4 题。

(　　) 3. What does Sid think small dinosaurs should eat to grow big and strong?

A. Meat.　　B. Vegetables.　　C. Fish.

(　　) 4. How is the food the mother dinosaur gives to them?

A. Well-cooked.　　B. Alive.　　C. Dead.

听第三个电影片段，回答5 ~6 题。

(　　) 5. What is Uncle Ian going to have?

A. A wedding ceremony.　　B. A new baby.　　C. A launch party.

(　　) 6. What time is it?

A. Christmas.　　B. Halloween.　　C. Easter.

听第四个电影片段，回答7 ~8 题。

(　　) 7. Where are the eggs from?

A. Underground, in ice.　　B. In a bird-nest.　　C. Under a tree.

(　　) 8. Manny says Sid is going to meet a ________ girl.

A. beautiful　　B. nice　　C. tall

三、听短文，填补所缺的内容。

Vivian's friends

NAME	JOB	LIKES	WHEN TO MEET	WHAT TO TALK ABOUT

四、听写。

____

____

____

____

____

____

____

____

Unit 11

Section 1

live *v.* 生存	never *adv.* 从不	bored *adj.* 无聊的
mind *v.* 介意	look forward to 期待	

一、听写单词。

1. ________ 2. ________ 3. ________ 4. ________
5. ________ 6. ________ 7. ________ 8. ________
9. ________ 10. ________ 11. ________ 12. ________
13. ________ 14. ________ 15. ________ 16. ________
17. ________ 18. ________ 19. ________ 20. ________

二、听下面的十个谜语，选出代表谜底的图片。

(　　) 1. A.  B.  C. 

(　　) 2. A.  B. 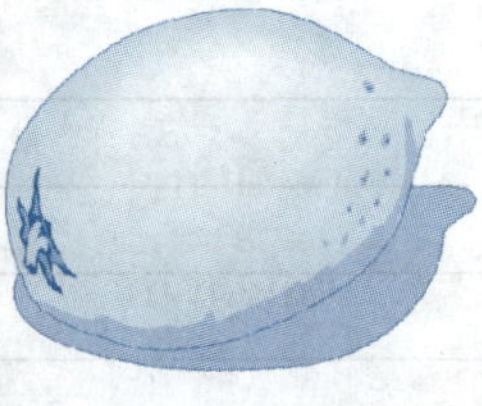 C. 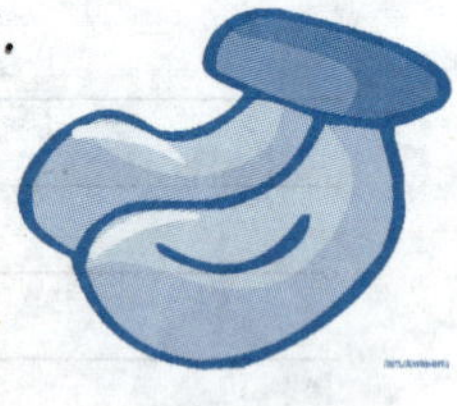

(　　) 3. A.  B.  C. 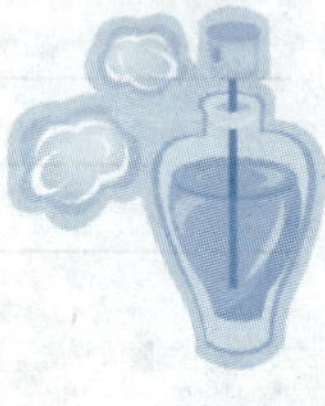

( ) 4. A.  B.  C. 

( ) 5. A.  B.  C. 

( ) 6. A.  B.  C. 

( ) 7. A.  B.  C. 

( ) 8. A.  B. 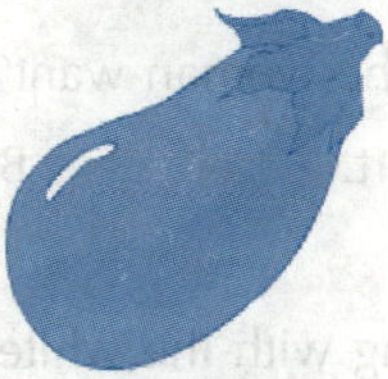 C. 

( ) 9. A.  B.  C. 

( ) 10. A.  B.  C. 

三、听下面的六段对话，根据对话内容选出最佳答案。

听第一段对话，回答1～3题。

(　　) 1. Where is Frank?

A. Miami. B. Tahiti. C. British Columbia.

(　　) 2. How is the weather there?

A. Cool. B. Awful. C. Hot.

(　　) 3. Where are they talking?

A. In a hotel room. B. On the phone. C. In the letter.

听第二段对话，回答4～6题。

(　　) 4. Who is sick in hospital?

A. Helen. B. Judy. C. Lisa.

(　　) 5. What's wrong with her?

A. She has a headache.

B. She has a stomachache.

C. She has a toothache.

(　　) 6. What does Kevin bring to the hospital?

A. Some toys. B. Some books. C. Some cakes.

听第三段对话，回答7～9题。

(　　) 7. Where are they talking?

A. In a cinema. B. In a shop. C. In a bookstore.

(　　) 8. What does the woman want?

A. A T-shirt. B. A dress. C. A book on English.

(　　) 9. What's wrong with the white one?

A. It's too long.

B. It's the wrong color.

C. It's too expensive.

听第四段对话，回答10～12题。

(　　) 10. What are they doing?

A. Listening to radio. B. Watching TV. C. Making a video.

(　　) 11. The quiz show will be on ________.

A. HBTV 4 B. CCTV 6 C. WHTV 7

(　　) 12. Which program does the woman like?

A. CCTV News. B. The 007 movie. C. The quiz show.

四、听短文，填补所缺内容。

Linton Zoo

Open Time	________ – ________ on weekdays. ________ – ________ on weekends.
Ticket Price	________ for an adult. ________ for children over 1. 20m. ________ for children under 1. 20m.
Attention	Do not give food to the animals. Do not get too ________ ________ or touch the animals. Keep the zoo ________.

Section 2

underneath *prep.* 在……下面	gardener *n.* 园丁；花匠
exchange *v.* 交换；兑换	allow *v.* 允许
reserved *v.* 保留的；预订的	permit *v.* 允许
except *prep.* 除……之外	staff *n.* 员工
activity *n.* 活动	improve *v.* 提高

一、听下面的一段英文歌，填补所缺的内容。

I don't want a lot for Christmas. There is just (1) ____________ I need.
I don't care about the (2) ____________ underneath the Christmas tree.
I don't need to hang my stocking there upon the fireplace.
Santa Claus won't (3) ____________ with a toy on Christmas day.
I just want you for my own. More than you could ever know.
Make my (4) ____________. All I want for Christmas is you.

I won't ask for much this Christmas. I won't even wish for (5) ____________.
I'm just gonna keep on (6) ____________ underneath the mistletoe.
I won't (7) ____________ and send it to the North Pole for Saint Nick.
I won't even stay awake to hear those magic (8) ____________ click.
'Cause I just want you (9) ____________ tonight holding on to me so tight.
What more can I do? Ooh baby, all I want for (10) ____________ is you.

二、听下面的六段对话，选出与所提问题相关的最佳图片。

( ) 1. A.  B.  C. 

( ) 2. A.  B.  C. 

( ) 3. A.  B.  C. 

( ) 4. A.  B.  C. 

( ) 5. A.  B.  C. 

( ) 6. A.  B.  C. 

三、听对话，在图书馆里允许做的事情前画圈（○），否则画叉（×）。

( ) 1. Food and drink.

( ) 2. Smoking in the reading rooms.

( ) 3. Borrowing magazines.

(　　) 4. Keeping six books at a time.

(　　) 5. Borrowing CDs and tapes.

(　　) 6. Copying articles and parts of books for personal use.

(　　) 7. Pets.

(　　) 8. Wearing T-shirts or shorts.

四、听对话，根据对话内容选出最佳答案。

(　　) 1. How does Susie like the trip?

A. Very enjoyable.　　B. Tiring.　　C. Expensive.

(　　) 2. What was the weather like in Switzerland?

A. Very cold.　　B. Cool.　　C. Warm.

(　　) 3. The hotels there were ________.

A. uncomfortable but not expensive

B. good but expensive

C. excellent and not expensive

(　　) 4. What did she say about the hotel staff?

A. Not helpful at all.

B. Busy and hardworking.

C. Friendly and helpful.

(　　) 5. Are there any language problems?

A. Yes, there are.　　B. No, there aren't.　　C. We don't know.

(　　) 6. What did she buy?

A. Clothes.　　B. Small gifts.　　C. Leather things.

五、听短文，填补所缺内容。

2010 Summer Camp

Opening time	________ to ________ (July ________ to July ________)
Members	Children aged ________
Fee & Pay time	________/ person; pay before ________
Activities	1. ________; 2. ________; 3. ________
Telephone	________________________
Email address	________________________

Section 3

waste *n.* 废弃物	suggestion *n.* 建议
mayer *n.* 市长	especially *adv.* 特别地
guard *v.* 守卫	director *n.* 导演
part-time *adj.* 兼职的	

一、听对话，填补所缺的内容。

M：Excuse me，may I borrow your (1) ________，please?
W：(2) ________.
M：Where is it?
W：Over (3) ________，under the tall (4) ________.
M：Oh，I see it.
W：(5) ________ are you going，may I ask?
M：I'm going (6) ________. I (7) ________ to buy some vegetables.
W：Is that so? Can you (8) ________ some tomatoes for me?
M：Sure.
W：Here is the (9) ________. Thanks.
M：Well，I must (10) ________ now. See you later.
W：See you.

二、听对话，完成地图并画好路线图。

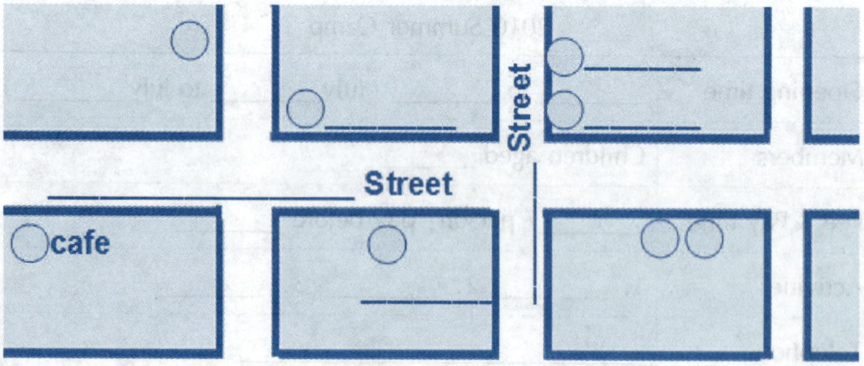

三、听下面的十个句子，选出与所听到的句子意思相同或最相近的句子。

(　　) 1. A. Is this pencil yours?
B. Whose pencil is this?
C. Who's got a pencil?

(　　) 2. A. What is his father?
B. Where does his father come from?
C. How is his father?

(　　) 3. A. It doesn't matter.
B. You are welcome.
C. The same to you.

(　　) 4. A. What an interesting game it is!
B. Is the game interesting?
C. I don't think much of the interesting game.

(　　) 5. A. Do you want to have some water?
B. I need a glass of water.
C. There isn't any glass of water.

(　　) 6. A. Don't write any email.
B. I'm going to write you a letter.
C. Write a letter to me, please.

(　　) 7. A. Which place do you usually come?
B. Where are you from?
C. Do you come from China?

(　　) 8. A. Do you have brothers or sisters?
B. How many children do you have?
C. Have you any friends?

(　　) 9. A. I don't like the food.
B. I don't want to eat.
C. I want something to eat.

(　　) 10. A. Do you have anything to say?
B. Where does it hurt?
C. What's wrong with you?

四、听下面的三段对话，根据对话内容选出最佳答案。

听第一段对话，回答 1 ~3 题。

(　　) 1. What problem are they discussing about?
A. Final Exams. 　　B. Wastes. 　　C. Shopping.

(　　) 2. Where are they?

A. In the park.　　B. At the Mayer's office.　　C. At school.

(　　) 3. What do they think the workers should do?

A. Put up a notice.　　B. Write a report.　　C. Call the police.

听第二段对话，回答4~6题。

(　　) 4. Which of the following is NOT mentioned in the dialogue?

A. The British Museum.

B. The Tower of London.

C. The Tower Bridge.

(　　) 5. What do the Beefeaters do?

A. Tell stories.　　B. Guard the tower.　　C. Eat beef.

(　　) 6. Why are they called Beefeaters?

A. Because they have beef as their food.

B. Because they are as strong as an ox.

C. Because they used to have beef as part of their salary.

听第三段对话，回答7~10题。

(　　) 7. Where does the woman want to go?

A. The USA.　　B. The UK.　　C. The PRC.

(　　) 8. What is she going to learn?

A. English.　　B. Science.　　C. Filming.

(　　) 9. The woman's English is ________.

A. very good　　B. just so so　　C. poor

(　　) 10. How does she got enough money for her study?

A. By asking parents for help.

B. By saving money every day.

C. By doing part-time jobs.

五、听短文，完成下面两组练习。

(一) 根据所听内容给下面的句子排序。

(　　) Get some skills.

(　　) Never be the last to leave.

(　　) Get a gimmick.

(　　) Don't over-advertised.

(　　) Don't do everything you're told.

(二) 填补所缺的内容。

1. Quit hiding your cool. ________ ________ ________.

2. ________, ________, ________, anything. Being good at something makes you

interesting.

3. Following the fads is a _______ _______.
4. Over-advertising _______, or your _______, or your _______ _______ is not cool.
5. Don't do everything you're told. Really _______ _______ _______.

Section 4

airline	*n.*	航空公司	flight	*n.*	航班
destination	*n.*	目的地	pyramid	*n.*	金字塔

一、听写单句。

1. ________________________________
2. ________________________________
3. ________________________________
4. ________________________________
5. ________________________________
6. ________________________________
7. ________________________________
8. ________________________________
9. ________________________________
10. ________________________________

二、听下面的五段对话，填补所缺内容。

Airline	Flight	Destination	Depart	Arrive
Pan Am	_______	Amsterdam	_______	_______
Quantas	_______	Sydney	_______	_______
Lufthansa	_______	Frankfurt	_______	_______
Air France	_______	Paris	_______	_______
Japan Air Lines	_______	Tokyo	_______	_______

三、拼写游戏。你将听到一些单词，这些单词都是由图片上物品的拼写加上或者减去一些字母组成的。先在横线上写下你所听到的单词，然后选出算式中问号所代表的图片。

(　　) 1. ? + C + H = ________

A. 
B. 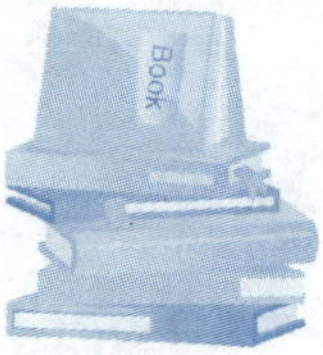

C. 

(　　) 2. S + L + ? − J = ________

A. 
B. 
C. 

(　　) 3. ? − B − K − E = ________

A. 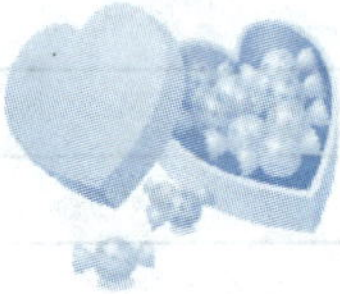
B. 
C. 

(　　) 4. F − T + ? = ________

A. 
B. 
C. 

(　　) 5. ? + D + A + Y = ________

A. 
B. 
C. 

(　　) 6. ? − N − G + X = ________

A. 
B. 
C. 

(　　) 7. O + ? − R − U = ________

A. 
B. 
C. 

(　　) 8. ? − B + E = ________

A. 

B. 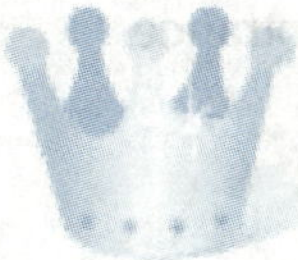
C. 

四、听短文，完成下面的两组练习。

（一）判断下列句子是否正确，正确用 T（True）表示，错误用 F（False）表示。

(　　) 1. Many people go online to a mailbox if they have a question about something.
(　　) 2. Question Box is a service for free.
(　　) 3. The service began three years ago.
(　　) 4. The operators can speaks English, French and Chinese.
(　　) 5. Workers go around telling people about Question Box service in North America.
(　　) 6. The Internet service in Uganda is quite slow.
(　　) 7. Nobody wants to know how long the Nile River is.
(　　) 8. The pyramids never moved to another place.
(　　) 9. You are listening to CNN Special English.
(　　) 10. June Simms is the writer of this program.

（二）填补所缺的内容。

1. They might not be able to ________, or they simply have ________ access.
2. You just push a button, a big ________ button, and that will connect you directly to our operators who are sitting in front of ________.

3. You can ask them any sort of ________ you want, and they'll look it up in ________ or in Hindi.
4. The idea was to make a technology that even ________ could use.
5. Question Box is a project of ________ Mind.

Section 5

elevator	*n.* 电梯	souvenir	*n.* 纪念品	subject	*n.* 学科，科目

一、听下面的五段对话，根据所听到的内容连线。

	near the entrance	bank
	next to the elevator	tour desk
	next to the coffee shop	restaurant
	opposite the souvenir shop	mail box
	at the end of the hall	magazine shop

二、听下面的四段电影片段，根据你所听到的内容选出最佳答案。

听第一个电影片段，回答1～2题。

( ) 1. When is it in a day?

A. In the morning.

B. In the afternoon.

C. In the evening.

( ) 2. Barry doesn't use the stairs because ________.

A. his Mom told him to fly in the house

B. his father paid good money for it

C. he is too excited

听第二个电影片段，回答3～4题。

( ) 3. Why is the woman so surprised?

A. The bee is talking to her.

B. She is walking while she is dreaming.

C. She wants to drink coffee.

( ) 4. What does she want to do?

A. Wash all the dishes again.

B. Get him something.

C. Make some coffee.

听第三个电影片段，回答5～6题。

( ) 5. Puppy Paws wishes to ________.

A. send all the gifts to good puppies

B. work hard to get

C. be an ordinary puppy

( ) 6. What does Puppy Paws have to understand?

A. His father is proud of him.

B. He is the future of Christmas.

C. How important Christmas is.

听第四个电影片段，回答7～8题。

( ) 7. ________ is a rule.

A. No eating B. No reading C. No running

( ) 8. The fair princess is locked in a ________.

A. light tower B. faraway castle C. dark cave

三、听下面一段短文，填补所缺的内容。

PERSONAL CHART

NAME: ________________

AGE: ________________

GENER: ________________

NATIONALITY: ________________

FAMILY: ________________

CITY: ________________

SCHOOL: ________________

FAVOURITE SUBJECT: ________________

HOBBIES/ INTERESTS: ________________

四、听写。

____

____

____

____

____

____

____

____

Unit 12

Section 1

seat *n.* 座位	together *adv.* 一起
thief *n.* 小偷	ought to 应该

一、单词听写。

1. ________ 2. ________ 3. ________
4. ________ 5. ________ 6. ________
7. ________ 8. ________ 9. ________
10. ________ 11. ________ 12. ________
13. ________ 14. ________ 15. ________
16. ________ 17. ________ 18. ________
19. ________ 20. ________

二、听下面的八个句子，选出与句子内容相关的图片。

( ) 1. A.  B.  C. 

( ) 2. A.  B.  C. 

( ) 3. A.  B. 

C. 

( ) 4. A.

B.

C.

( ) 5. A.

B.

C.

( ) 6. A.

B.
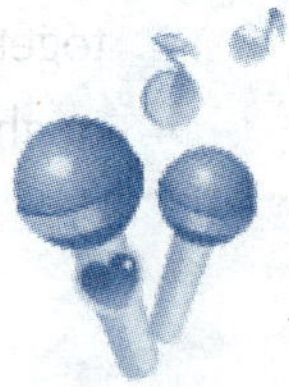
C.

( ) 7. A.
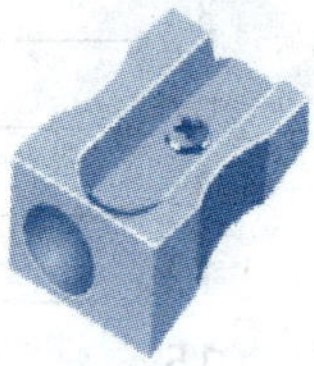
B.
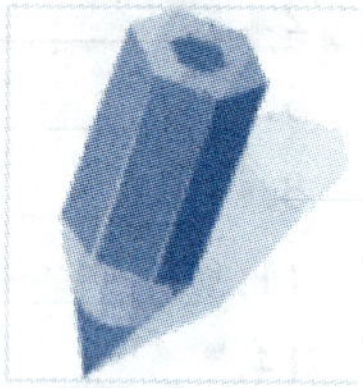
C.

( ) 8. A.

B.

C.
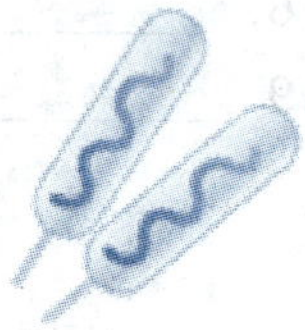

三、听下面的六段对话，根据对话内容选出最佳答案。

( ) 1. Whose ruler is this?
A. Lisa's. B. Angela's. C. Linda's.

( ) 2. How many members are there in a group?
A. Three. B. Seven. C. Eight.

( ) 3. What is the woman's email address?
A. WFLS@126. com.
B. WEFLS@163. com.
C. WEFLS@126. com.

( ) 4. Where is the map?
A. On the wall in the classroom.
B. On the blackboard in the classroom.

C. On the wall outside the classroom.

(　　) 5. Which phone number does the man want to dial?

A. 87395127.　　B. 87365127.　　C. 87425127.

(　　) 6. Where are they talking?

A. In a KFC.　　B. At home.　　C. On the street.

四、听短文，判断下列句子是否正确，正确用 T（True）表示，错误用 F（False）表示。

(　　) 1. The story happened two weeks ago.

(　　) 2. They found a gold stick on the ground.

(　　) 3. The first traveler wanted to give it back to the owner.

(　　) 4. At last the two men decided to share it.

(　　) 5. The strong man was the real owner.

(　　) 6. The second traveler left the first one alone.

(　　) 7. The first man put the gold stick in a hole.

(　　) 8. The strong man caught the first traveler.

五、听短文，填补所缺的内容。

1. Emily's company is ________ ________ from her home.

2. The bus stop is in front of ________ ________ ________.

3. The bus stop is about ________ ________ from her home.

4. She catches the number ________ bus to work, but sometimes she goes ________ ________.

5. Her work finishes at ________, and Emily gets back home at ________.

6. Every day she does the ________ thing.

Section 2

plastic *n.* 塑料	flightless *adj.* 不能飞的
cop *n.* 巡警，警官	jealous *adj.* 嫉妒的
loom *v.* 隐约可见	blunt *adj.* 钝的
exhibition *n.* 展览	service *n.* 服务

一、听下面的一段英文歌，填补所缺的内容。

I was a quick wet (1) ________, diving too deep for (2) ________

All of your street light eyes wide on my plastic (3) ________
Then when the cops closed the fair, I cut my (4) ________
Stole me a dog-eared map and called for you everywhere
Have I found you? Flightless bird, jealous, weeping
Or lost you? American mouth. Big pill looming
Now I'm a (5) ____________, nursing my sore blunt tongue
Watching the warm poison rats curl through the wide fence cracks
Pissing on (6) ________ photos
Those fishing lures thrown in the (7) ________
blood of Christ mountain stream

二、听下面的十段对话，选出与所提问题相关的最佳图片。

(　　) 1. What is Rosemary going to do?

A. 

B. 

C. 

(　　) 2. What does Mandy want?

A. 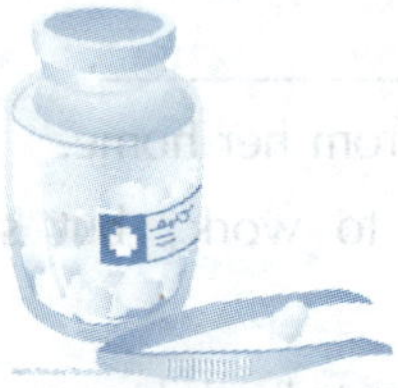

B. 

C. 

(　　) 3. What are they talking about?

A. 

B. 

C. 

(　　) 4. Where are they talking now?

A. 

B. 

C. 

(　　) 5. Where did the woman get the news?

A. B. C.

(　　) 6. What is she going to have for lunch?

A. B. C.

(　　) 7. What is Mary good at?

A. B. C.

(　　) 8. What is the boy looking for?

A. B. C.

(　　) 9. How did the woman get to Nanjing?

A. B. C.

(　　) 10. Which job does the girl want to have?

A. B. C.

三、听下面的十个句子，选出与你所听到的句子意思相同或最相近的句子。

(　　) 1. A. There is some milk in the glass.

B. There isn't any milk in the bottle.

C. The glass is empty.

( ) 2. A. Where is his schoolbag?
B. His schoolbag is under the desk.
C. There is a schoolbag in the desk.

( ) 3. A. What is the number of the kites in the sky?
B. Can you see the kites in the sky?
C. How do you like the kites in the sky?

( ) 4. A. I like this shirt.
B. This is my shirt.
C. The shirt is very cheap.

( ) 5. A. My father usually gets home at 6:15.
B. My father goes to work at 7:50.
C. My father often arrives home at 6:50.

( ) 6. A. Mr. Lee is one of my friends.
B. Mr. Lee and I live together.
C. Mr. Lee lives next to me.

( ) 7. A. Do you drink any coffee?
B. How do you like the coffee?
C. What is the name of that coffee?

( ) 8. A. Thank you for your email.
B. I'm glad to send you an email.
C. The email is full of thanks.

( ) 9. A. They like playing football.
B. They play basketball after class.
C. Volleyball is their favourite game after school.

( ) 10. A. Computer games is of great fun.
B. Do you like playing computer games?
C. I usually play computer games.

四、听对话，选出表格内所缺的内容。

RENTAL APPLICATION FORM

Name: (1) ________

Address: No. (2) ________ Lindon Street, (3) ________ City

Telephone: (4) ________

Job: engineer

Employer: (5) ________

(　　) 1. A. Smith Johnson　　B. Alice Moore　　C. Albert Enakei
(　　) 2. A. 1267　　B. 1466　　C. 1737
(　　) 3. A. Los Angeles　　B. Chicago　　C. San Francisco
(　　) 4. A. 935-8933　　B. 364-9758　　C. 285-9841
(　　) 5. A. IBM　　B. APPLE　　C. DELL

五、听短文，填补所缺的内容。

1. Linda is an ________ doctor.
2. She works in a ________ ________ in Wuhan.
3. She works hard for the ________ during the day and reads books about Chinese ________ at night.
4. She says Chinese people are ________ and ________.
5. Now, Linda can ________ and even ________ some Chinese.

Section 3

awful *adj.* 不舒服的	relationship *n.* 关系
stomachache *n.* 胃疼	interview *n.* 面试；采访
require *v.* 要求	temperature *n.* 温度
havaianas *n.* 人字拖	

一、听句子，填补所缺的单词。

1. He often walks home ________ school.
2. I can see some ________ on the table.
3. There aren't any students in the ________.
4. ________ ________ the map on the wall.
5. Is it OK to call you at ________?
6. How many ________ ________ does Timmy have?
7. Today is ________, and it is windy.
8. ________ in my family is happy at this time.
9. What do you want to have for ________?
10. Who's that girl in the ________ ________?

二、听下面的六个句子，选出最佳答语。

(　　) 1. A. Where is it?　　B. I'm coming.　　C. Good morning.

( ) 2. A. Next Sunday. B. In the drawer. C. Certainly.
( ) 3. A. Yes, thank you. B. It's delicious. C. Fine.
( ) 4. A. It's Feb. 21th. B. It's 4 o'clock. C. It's Monday.
( ) 5. A. I'd love to. B. It's a pleasure. C. Sorry, I won't.
( ) 6. A. Thank you. B. The same to you. C. It doesn't work.

三、听下面的四段对话，根据对话内容选出最佳答案。

听第一段对话，回答1 ~2 题

( ) 1. What's the matter with the man?
A. He has a toothache.
B. He has a fever.
C. He has a headache.

( ) 2. What is the relationship between the two speakers?
A. Mother and son.
B. Teacher and student.
C. Doctor and patient.

听第二段对话，回答3 ~4 题。

( ) 3. What is the woman?
A. A tennis fan. B. A nurse. C. A tennis player.

( ) 4. What is the relationship between the two speakers?
A. Doctor and patient. B. Coach and player. C. Co-workers.

听第三段对话，回答5 ~6 题。

( ) 5. What is the name of the hotel?
A. Plane Hotel. B. Planet Hotel. C. Play Hotel.

( ) 6. What is the relationship between the two speakers?
A. Customer and receptionist.
B. Father and daughter.
C. Fireman and caller.

听第四段对话，回答7 ~8 题。

( ) 7. Where are they talking now?
A. On the phone. B. In the street. C. In an office.

( ) 8. What is the relationship between the two speakers?
A. Interviewer and interviewee.
B. Manager and clerk.
C. Teacher and student.

四、听英文歌，完成下面两组练习。

(一) 判断下列句子是否正确，正确用 T (True) 表示，错误用 F (False) 表示。

( ) 1. The story happened at night.

( ) 2. I went out to the backyard to look for my naughty son.
( ) 3. Peter was a neighbour of mine.
( ) 4. Peter and I built a time machine together.
( ) 5. Not much has changed in the year 3000.
( ) 6. The great great great grandchild is doing her homework.

(二)根据所听内容选出最佳答案。

( ) 1. What did I hear when I came home?
A. A funny noise. B. A bird singing. C. A girl crying.

( ) 2. Where can we see time machines?
A. In the magazine. B. In the film. C. On TV.

( ) 3. Where does people live in the year 3000?
A. On trees. B. In the ground. C. Under water.

( ) 4. Who does Peter see in the year 3000?
A. His great great granddaughter.
B. His great great great grandson.
C. His great great great granddaughter.

( ) 5. What do the girls look like in the year 3000?
A. They have long hair.
B. They have round hair.
C. They have no hair.

五、听一段天气预报,给图片排序并写出相应的天气和温度。

( ) ( ) ( ) ( ) ( ) ( ) ( )

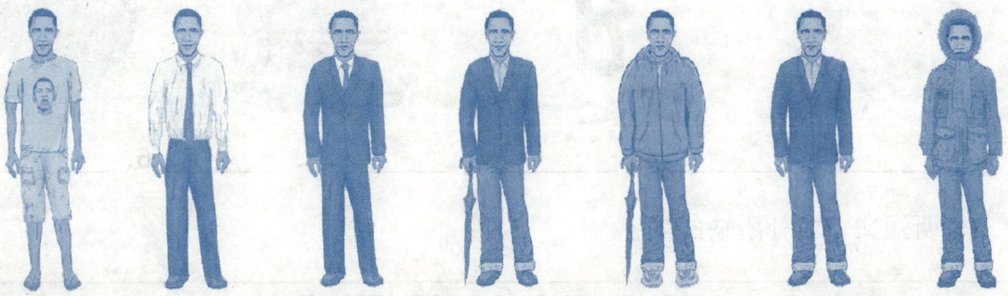

______ ______ ______ ______ ______ ______ ______
______ ______ ______ ______ ______ ______ ______

Section 4

trouble	*n.* 麻烦	believe	*v.* 相信
chance	*n.* 机会	order	*n.* 顺序
brand	*n.* 品牌	sometime	*adv.* 某个时候;日后

一、听写单句。

1. ________________
2. ________________
3. ________________
4. ________________
5. ________________
6. ________________
7. ________________
8. ________________
9. ________________
10. ________________

二、听下面的六段对话和问题，根据你所听到的内容选出与所提问题相关的最佳图片。

A. 

B. 

C. 

D. 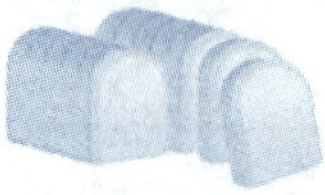

E. 

F. 

G. 

H. 

1. ________ 2. ________ 3. ________ 4. ________ 5. ________ 6. ________

三、听短文，填补所缺的内容。

TOUR BUS 77 SCHEDULE	
Terminal	8:30 am
City Hall	
Shopping Center	
Swimming Pool	
No. 2 Middle School	
Sports Stadium	
	10:30 am
People's Hospital	
May's Garden	11:30 am

四、听下面的五段对话，根据对话内容选出最佳答案。

听第一段对话，回答 1 ~2 题。

(　　) 1. Who broke the window?

A. Steven.　　B. Cissy.　　C. Peter.

(　　) 2. What was Steven doing just now?

A. Playing with Cissy.　　B. Playing baseball.　　C. Watching TV.

听第二段对话，回答 3 ~4 题。

(　　) 3. Where did Ted go on holiday?

A. Japan.　　B. Germany.　　C. Australia.

(　　) 4. How did he come back?

A. By ship.　　B. By plane.　　C. By train.

听第三段对话，回答 5 ~6 题。

(　　) 5. What is the man doing now?

A. Cleaning up his room.

B. Looking for his wallet.

C. Doing sports.

(　　) 6. When are they going to see a film?

A. In the afternoon.　　B. In the evening.　　C. Tomorrow.

听第四段对话，回答 7 ~8 题。

(　　) 7. Who is the present for?

A. His mother.　　B. His father.　　C. His teacher.

(　　) 8. How long did the boy spend in shopping?

A. Three days.　　B. Four days.　　C. Five days.

听第五段对话，回答 9 ~10 题。

(　　) 9. What does the man do each morning?

A. Running.　　B. Playing basketball.　　C. Swimming.

(　　) 10. When does the woman play tennis?

A. Every day in the morning.

B. After work.

C. Every weekend.

五、听短文，完成下面两组练习。

(一) 根据所听到的内容选择最佳答案。

(　　) 1. What is the name of this program?

A. Development Report.

B. Health Report.

C. Education Report.

( ) 2. What is the name of the contest?

A. The battle of the hands.

B. The battle of the brains.

C. The battle of the eyes.

( ) 3. Where did the contest take place?

A. Palo Alto, California.

B. Harbin, China.

C. Vancouver, Canada.

( ) 4. How many members are there in a team?

A. Three. B. Four. C. Six.

( ) 5. Which of the following in not a problem in the context?

A. Chocolate bars. B. Robots. C. Cakes.

( ) 6. Which team was the winner?

A. Stanford University.

B. Shanghai Jiaotong University.

C. Oxford University.

( ) 7. What is the contest about?

A. Computer programming.

B. Online games.

C. Public services.

(二) 填补所缺的内容。

1. Last month, students from ________ universities in ________ countries took part in the contest.
2. Each school team had ________ hours to solve ________ real world problems.
3. Stanford was one of ________ American universities that took part in the contest this year.
4. The first ACM contest began in the year ________.
5. The first final competition was held in ________.

Section 5

roasted *adj.* 烧烤的	cereal *n.* 谷物
dressing *adj.* 沙拉酱	palace *n.* 宫殿
nervous *adj.* 紧张的	natural *adj.* 自然的

一、听对话，在 Laura 和 Allen 要买的东西图片下画○，否则画×。

(　　)

(　　)

(　　)

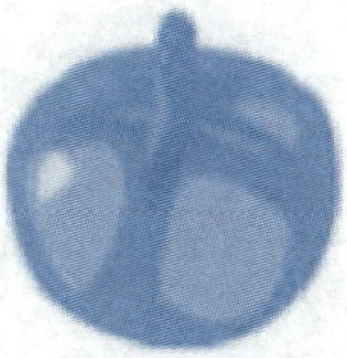
(　　)

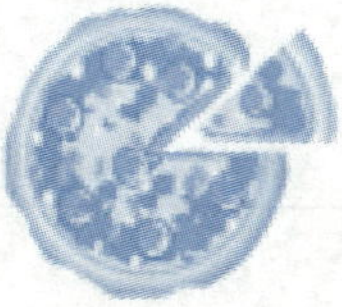
(　　)

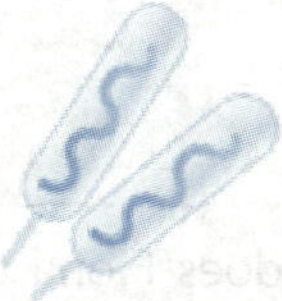
(　　)

(　　)

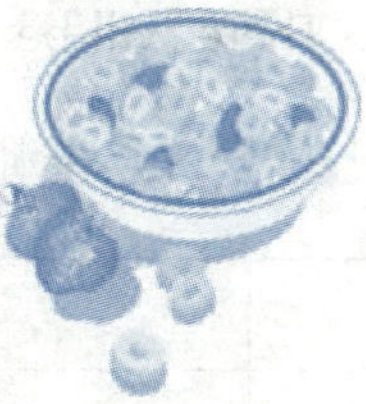
(　　)

(　　)

二、听下面的四段电影片段，根据你所听到的内容选出最佳答案。

听第一个电影片段，回答 1 ~2 题。

(　　) 1. What is the difference between her real mother and the "other mother"?

A. The voice.　　B. The button eyes.　　C. The piano.

(　　) 2. How does the "other father" play the piano?

A. By using his left hand only.

B. The piano plays him.

C. By writing a new song.

听第二个电影片段，回答 3 ~4 题。

(　　) 3. Why has the boy never been inside the pink palace?

A. Because his mother would kill him.

B. Because his grandmother lived there.

C. Because it was dangerous.

(　　) 4. __________ disappeared when she was a kid.

A. The boy's grandma

B. His grandmother's twin sister

C. The girl's grandmother

听第三个电影片段，回答 5 ~6 题。

(　　) 5. What will there be tonight?

A. A dancing party.　　B. An open mike.　　C. A football match.

(　　) 6. What do they cook for dinner?

A. Hamburgers.　　B. Noodle.　　C. Chicken.

听第四个电影片段，回答7～8题。

( ) 7. Flies, sweat and Monday mornings are ________.

A. natural parts of nature

B. things people love much

C. terrible sadness

( ) 8. What does the princess wish?

A. There will be a prince, too.

B. It will be rainy.

C. There will be light.

三、听下面的一段短文，填补所缺的内容。

Time	What does Fiona do?
6:00	Get up, ________
7:15	________, ________ and have classes
12:10	________
16:00	________, do homework, ________; Sometimes ________
19:00	Have dinner, then ________
21:00	Go to bed

四、听写。

____

____

____

____

____

____

____

____

____

____

Unit 13

Section 1

一、听词组，把你所听到的词组写在下面的横线上。

1. ______ 2. ______ 3. ______
4. ______ 5. ______ 6. ______
7. ______ 8. ______ 9. ______
10. ______

二、听下面的十句话，选出与你所听到的句子一致的答案，并将代表该答案的字母填在题前的括号内。

( ) 1. A. My parents are planning their vacation.
B. My parents are going on a vacation.
C. My parents are going to plan a vacation.

( ) 2. A. We live at the bus stop.
B. We live near the bus stop.
C. The bus doesn't stop near here.

( ) 3. A. Did you bring your books?
B. Don't bring your books.
C. Don't forget to bring your books.

( ) 4. A. Let's work for our jacket tomorrow.
B. Let's work on our project tomorrow.
C. Let's finish our project now.

( ) 5. A. Is the girl a new student?
B. Is the girl your sister?
C. Is the new boy a student?

( ) 6. A. Write your name on the bottom of the page.
B. Write your name at the top of the page.
C. Don't write your name on the paper.

( ) 7. A. I'm interested in going to the concert.

B. I'm not interested in going to the concert.

C. I'm not interested in joining the concert.

( ) 8. A. Paul is older than Simon but younger than Tom.

B. Paul is older than Tom but younger than Simon.

C. Paul is younger than Simon but older than Tom.

( ) 9. A. Is the gym open every day?

B. Have you been to the gym yet?

C. Has the gym opened yet today?

( ) 10. A. The teacher's students use the school library.

B. Only the students can use the school library.

C. The teacher's students use the school computers.

三、听下面的三段材料，在你所听到的物品下面的方框内打钩。

1.

☐

☐

☐

☐

☐

☐

2.

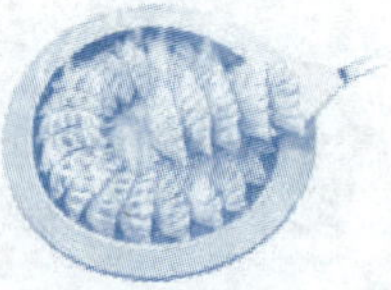
☐

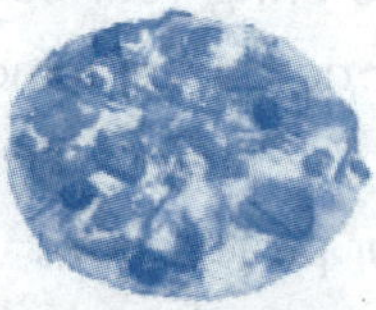
☐

☐

☐

☐

☐

3.

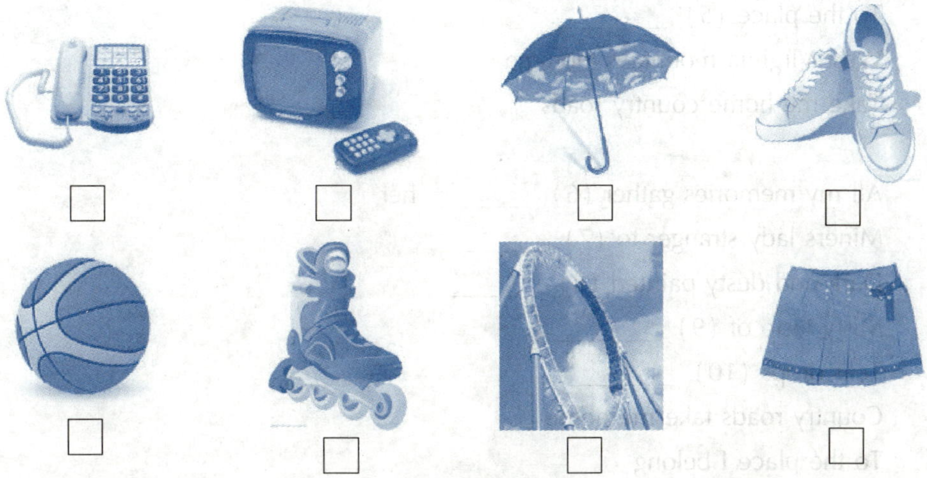

四、听下面的一段材料，根据内容判断下列句子的正误，将 T（正确）或 F（错误）填入题前的括号内。

(　　) 1. This sports center is small.
(　　) 2. Only sportsmen can go there.
(　　) 3. People can go there to build up their health.
(　　) 4. Tennis is open from 10 o'clock in the morning till 5 o'clock in the afternoon.
(　　) 5. Volleyball is arranged in the evenings.
(　　) 6. Football is at the weekdays.
(　　) 7. We don't have baseball classes because it is too exciting.
(　　) 8. We only provide ball games for people.
(　　) 9. You are always welcome at any time.
(　　) 10. Very few people like playing baseball.

Section 2

一、听下面的一首歌，根据歌词填空。

Almost heaven west Virginia
Blue ridge mountains Shenandoah River
(1) ________ is old there older than the trees
(2) ________ than the mountains
(3) ________ like a breeze
Country roads (4) ________

To the place (5) ________
West Virginia mountain momma
Take me home country roads

All my memories gather (6) ________ her
Miners lady stranger to (7) ________
Dark and dusty painted (8) ________
Misty taste of (9) ________
Tear drops (10) ________
Country roads take me home
To the place I belong
West Virginia mountain momma
Take me home country roads

二、看下面的十五幅图，每幅图你都会听到三个描述此图的句子 A，B 和 C，请选出正确描述此图的句子。

(　　) 1.

(　　) 2.

(　　) 3.

(　　) 4.
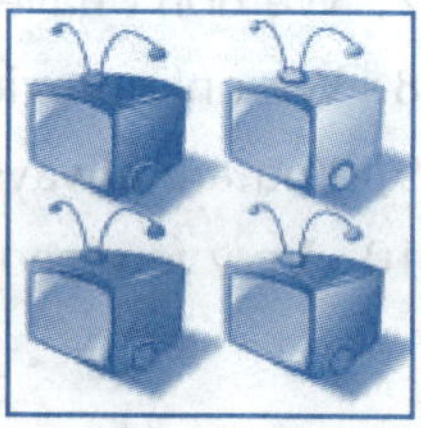

(　　) 5.

(　　) 6.

(　　) 7.

(　　) 8.

(　　) 9.

(　　) 10.

(　　) 11.

(　　) 12.

(　　) 13.

(　　) 14.

(　　) 15.

三、听短文，根据所听内容填写下列表格。

	City	Weather	Temperature
1.	London		
2.		Rainy	
3.	Washington		18℃ to 28℃
4.		Sunny	
5.	Wuhan		15℃ to 26℃

Section 3

一、听下面的十个句子，把你所听到的句子写在下面的横线上。

1. ____

2. ____

3. ____

4. ____

5. ____

6. ____

7. ____

8. ____

9. ____

10. ____

二、听下面的十个问题，根据问题选出最佳答语，并将答语排序。将代表答语的序号写在横线上。

A. Because I can't swim.

B. Well, I had it yesterday. Let's have something else.

C. Because I don't like vegetables.

D. It's starting to rain. Let's go later.

E. We can't. We don't have a ball.

1. ________ 2. ________ 3. ________ 4. ________ 5. ________

F. I am watching TV. This is my favourite TV program.

G. Red. It means passion.

H. I'm too tired to do anything else except sleeping.

I. April the first. Oh! Today is April Fools' Day.

J. There are two kites flying in the sky.

6. ________ 7. ________ 8. ________ 9. ________ 10. ________

三、听下面的十段小独白，根据独白内容选择相应的图片，并将代表该图片的字母填在题前的括号内。

(　　) 1. A.  B.  C. 

(　　) 2. A.  B.  C. 

(　　) 3. A.  B.  C. 

(　　) 4. A.  B.  C. 

(　　) 5. A.  B.  C. 

(　　) 6. A.  B.  C. 

(　　) 7. A.  B.  C. 

(　　) 8. A.  B.  C. 

(　　) 9. A.  B.  C. 

(　　) 10. A.  B.  C. 

四、听下面的一段独白，根据独白内容完成下列各小题。

1. I am a teacher, but my sister is ________________________.

2. I live in New York, but she lives in ____________________.

3. I have a large house in the suburbs, but she ______________.

4. I ________, but she is single.
5. I play golf, but she ________________________________.
6. I play the piano, but she ______________________________.
7. On the weekend I usually watch videos, but she ______________.
8. On the weekend I rarely go out, but she ________________.

Section 4

一、听下面的一段对话，用你所听到的单词或句子补全对话。

Sindy: (1) ________ the National Park?
Guide: It is about (2) ________.
Sindy: (3) ______________?
Guide: About an hour.
Sindy: Look at that high mountain! (4) ________ is it?
Guide: It's a volcano. It's about (5) ________.
Sindy: (6) ______________?
Guide: It's about (7) ________.
Sindy: (8) ________ is the hole?
Guide: It's about (9) ________ feet deep.
Sindy: Oh! There is a temple. (10) ________ is this temple?
Guide: It's about (11) ________.
Sindy: Is that the beach? (12) ________ is it?
Guide: I'm not sure, but it's probably (13) ________.

二、听下面的一段独白，根据独白内容完成下列表格。

Monday	Tuesday	Wednesday	Thursday	Friday	Saturday	Sunday
Italian food						

三、听下面的一段长对话，根据对话内容选择最佳答案，并将代表该答案的字母写在题前的括号内。

(   ) 1. What's the relationship between the two people?
A. Classmates. B. Relatives. C. Neighbours.

(   ) 2. What did the girl buy for her mother?
A. She bought a beautiful silver necklace.

B. She bought a beautiful gold necklace.

C. She bought a beautiful Italian necklace.

(　　) 3. Why did she buy a present for her mother?

A. Because she loves her mother.

B. Because her mother's birthday is coming.

C. Because Mother's Day will come.

(　　) 4. What is her father's hobby?

A. Playing tennis.　　B. Playing basketball.　　C. Running.

(　　) 5. What did she buy for her birthday?

A. Some vegetables, some drinks and a birthday cake.

B. Some snacks, some drinks and a birthday cake.

C. Some snacks, some drinks and a big pizza.

四、听下面的一段独白，根据要求完成各个小题。

（一）根据独白的内容，把代表地点的字母写在图片下的横线上。

A. Mann's Chinese Theater　　B. Beverly Hills　　C. Universal Studios

D. The Walk of Fame　　E. The Hollywood Bowl

1. ____________

2. ____________

3. ____________

4. ____________

5. ________

（二）根据独白的内容填空。

1. Mann's Chinese Theater was built in ________.

2. There are so many ________ shops in Beverly Hills.

3. People will see ________ from the movie *Jurassic Park* in Universal Studios.

4. The Walk of Fame is a ________ road.

5. The Hollywood Bowl is in ________.

Section 5

一、听下面的五段对话，根据对话内容判断其发生地点，并与相应的图片连线。

1.

2.

3.

4.

5.

二、听下面的一段独白，根据独白内容完成下列表格。

Monday	Tuesday	Wednesday	Thursday	Friday	Saturday	Sunday
jog						

三、听下面的两段材料，根据所听内容完成各个小题，并将代表最佳答案的字母填在题前的括号内。

听下面的录音，回答1 ~3 题。

(　　) 1. Who is the host（主持人）of this year's Academy Awards?

A. Hugh Grant.　　B. Hugh Jackman.　　C. Robert Downey.

(　　) 2. Which of the following star didn't the host introduce in the recording?

A. Brad Pitt.　　B. Kate Winslet.　　C. Robert Downey Jr.

(　　) 3. What nationality is the host?

A. British.　　B. American.　　C. Australian.

听下面的一段歌曲，回答4 ~6 题。

(　　) 4. This song is for ________.

A. the Olympic Games

B. the Olympic Torch Relay

C. a party

(　　) 5. What do you think is the name of the song?

A. *Together.*　　B. *Unite the Words.*　　C. *Pass the Flame.*

(　　) 6. Which of the following sentence is NOT in the song?

A. It's the time to celebrate, let our voices be heard.

B. We can grow a forest on a dried-up river bed.

C. Reach you, hold out your hands.

四、听下面的一段独白，请把独白中的每一句话完整地记录下来。

____

____

____

____

____

____

Unit 14

Section 1

一、听下面的十个句子，用英语写出句子中所提到的日期。

1. ________ 2. ________ 3. ________
4. ________ 5. ________ 6. ________
7. ________ 8. ________ 9. ________
10. ________

二、听下面的十个问句，根据所听到的内容选出相应的答语，并将代表该答案的字母填在题前的括号内。

(　　) 1. A. She does well. B. She is a doctor. C. She likes basketball.
(　　) 2. A. It's Mery. B. It's her. C. It's his.
(　　) 3. A. 2 days ago. B. In 3 days. C. For 4 days.
(　　) 4. A. This is John speaking. B. I am John. C. It is John.
(　　) 5. A. Sunning. B. Morning. C. Early.
(　　) 6. A. A worker. B. In a factory. C. A doctor.
(　　) 7. A. Very busy. B. One week. C. Once a month.
(　　) 8. A. It's hot. B. It's summer. C. It's orange.
(　　) 9. A. It's interesting. B. It's difficult. C. It's wonderful.
(　　) 10. A. Monday. B. March 10th. C. Today is rainy.

三、听下面的一段独白，根据独白的内容将以下人物的名称写在相应图片下的横线上。

Mary　Betty　Peter　Ben　Helen

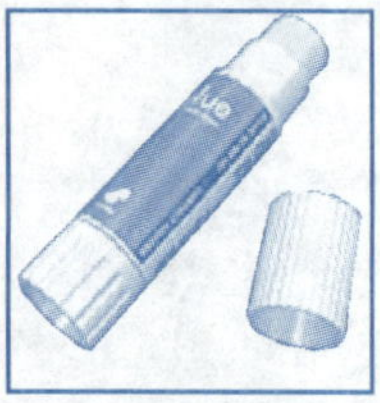

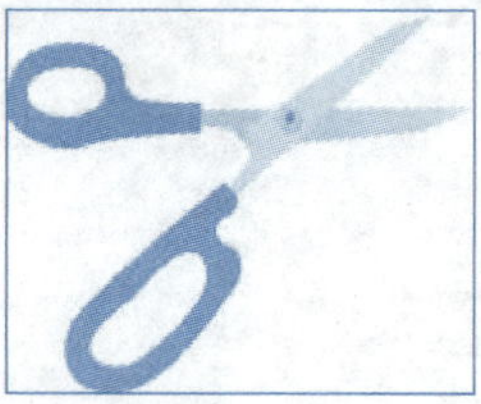

________ ________ ________

________　　________

四、听下面的一段独白，根据独白内容完成下列各题。

（一）根据独白的内容填写以下时间表。

Peter's Time Table

7:30	Get up
8:00	
9:30	
13:00	
14:00	
15:45	School finishes
18:00	
19:30	
22:00	

（二）根据独白的内容，判断下列句子正误，将 T（正确）或 F（错误）填入题前的括号内。

(　　) 1. At school he wears school uniform.

(　　) 2. He likes French and Art.

(　　) 3. After doing homework he usually plays games.

Section 2

一、听下面的一首诗，请将诗中所缺的内容补充完整。

I listen to the (1) ________, and they say:

"Be true to yourself.

Stand alone, and stand together.
Be (2) _______.
Be (3) _______.
With time, you will grow."

I listen to the (4) _______, and it says:
"Breathe.
Take care of yourself—body, mind, and spirit.
Take time.
Be (5) _______.
Listen from your (6) _______.
Forgive."

I listen to the (7) _______, and they say:
"Be there.
Be (8) _______.
Be trustworthy.
Do what you say (9) _______.
Be true, genuine, and real.
Speak from the heart.
Don't cheat."

I listen to the (10) _______, and they say:
"Be humble.
Be (11) _______.
Respect the beauty of small things.
Respect the beauty of humility and truth.
Let go of perfectionism.
Love yourself as you are; it opens the door to (12) _______.
Practice acceptance."

I listen to the (13) _______, and it says:
"Love.
(14) _______.
Make love.
Be romantic—touch and caress.
Allow yourself to be loved.
Be gentle, kind, and (15) _______."

I listen to the (16) _______, and it says:

"I am your mother.
(17) ________.
Respect all that is (18) ________ you."

二、听句子，然后从A，B，C三个选项中选出一个与你所听到的句子意思一致或最接近的选项。

( ) 1. A. I know that he will come.
B. I know that he won't come.
C. I don't know whether he will come or not.

( ) 2. A. How fine the weather is!
B. How is the weather?
C. What is the weather like?

( ) 3. A. Tom wished his classmate a happy birthday.
B. It's Tom's birthday.
C. Tom's classmate sent him a card.

( ) 4. A. John doesn't like his father.
B. John's father doesn't like him.
C. John and his father look different.

( ) 5. A. Robert has as many books as pencils.
B. Robert has more pencils than books.
C. Robert has no books or pencils.

三、听下面的一段对话，根据对话内容选择最佳答案，并将代表该答案的字母填在题前的括号内。

( ) 1. Where didn't Jack go?
A. Shanghai. B. Guilin. C. Guangzhou.

( ) 2. Where is always crowded in Shanghai?
A. The stores. B. The downtown area. C. The green hills.

( ) 3. When is the woman going to visit the two cities?
A. Next year. B. Next week. C. Next month.

四、听下面的一段材料，完成各个小题。

（一）请把所听到的数字填入下表中。

Spain	Date	Ship(s)	People
Leaving			
Returning			

（二）根据独白内容，判断下列句子的正误，将 T（正确）或 F（错误）填入题前的括号内。

(　　) 1. Most of the planes can fly at 600 miles an hour.

(　　) 2. People can have breakfast and supper both in Tokyo and in Paris.

(　　) 3. Magellan was killed in the Philippines.

(　　) 4. The trip taught people that the world is round.

Section 3

一、听下面一篇短文，按要求完成各个小题。

（一）请将短文中所缺内容补充完整。

The best way of learning a language is (1) ________. The best way of learning English is (2) ________. There may be times (3) ________ and you cannot understand them, and you may get your words mixed up in answering them and they (4) ________. Don't be unhappy if people seem to (5) ________. If you keep your sense of humor, you can always have a good laugh over the mistakes you make. It's (6) ________ to laugh at your mistakes than (7) ________ because they don't understand (8) ________. The most important rule for learning English is "Don't (9) ________." Everyone makes mistakes.

（二）请用刚才填空中所用到的形容词补全句子。

1. My mother is always ________ with me when I do something wrong.
2. We should try to speak as much English as ________ after class.
3. You are a brave boy so don't be ________ of the dark.
4. Heal the world and make it a ________ place.

二、听下面五段对话，根据对话内容选择相应的图片，并将代表该答案的字母填在题前的括号内。

(　　) 1. Where does the man want to go?

A. 

B. 

C. 

(　　) 2. How is the weather now?

A.  B.  C. 

(　　) 3. When will they talk with each other?

A.  B. 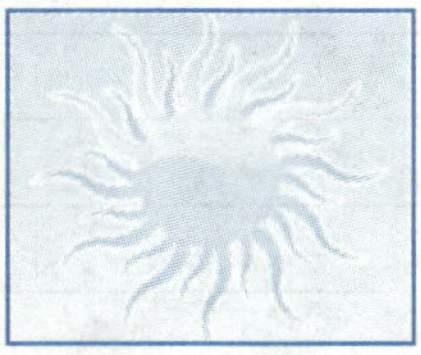 C. 

(　　) 4. How does the man go to Beijing?

A.  B.  C. 

(　　) 5. Which pet does the girl keep?

A.  B.  C. 

三、听下面一篇短文，按要求完成各个小题。

（一）根据短文顺序将下列句子排序。

a. They plant the seeds in a greenhouse in the spring.

b. They put little plants in the ground and water them.

c. In the autumn the pumpkins are big enough and farmers pick them.

d. The seeds grow into little plants.

e. The pumpkins grow very quickly.

f. The flowers grow into little pumpkins.

g. The plants grow bigger and bigger. Yellow flowers begin to grow on the plants.

____

（二）根据短文内容填空。

1. After listening to the passage we will know ____________.

2. Before the seeds grow into little plants, farmers will wait for ____________.

3. A pumpkin leaf looks like ____________.

Section 4

一、听下面十个句子，把所听到的句子写在下面的横线上。

1. ______________________________
2. ______________________________
3. ______________________________
4. ______________________________
5. ______________________________
6. ______________________________
7. ______________________________
8. ______________________________
9. ______________________________
10. ______________________________

二、听下面五段对话，根据对话内容选择相应的图片，并将代表该对话的序号写在图片下的括号内。

( )

( )

( )

( )

( )

三、听下面一段短文，根据短文内容选择最佳答案。

( ) 1. What are scientists trying to do?
A. They are trying to make more deserts.
B. They are trying to make deserts into useful land.
C. They are trying to take water from deserts.

(　　) 2. Why do people want to bring water to desert?

A. Because they can live and grow food.

B. Because many animals can live there.

C. Because they want to drink it.

(　　) 3. How about deserts on the earth now?

A. There are fewer and fewer deserts because of scientists.

B. More and more of the earth is becoming deserts.

C. Scientists can change deserts.

(　　) 4. How do people make deserts?

A. By doing bad things to the earth.

B. By taking water from the earth.

C. By planting trees and grass.

(　　) 5. Which of the following is true?

A. Without much rain some places will become deserts.

B. Plants let the wind blow the dirt away easier.

C. Plants can stop the land from becoming a desert.

四、听下面一段电影录音，完成下列各题。

(　　) 1. Which movie is it?

A. 

B. 

C. 

(　　) 2. What is a Dementor?

A. A prisoner in Azkaban.

B. A guard in Azkaban.

C. A guard in Hogwarts.

(　　) 3. Which page does the teacher ask the students to turn to?

A. Page 384.　　B. Page 494.　　C. Page 394.

Section 5

一、听下面一段对话，根据对话内容选择最佳答案，并将代表该答案的字母填在题前的括号内。

(　　) 1. What are they talking about?

A. How to open the door in the future.

B. The home in the future.

C. The activities in the future.

( ) 2. Who can use the fingerprints to open your door?

A. Your close friends. B. The policeman. C. Your grandfather.

( ) 3. What needn't we do in the future?

A. Put our fingers on the button to open the door.

B. Clean up the rooms.

C. Study and join the activities.

二、听下面一段短文，根据短文内容选出最佳答案。

( ) 1. Which sport does the speaker like best?

A.  B.  C. 

( ) 2. Swimming can make people ________.

A. hot, relaxed and comfortable

B. cool, tired and comfortable

C. cool, relaxed and comfortable

( ) 3. Who likes swimming?

A. The young.

B. The old.

C. Both the young and the old.

( ) 4. Swimming is the best and the most popular sport ________.

A. in summer B. in winter C. in spring

( ) 5. Swimming provides an opportunity for people to ________.

A. get enough money B. get enough exercise C. get fresh air

三、听下面两段材料，根据所听内容完成各个小题，并将代表最佳答案的字母填在题前的括号内。

听下面一段电影片段，完成1~3题。

( ) 1. What is Alex, the King of New York?

A.  B.  C. 

(　　) 2. The old lady said that the animal was a very bad ________.

A. puppy　　B. doggy　　C. kitty

(　　) 3. Which place did people want to send the animals to?

A. Asia.　　B. Africa.　　C. America.

听下面的原声录音，完成4～6题。

(　　) 4. Which of the following famous people is NOT mentioned in the passage?

A. Albert Einstein.　　B. Douglas McArthur.　　C. Isaac Newton.

(　　) 5. When did Winston Churchill become the Prime Minister of Britain?

A. When he was 42.　　B. When he was 52.　　C. When he was 62.

(　　) 6. Who was cut from the basketball team when he was in high school?

A. Michael Jordan.　　B. Kobe Bryant.　　C. Lebrown James.

四、听下面一段独白，请把独白中的每一句话完整地记录下来。

____

____

____

____

____

____

____

Unit 15

Section 1

一、听下面关于职业的十个单词，并将它们写在横线上。

1. ________ 2. ________ 3. ________ 4. ________ 5. ________
6. ________ 7. ________ 8. ________ 9. ________ 10. ________

二、听下面的十个句子，根据所听内容选出相应的答语，并将代表该答案的字母填在题前的括号内。

( ) 1. A. Thank you. B. The same to you. C. So kind of you.
( ) 2. A. Very early. B. Very late. C. At 8:30.
( ) 3. A. By bike. B. On time. C. Very happy.
( ) 4. A. He likes watching TV.
B. He is a doctor.
C. He works in a factory.
( ) 5. A. I'm sorry. B. Good idea. C. Pardon?
( ) 6. A. Physics. B. Red. C. Watermelon.
( ) 7. A. He is a good student. B. He works hard. C. He is 15.
( ) 8. A. It doesn't matter. B. Of course not. C. Certainly.
( ) 9. A. It's my pleasure. B. That's all right. C. Excuse me.
( ) 10. A. It's her. B. It's hers. C. It's Mary.

三、听下面的十句话，根据句意选出相应的图片，并将代表该图片的字母填在题前的括号内。

( ) 1. A. 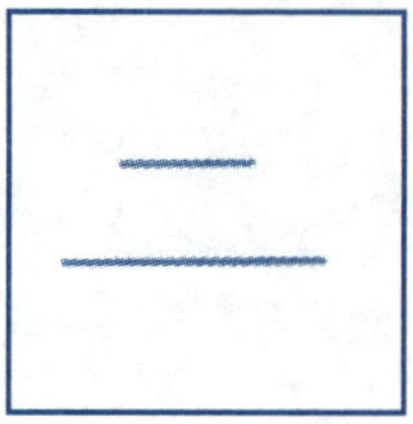 B.  C. 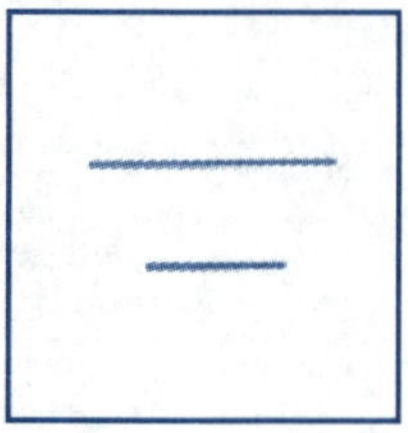

( ) 2. A.

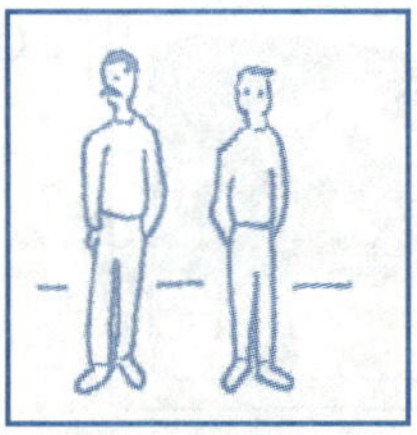

B.

C.

( ) 3. A.

B.

C.

( ) 4. A.

B.

C.

( ) 5. A.

B.

C.

( ) 6. A.

B.

C.

( ) 7. A.

B.

C.

( ) 8. A.

B.

C.

( ) 9. A. 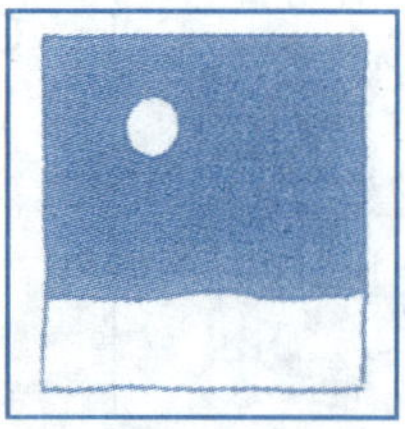 B.  C. 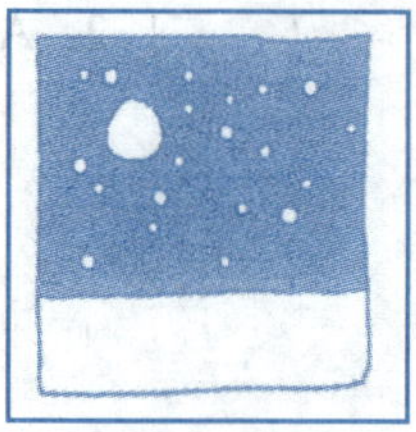

( ) 10. A. 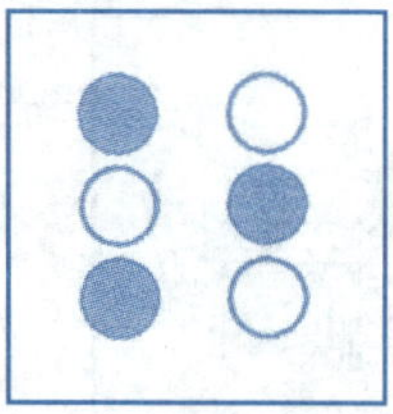 B. 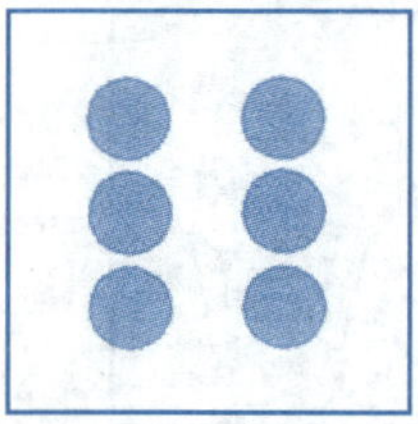 C. 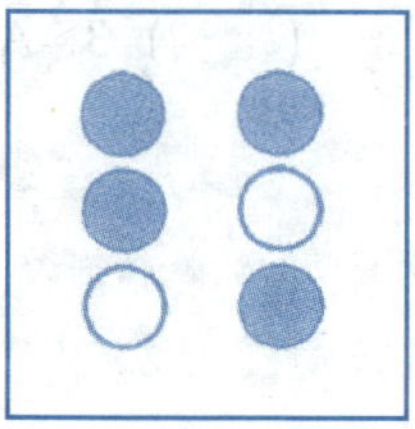

四、听下面三段独白，根据独白内容回答问题。

听第一段独白，回答1 ~2 题。

1. Does Mr. White drink coffee for dinner?

____

2. How many cups of coffee does he drink every day?

____

听第二段独白，回答 3 ~4 题。

3. Does Hebie have Japanese stamps?

____

4. How many stamps does Hebie have now?

____

听第三段独白，回答 5 ~6 题。

5. How many pieces of candy does Kathy eat every day?

____

6. How many times does she eat candy every day?

____

Section 2

一、听下面一首歌，根据歌词填空。

Lemon Tree

I'm sitting here in the (1) ________

It's just another rainy (2) ________

I'm wasting my time, I got nothing to do

I'm hanging around, I'm (3) ________
But nothing ever happens, and I wonder
I'm driving (4) ________
I'm driving too fast, I'm driving too far I'd like to (5) ________
I feel so (6) ________, I'm waiting for you
But (7) ________, and I wonder
I wonder (8) ________, I wonder (9) ________
Yesterday you told me about the blue-blue sky
And all that I can see is (10) ________
I'm turning my head (11) ________
I'm turning, turning, turning, turning, turning around
And all that I can see is just (12) ________

二、听下面七段独白，根据独白内容依次写出七种职业。

1. ____________ 2. ____________ 3. ____________
4. ____________ 5. ____________ 6. ____________
7. ____________

三、听下面五段小对话，根据对话内容回答相应的问题，并将代表该答案的字母填在题前的括号内。

( ) 1. When will the man see the dentist?
A. On Friday. B. On Saturday. C. On Sunday.

( ) 2. Why is the man in a hurry?
A. He is going to catch the plane.
B. He is going to drive the car.
C. He is going to catch the train.

( ) 3. Which box does the man like?
A. The bigger one. B. The smaller one. C. Both of them.

( ) 4. What does the girl's sister do?
A. A teacher. B. A reporter. C. A doctor.

( ) 5. What is the weather like in Tianjin?
A. Windy. B. Cloudy. C. Sunny.

四、听下面一段独白，在图片人物上方标出其名字所属序号。

1. grandfather 2. grandmother 3. I 4. Jack 5. Sophie 6. Tim

Section 3

一、听下面一篇文章，根据文章内容填空。

Early Monday morning is (1) ________ in Cambridge. Men and women usually (2) ________. Some people (3) ________, some people (4) ________, and others (4) ________. Children usually (6) ________. Some children (7) ________, some children (8) ________, and others (9) ________. The city is usually very busy. Trucks deliver food to (10) ________, mail carriers deliver mail to (11) ________, and police officers direct traffic (12) ________.

二、听下面六段独白，根据独白内容选择相应的图片。

A. 

B. 

C. 

D. 

E. 

F. 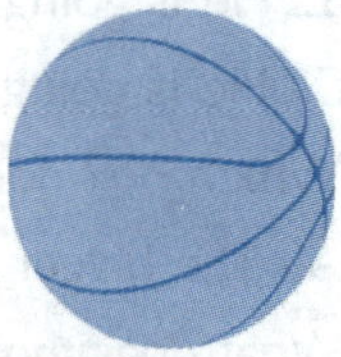

1. ________ 2. ________ 3. ________
4. ________ 5. ________ 6. ________

三、听下面一篇短文，根据短文内容将下列活动排序。

A. Go to the airport. B. Get up early. C. Have lunch.
D. Go to a concert. E. Drive her to Boston. F. Visit Harvard University.
G. Visit places of interest.

1. ______ 2. ______ 3. ______ 4. ______ 5. ______ 6. ______ 7. ______

四、听下面一段短文，根据短文内容判断下列句子的正误，将 T（正确）或 F（错误）填入题前的括号内。

(　　) 1. There are two hills far from his home.
(　　) 2. The school is next to the valley.
(　　) 3. He walks to school every day.
(　　) 4. There is a small river next to school, over which there is a stone bridge.
(　　) 5. The playground in front of the teaching building is small.
(　　) 6. Children often climb the trees after school.
(　　) 7. When autumn comes, all the teachers and students will help farmers with their harvest.

Section 4

一、听下面一篇短文，请把短文中空缺的部分补充完整。

We usually say that people have five senses. Senses are the way that (1) __________. The five main senses are (2) __________. Each sense usually depends on one organ of the body. (3) __________ and then the nerves (4) __________. For example, eyes control sight, (5) __________ and (6) __________. Taste depends on the tongue and (7) __________. There are also other important senses. There is the sense of balance, (8) __________. (9) __________.

二、听下面三段小对话，回答 1 ~6 题。

听第一段对话，回答 1 ~2 题。

1. What is the man going to do at five?

____

2. Where is the girl going?

____

听第二段对话，回答 3 ~4 题。

3. What does his mother do?

____

4. What will the son do if his father comes back as usual?

____

听第三段对话，回答5 ~6 题。

5. What is the woman?

____

6. How many books can the man borrow at a time?

____

三、听下面一段独白，选出独白内容所涉及活动的图片，并将图片的序号排序。

A. 

B. 

C. 

D. 

E. 

F. 

G. 

H. 

I. 

J. 

1. 你所听到的内容涉及的图片：______________________________

2. 图片的顺序：______________________________

四、听下面一段电影录音，完成下列各题。

(　　) 1. What is the prince's name?

A. Prince Handsome. B. Prince Charming. C. Prince Cool.

(　　) 2. What is the prince trying to do?

A. He is trying to save a princess.

B. He is fighting a dragon.

C. He is meeting a man.

(　　) 3. What is the princess' name?

A. Sandra.　　B. Fiona.　　C. Christina.

(　　) 4. Where is the princess when the prince arrives?

A. She is sleeping in the bed.

B. She is on her honeymoon.

C. She is died.

Section 5

一、听下面一段对话，根据对话内容选择最佳答案，并将代表该答案的字母填在题前的括号内。

(　　) 1. How long will Alan go overseas?

A. For a week.　　B. For a month.　　C. For a year.

(　　) 2. What can Alan do in Hong Kong if she goes there?

A. 　B. 　C. 

(　　) 3. Which places is Alan allowed to go?

A. She is allowed to go to Paris, Hong Kong and Rome.

B. She is allowed to go to Switzerland, Beijing and Rome.

C. She is allowed to go to Paris, Beijing and Rome.

(　　) 4. Where does Alan decide to go at last?

A. 　B. 　C. 

二、听下面十段小独白，分辨是下图中 A，B，C，D 哪个人所说的话，并将独白序号写在下面横线上。

A：__________ B：__________

C：__________ D：__________

三、听下面两段材料，根据所听内容完成各个小题，并将代表最佳答案的字母填在题前的括号内。

听下面一首歌，回答 1 ~3 题。

(　　) 1. This song is about ________.

A. a town　　B. New Year's Day　　C. Christmas

(　　) 2. In the song, the presents for the children are packed in ________.

A. red　　B. green　　C. red and green

(　　) 3. No one will be sleeping on the Christmas Eve because ________.

A. they are having dinner with their parents

B. they are waiting for Santa Clause

C. they are playing with each other

听下面一则录音，回答 4 ~7 题。

(　　) 4. Where did the story take place?

A. America.　　B. Britain.　　C. Australia.

(　　) 5. Who is the writer of the story?

A. Mark Twin.　　B. Shep O'Neal.　　C. O. Henry.

(　　) 6. What was the weather like at the beginning of the story?

A. 　　B. 　　C. 

( ) 7. What did the man that the writer met look like?

A. Tall and thin. B. Tall and fat. C. Fit.

四、听下面一段独白，请把独白中的每一句话完整地记录下来。

____

____

____

____

____

____

____

Unit 16

Section 1

一、听下面一段独白，根据独白内容填上所缺的单词。

I live in a small (1) ________ near South London. Lots of (2) ________ in this town do the (3) ________ thing at the same time every (4) ________. Every morning, Mr. Brain (5) ________ past the town bank at 7 o'clock. He's on his way to his job at the (6) ________ station. He must get (7) ________ for the first morning train. And just when he walks past the bank, John Smith's (8) ________ shop is open. I can always see them (9) ________ hello to (10) ________ other.

二、听下面五段对话，根据所听到的内容填写下列表格。

	Place to go	Bus number
1.		
2.		
3.		
4.		
5.		

三、听下面四段对话，根据对话内容选出最佳图片，并将代表该图片的序号填在题前的括号内。

听第一段对话，回答1~2题。

(　　) 1. Where is the woman going?

A. 

B. 

C. 

(　　) 2. How will the woman go there?

A.  B.  C. 

听第二段对话，回答 3 ~4 题。

(　　) 3. Where is the woman going?

A.  B.  C. 

(　　) 4. How will the man's friend come?

A.  B.  C. 

听第三段对话，回答 5 ~6 题。

(　　) 5. Where will the woman go?

A.  B.  C. 

(　　) 6. Where does the conversation take place?

A. 

B. 

C. 

听第四段对话，回答 7 ~8 题。

(　　) 7. Where will Linda's friend meet Jim?

A.  B.  C. 

(　　) 8. What does Linda's friend look like?

A.  B.  C. 

四、听下面一段材料，根据内容判断下列句子的正误，将 T（正确）或 F（错误）填入题前的括号内。

(　　) 1. Joe and Bob are good friends.

(　　) 2. Bob gets up late.

(　　) 3. Joe plays the piano well.

(　　) 4. Bob doesn't draw pictures beautifully.

(　　) 5. Bob does his homework carefully.

(　　) 6. Joe eats slowly.

(　　) 7. Joe hates housework.

Section 9

一、听下面一首诗，请将诗中所缺内容补充完整。

What is pink? (1) ________
By the fountain's brink.
(2) ________? A poppy's red
In its barley bed.
What is blue? (3) ________
Where the clouds float through.
What is white? (4) ________
Sailing in the light.

What is yellow? (5) ________
Rich and ripe and mellow.
What is green? (6) ________
With small flowers between.
What is violet? (7) ________
In the summer twilight.
What is orange? Why, an orange,
(8) ________!

二、看下面的图片，你将听见十句描述本图片的句子。根据图片判断句子的正误，将 T（正确）或 F（错误）填在横线上。

1. ________ 2. ________ 3. ________ 4. ________ 5. ________
6. ________ 7. ________ 8. ________ 9. ________ 10. ________

三、听下面十段小对话，根据对话内容选择最佳答案，并将代表该答案的字母写在题前的括号内。

(　　) 1. How does the color red make people feel?
A. Angry.　　B. Hungry.　　C. Relaxed.

(　　) 2. Where does the conversation take place?
A. In a cinema.　　B. In a shop.　　C. In a restaurant.

(　　) 3. How is the weather now?
A. Rainy.　　B. Windy.　　C. Sunny.

(　　) 4. What is Linda doing?
A. Listening to music.

B. Reading a newspaper.

C. Watching TV.

(　　) 5. When did she start diving?

A. In 1985.　　B. In 1991.　　C. In 1998.

(　　) 6. How does David often go to school?

A. On foot.　　B. By bus.　　C. By bike.

(　　) 7. What is the relationship between them?

A. Strangers.　　B. Good friends.　　C. Father and daughter.

(　　) 8. What does the woman want to have?

A. A cup of coffee.　　B. A cup to tea.　　C. A cup of juice.

(　　) 9. When does the concert begin?

A. 9:00.　　B. 9:15.　　C. 8:45.

(　　) 10. What will the girl do tomorrow?

A. She will go boating.

B. She will go skating.

C. She will go fishing.

四、听下面一段长对话，根据对话内容填空。

1. The woman would like to book a ________ room with a ________ and a ________ bed.

2. Her full name is ____________________.

3. Her nationality is ________.

4. The woman will stay ________.

5. She will pay ________ dollars in all.

6. Her passport number is ________.

7. She will pay with ________.

8. The room number is ________, on ________ floor.

Section 3

一、听下面十个句子，把你所听到的句子写在下面的横线上。

1. ____

2. ____

3. ____

4. ____

5. ____
6. ____
7. ____
8. ____
9. ____
10. ____

二、听下面一段长对话，根据对话内容将对话中的地点写在食物下的横线上。

A. San Francisco B. Seattle C. Chicago D. New York E. Boston

1. 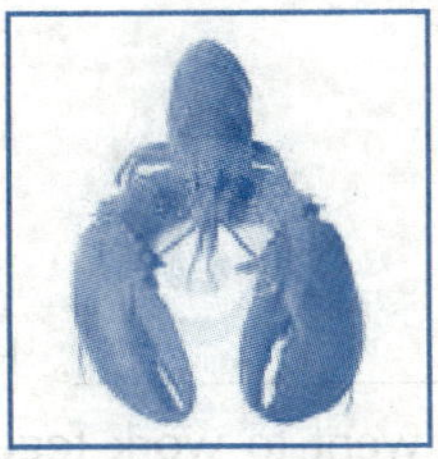 ____________
2.  ____________
3.  ____________

4.  ____________
5. 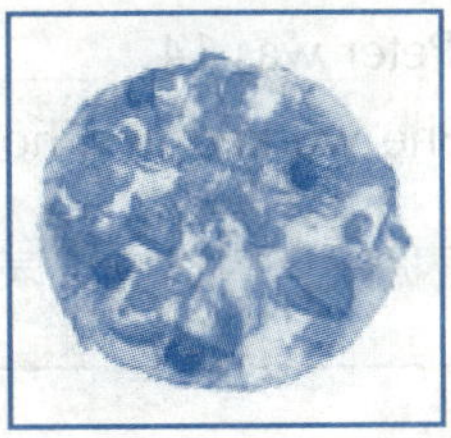 ____________
6.  ____________

三、听下面两篇短文，根据短文内容选择最佳答案。

听第一篇短文，完成1～4题。

( ) 1. What happened when I was sleeping?

A. I couldn't fall asleep.

B. I was woken up by wind.

C. I was woken up by some noise.

( ) 2. What did I see when I went into the living room?

A. I saw something black. B. I saw nothing. C. I saw a thief.

( ) 3. Where did I take out a gun?

A. From a desk. B. From my bed. C. From a drawer.

( ) 4. What did I do at last?

A. I shot it. B. I dropped my gun. C. I was afraid.

听第二篇短文，完成5～8题。

( ) 5. What isn't the White family doing?

A. Sitting in the yard. B. Drinking coffee. C. Eating fruit.

( ) 6. Who is going to study in Cambridge University?

A. Abby. B. Jason. C. Ben.

( ) 7. What is Jimmy going to buy?

A. A new car. B. A toy car. C. A used car.

( ) 8. How will Mr. and Mrs. White go to Hawaii?

A. By air. B. By car. C. By ship.

Section 4

一、听下面一篇短文，填上所缺内容。

20 years ago, Mr. and Mrs. Brown lived in London. ____________. His wife worked in a school. ____________. Mr. and Mrs. Brown went to work together by car. Mrs. Brown drove ____________. There were three children in the Brown family. ________________. Peter was 14. ________________. Susan was the oldest. ________________. She worked in a hotel.

二、听下面一段采访对话，根据对话内容完成表格。

Name: ________

Job: ________

Major events:

________ Born in ________

________ Started wushu training when he was ________ years old

1970s Won ________ national gold medals

________ Made his first film

________ Made his first Hollywood film

三、听下面一篇短文，根据短文内容选出代表 Sam 和 Lily 周末活动的图片，并填在相应的横线上。图片可以循环使用。

A. 

B. 

C. 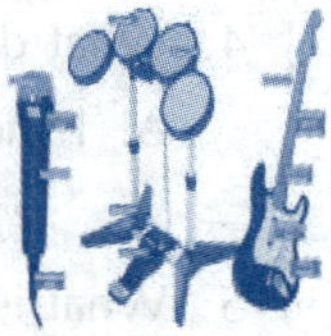

D. 

E. 

F. 

G. 

H. 

I. 

J. 

K. 

L. 

M. 

N. 

On Fridays: ________________

On Saturdays: ________________

On Sundays: ________________

四、听下面两段材料，根据所听内容完成各个小题，并将代表最佳答案的字母填在题前的括号内。

听下面一则录音，回答1～4题。

(　　) 1. What is the time?

A. A morning on April 20, 1990.

B. A morning on April 20, 1999.

C. An evening on April 20, 1990.

(　　) 2. What did the milkman do on that morning?

A. He slept very late.

B. He made his delivery as usually.

C. He went to feed his cows.

(　　) 3. Where does Mrs. Hughes come from?

A. Florida.　　B. Texas.　　C. Michigan.

(　　) 4. In Colorado, two boys went bowling at ________.

A. 5:00 am　　B. 6:00 am　　C. 7:00 am

听下面一段电影片段，回答5～7题。

( ) 5. When did the story begin?

A. A July twenty years ago.

B. A January twenty years ago.

C. A June twenty years ago.

( ) 6. What happened in that afternoon?

A. There was a wedding.

B. Someone borrowed something.

C. The two girls got married.

( ) 7. What did the two little girls dream of?

A. Playing bride and groom.

B. Getting married at the Plaza Hotel in June.

C. Drinking tea at the Plaza Hotel.

Section 5

一、听下面一段介绍华盛顿的材料，完成下列各小题。

(一) 请按材料介绍的顺序将下列图片排序。

A. 

B. 

C. 

D. 

E. 

1. ________ 2. ________ 3. ________ 4. ________ 5. ________

(二) 根据材料内容选出最佳答案。

1. The person is ________.

A. a driver B. a guide C. a teacher

2. He is telling something about ________.

A. London B. Paris C. Washington, D. C.

3. The tour will take ________.

A. 2 hours　　　　B. 3 hours　　　　C. a day

二、听下面一段长对话，根据对话内容回答下列各题。

1. How many times does Sam go to Los Angeles?

____

2. Where will Sam go after visiting Los Angeles?

____

3. Where are Sam's plane tickets?

____

4. What kind of room has Sam booked?

____

5. What does Sam ask Lily to do?

____

三、听下面两段材料，根据所听内容完成各个小题，并将代表最佳答案的字母填在题前的括号内。

听下面一段电影片段，回答1~3题。

(　　) 1. Which of the following movies do you think it is?

A. 

B. 

C. 

(　　) 2. What did the man ask the woman to eat?

A. Fruit.　　　　B. Chocolate.　　　　C. Vegetables.

(　　) 3. What did his Mom always say to him?

A. Life was like a magician's box, you never know what you're gonna get.

B. Life was like a box of chocolates, you never know what you're gonna get.

C. Life was like a box of presents, you never know what you're gonna get.

听下面一则录音，回答4~6题。

(　　) 4. What is this activity?

A.

B.

C.

(　　) 5. Where are these people?

A. In Beijing.　　B. In Paris.　　C. In L. A.

(　　) 6. Which is NOT the sponsor（赞助商）of this activity?

A. diet Coke　　B. Sprint　　C. Plymouth Rock assurance

四、听下面一段独白，请把独白中的每一句话完整地记录下来。

____

____

____

____

____

____

____

Test 1

一、听下面几段录音片断，根据所听内容完成各个小题，并将代表最佳答案的字母填在题前的括号内。每段片断仅播放一遍。

听下面一段录音，完成 1 ~4 题。

(　　) 1. What is this movie?

A. *The Lord of the Rings.*　B. *Troy.*　C. *Sparta.*

(　　) 2. What is the weather like?

A. 　B. 　C. 

(　　) 3. Where are the two brothers from?

A. Sparta.　B. Greece.　C. Troy.

(　　) 4. What are they quarrelling (争吵) for?

A. For their father.　B. For a woman.　C. For a war.

听下面的录音，回答 5 ~7 题。

(　　) 5. Where did President Obama make the speech?

A. In Egypt.　B. In Dubai.　C. In Istanbul.

(　　) 6. Where is the President going later?

A. Egypt.　B. Germany.　C. France.

(　　) 7. What will he do after he leaves Germany?

A. To meet some Asian leaders (领导人).

B. To join the 65th anniversary of D-Day.

C. To go back to America.

听下面的录音，回答 8 ~11 题。

(　　) 8. What is the name of the show?

A. Who wants to be a billionaire?

B. Who wants to be a millionaire?

C. Who wants to be rich?

(　　) 9. How much can the contestant (选手) win if he answers the final question correctly?

A. 10, 000, 000 rupees.

B. 20,000,000 rupees.

C. 2,000,000 rupees.

(　　) 10. Which of the following books is the question about?

A. 

B. 

C. 

(　　) 11. What does the contestant want to do to look for help?

A. Cross out two wrong answers.

B. Ask the audience (观众) for help.

C. Call a friend for help.

二、听下面五个问句，根据所听内容选出相应的答语，并将代表该答案的字母填在题前的括号内。每个问题仅读一遍。

(　　) 1. A. He is tall. B. He is reading. C. He is at home.

(　　) 2. A. It's OK! B. Thirty dollars. C. I like it very much.

(　　) 3. A. That's all right. B. You are welcome. C. Thanks a lot.

(　　) 4. A. Thanks! The same to you. B. I'm OK. C. Me, too.

(　　) 5. A. At times. B. At 8:10 am. C. Not long.

三、听下面五段对话，根据对话内容选择合适的图片，并将代表该图片的字母填在题前括号内。每段对话读一遍。

(　　) 1. How will they go to California?

A. 

B. 

C. 

(　　) 2. What does the man still need?

A. 

B. 

C. 

(　　) 3. What do they want to eat?

A. 

B. 

C. 

(　　) 4. What does the man do?

A.

B.

C.

(　　) 5. What does the girl think is the most popular game?

A.

B.

C.

四、听下面几段对话，每段对话后有一个小题，从题中所给的选项中选出正确答案填在题前括号内。每段对话仅读一遍。

(　　) 1. How is the weather when they are talking?

A. Rainy.　　B. Cloudy.　　C. Fine.

(　　) 2. What are they mainly talking about?

A. An English map.　　B. A stamp.　　C. England.

(　　) 3. Why didn't Linda go to Ann's birthday party?

A. She was ill.

B. She didn't want to go.

C. She had to stay with her uncle.

(　　) 4. What time did the concert start?

A. At 7:50.　　B. At 7:00.　　C. At 7:35.

(　　) 5. What does Mary mean?

A. She doesn't want to help Tom at all.

B. She can help Tom this evening.

C. She is busy with English now.

五、听下面一段独白，根据所听内容选择合适的答案填在题前的括号内。短文读一遍。

(　　) 1. What's the first thing I do in the morning?

A. Do some exercise.　　B. Have breakfast.　　C. Take a shower.

(　　) 2. How do I go to school?

A. Take a bus.　　B. Ride a bike.　　C. Walk.

(　　) 3. How many classes do I usually have in the afternoon?

A. One.　　B. Two.　　C. Four.

(　　) 4. Where do I usually go after my classes?

A. My teacher's office.　　B. My home.　　C. The library.

Test 2

一、听下面几段录音片断，根据所听内容完成各个小题，并将代表最佳答案的字母填在题前的括号内。每段片断仅播放一遍。

听下面一段录音，完成 1 ~3 题。

(　　) 1. Whose story is it?

A. Julius Caesar.　　B. Napoleon Bonaparte.　C. King Arthur.

(　　) 2. When did the hero live?

A. 600 years ago.　　B. 1, 600 years ago.　　C. 6, 000 years ago.

(　　) 3. Which of the following statements is NOT the same as it is in the passage?

A. My power shall be with you wherever you go.

B. On this day, if this be our destiny, so be it!

C. Remember my face; it will be the last thing you see on this earth.

听下面一段演讲，完成 4 ~6 题。

(　　) 4. Who made this speech?

A. 

B. 

C. 

(　　) 5. What happened to Ronald Reagan?

A. He died.　　B. He is hurt.　　C. He is ill.

(　　) 6. Which of the following qualities（品格）is NOT the same as in the speech?

A. The confidence that comes with conviction.

B. The strength that comes with character.

C. The gentleness that comes with humility.

听下面一首诗歌，完成 7 ~9 题。

(　　) 7. Which season is the poem about?

A. Spring.　　B. Summer.　　C. Autumn.

(　　) 8. Who was the writer of the poem?

A. John Keats.　　B. T. S. Eliot.　　C. William Yeats.

(　　) 9. Which of the following is NOT in the poem?

A. 
B. 
C. 

二、听下面五个句子，并从所给的选项中选出意思相同或相近的一项。每个句子仅读一遍。

(　　) 1. A. My number is 1009.
B. 1009 is my car's number.
C. 1099 is my car's number.

(　　) 2. A. Brad studies English in Class 8.
B. Brad teaches English in Class 9.
C. Brad teaches English in Class 8.

(　　) 3. A. Sandra gives Stanley a book.
B. Stanley gets a book from Sandra.
C. Sandra gives Stanley some books.

(　　) 4. A. I sit next to Jessie.
B. Jessie's seat is opposite mine.
C. Jessie's seat and mine are the same.

(　　) 5. A. It's time for lunch.
B. It's time for breakfast.
C. It's time to have dinner.

三、听下面几段对话，每段对话后有一个小题，从题中所给的选项中选出正确答案填在题前括号内。每段对话仅读一遍。

(　　) 1. Why is Amy sure that David is in his room?
A. Because he is singing in his room.
B. Because the light is on.
C. Because he is making some noise.

(　　) 2. What is the man?
A. A doctor.　　B. A soldier.　　C. A reporter.

(　　) 3. Why is Sally in a hurry?
A. She has a stomachache.
B. She has to meet her Mom.
C. She has to say goodbye to her Mom.

( ) 4. What are they talking about?

A. Eating healthy food. B. Weather. C. Exercise.

( ) 5. Where is Carla now?

A. In her room. B. In the cinema. C. In the street.

四、听下面的对话或短文，每段对话或短文后有几个问题。从题中所给的选项中选择最佳答案。每段对话或短文读两遍。

听第一段材料，回答1～2题。

( ) 1. Where does Barry's father work?

A. In a cinema.

B. In a movie company.

C. In a poster company.

( ) 2. Who has the poster at last?

A. Barry. B. Tina. C. Berry's father.

听第二段材料，回答3～5题。

( ) 3. What does the man want to drink?

A. Pop. B. Coffee. C. Lemonade.

( ) 4. How many children does the man have?

A. One. B. Two. C. Three.

( ) 5. How much does the man have to pay?

A. 10 yuan. B. 12 yuan. C. 20 yuan.

五、听下面一段对话，根据你所听到的内容完成各个小题。对话读两遍。

（一）根据你所听到的内容选择最佳答案。

( ) 1. Where did the man lose his thing?

A. In his hotel. B. On a train. C. On a bus.

( ) 2. How long is the man going to stay here?

A. A few days. B. A few weeks. C. A few months.

( ) 3. How will he get it if they found the thing he lost?

A. They will call him.

B. They will send it to him.

C. He will come and see by himself.

（二）根据你所听到的内容完成表格。

Lost Property Form

Name: Mark Adams	Nationality: American
Lost Property: (1) a ______________ (Samsung G302)	
Address: (2) ______________, Lyndon Drive, Leighton, Essex.	
Telephone: (3) ______________	

Tapescripts

Unit 1

Section 1

一、听对话，根据问题选出最佳答案。

1. W: What do we need to get from the supermarket?
   M: We need lots of things. I'll make a list. We need a bag of sugar, a loaf of bread and a crate of beer.
2. W: Let's go and get a coffee together. That will help you to wake up again!
   M: OK. I feel like sitting down and having a chat.
3. W: How have you been recently?
   M: Oh, you know me. I'm always happy! If I think I'm getting into a bad mood, I call some friends and socialize or have a chat.
   W: That's a good idea. I usually just sit at home alone and get increasingly moody.
4. W: Hello! What are you reading about in the newspaper?
   M: Hello! I was tired from studying, so I decided to read the newspaper to relax. Unfortunately, the news is so depressing. There has been another murder in the city center. I'm shocked that the police haven't caught the killer yet.
5. W: Do you like animals? I really like rabbits. They are so cute.
   M: So do I. But I don't like dogs.
   W: Why? I think dogs are cute, too.
   M: I can't bear being near dogs. They don't seem to like me either.
6. W: Have you bought a present for Jim's birthday yet?
   M: No, I haven't. I can't think of anything to get him.
   W: I'm having the same problem. I want to get something really special. Jim always seems to know exactly what to get people as a gift.
   M: I know. He bought me that beautiful sweater for my birthday. It was exactly what I wanted. And it fits me perfectly!
7. W: What do you hope to do when you finish university?

M: I'd like to go into management. I've applied for several jobs already and I'm hopeful that I'll get some job offers. How about you?

W: After I graduate, I have to do some more studies to pass exams to become a lawyer. I think I've got a good chance of passing.

8. W: My father wanted me to become a doctor, but I knew it would be impossible for me to be successful in that field.

M: I hope my parents don't try to interfere in my choice of career.

9. W: Are you good at making decisions?

M: Not really. Sometimes, I even let other people make key decisions for me.

W: What kinds of decisions do you leave to other people?

M: There are basic decisions like which restaurant to go to. I can never seem to choose.

10. W: Which countries have you been to?

M: I've been to most of the countries in Europe, several countries in Asia—China, Japan, and Thailand—and to the United States and Canada.

二、你将会听到一段关于世界各国人们的睡眠和饮食时间研究结果的新闻，讲述了世界各国的人花在睡眠和用餐上的不同时间。

（一）听说明，做出正确的选择。

True to their reputation as leisure-loving gourmets, the French spend more time sleeping and eating than anyone else among the world's wealthy nations, according to a study published on Monday.

The average French person sleeps almost 9 hours every night, 2 hours longer than the average Japanese and Korean, who sleep the least in the survey of 18 members of the Organization for Economic Cooperation and Development (OECD).

Despite their siesta habit, the German sleep 8 hours a day, rank only third in the poll after Americans, who sleep more than 8. 5 hours.

And while more and more French people grab a bite at fast-food chains these days or wolf down a sandwich at their desks, they still spend 3 hours a day eating.

That means their meals are twice as long as those of the average Mexican, who dedicate just 1. 5 hours a day to food.

The Japanese, working long hours, still manage to spend 2 hours a day eating and drinking, placing them third behind New Zealanders, who spend 2. 5 hours eating.

The moderate amount of time Americans spend eating each day is about 1. 25 hours.

The Japanese like to spend their free time watching television or listening to the radio. This takes up 47 percent of leisure time in Japan.

The Italian, on the other hand, spend more than a third of their leisure time entertaining friends.

Norwegians spend the most time at leisure, just over a quarter of their day, while at the low end, Mexicans spend just 16 percent of their time having fun.

The OECD has 30 members. The survey covers only the countries for which appropriate figures were available.

（二）再听一次研究结果，在图表的1、2、3、4、5处标注相应的国名。

Section 2

一、听一段关于胡萝卜的科普广播，根据你所听到的内容，在横线上填上所缺的单词。

Carrots are grown on farms and in family gardens throughout the world. Carrots are easy to raise and easy to harvest. They taste good. And they contain a lot of carotene, which the body makes into Vitamin A.

When people think of carrots, they usually picture in their mind a vegetable that is long, thin and orange in color. But carrots come in many different sizes and shapes. And not all carrots are orange.

For example, Paris Market carrots are about five centimeters around. Imperator carrots are thin and about twenty-five centimeters long. And Belgian White carrots are, as their name suggests, white.

二、听下面三段长对话，每段长对话后都有三至四个小题。从题中所给的A，B，C三个选项中选出最佳答案。

听第一段对话，回答1～3题。

W：Do you think children watch too much TV?

M：I only allow my child to watch up to an hour a day. I don't think that TV is bad for kids. I think that kids should be active and not become couch potatoes.

W：Perhaps I should impose a limit on how much TV my kids can watch. They don't do much else in their free time. At least they always do their homework first.

M：If you decide to put a limit on the amount of TV they can watch, remember to have something else for them to do. If you don't, they'll get bored and misbehave.

W：They could go out and play with their friends.

M：Sure. You could talk to other parents in our neighbourhood and plan it so that all the kids are free at the same time.

W：Perhaps I could ask my husband to teach them football or something. He watches too much TV, too.

M：That's a good idea. Remember that if the parents watch too much TV, the kids will probably follow them.

听第二段对话，回答4～6题。

W：Shall we go to cinema this evening? The new movie starring Mel Gibson is showing. It's supposed to be really good.

M：What kind of movie is it? I don't like many of his movies, actually.

W：It's a comedy. It has Julia Roberts playing the female lead.

M：I like comedy and I like Julia Roberts, so it might be interesting. I read a review today and the critic didn't seem to be very impressed.

W：What did the critic say?

M：He didn't say it was bad, but he said that it wasn't as good as it could have been, particularly as there were some good actors and actresses in it.

W：The movie starts at eight o'clock, so we have plenty of time to eat and get ready.

M：Good. Dinner is nearly ready and I'd like to watch the evening news before we go. The Oscars were last night and I want to see the results.

W：I won't spoil your enjoyment by telling you who won. There were a few surprises.

听第三段对话，回答7～10题。

W：London is such a historic city! There's history everywhere you look. There's Nelson's column, built as a monument to one of the Britain's great admirals and his important victory. He won the battle of Trafalgar in 1805.

M：I'm looking forward to seeing Westminster Abbey, where many historic figures are buried, like Isaac Newton, the great mathematician and Winston Churchill, the great wartime leader.

W：Nearby, on the banks of the Thames, there's the statue of Boudicea. She fought the Romans when they invaded Britain.

M：Women have often played an important role in British history. Queen Elizabeth Ⅰ built a navy strong enough to fight off the Spanish armada in 1588. More recently, Margaret Thatcher transformed British society in the 1980s.

W：She was a very controversial leader. Are we going to visit the famous Tower of London later?

M：There's a lot to see there. Perhaps we should go tomorrow.

三、你将听到一段关于胡萝卜的科普广播的后半段。根据你听到的内容完成练习。

（一）听录音，选出最佳答案。

（二）再听一次录音，根据你听到的内容，在横线上填上所缺的词或句子。

For the best results, carrots should be grown in sandy soil that does not hold water for a long time. The soil also should have no rocks.

To prepare your carrot garden, dig up the soil, loosen it and turn it over. Then, mix in some plant material or animal fertilizer.

Weather, soil conditions and age will affect the way carrots taste. Experts say warm days, cool nights and a medium soil temperature are the best conditions for growing carrots that taste great.

Carrots need time to develop their full sugar content. This gives them their taste. If they are harvested too early, they will not have enough sugar. But carrots loose their sweetness if you wait too long to pull them from the ground.

The best way to judge if a carrot is ready to be harvested is by its color. Usually, the brighter the color, the better the taste.

Most people do not know that carrots can be grown during the winter months. If the winter is not cold enough to freeze the ground, you can grow and harvest carrots the same way as during the summer months.

If the ground does freeze in your part of the world, simply cover your carrot garden with a thick layer of leaves or straw. This will prevent the ground from freezing. You can remove the ground cover and harvest the carrots as they are needed.

Carrots are prepared and eaten in many different ways. They are cut in thin pieces and added to other vegetables. They are cooked by themselves or added to stews. Or, once they are washed, they are eaten just as they come out of the ground.

Section 3

一、听歌曲 *The Climb*，根据你所听到的内容，在横线上填上所缺的单词。

I can almost see it
that dream I'm dreaming but
there's a voice inside my head saying
you'll never reach it
every step I'm taking
every move I make feels

lost with no direction
my faith is shaking
but I, I gotta keep trying
gotta keep my head held high

there's always gonna be another mountain
I'm always gonna wanna make it move
always gonna be an uphill battle
sometimes I'm gonna have to lose
aren't about how fast I get there
aren't about what's waiting on the other side
it's the climb

二、听下面三段长对话，每段长对话后都有三至四个小题。从题中所给的 A，B，C 三个选项中选出最佳答案。

听第一段对话，回答 1 ~3 题。

W：Hi，Samus！What's up?

M：Oh，not much. What have you been doing recently，Carlo?

W：I've been chatting online a lot with friends.

M：Where do you go to chat?

W：I usually use Yahoo Messager. What about you?

M：I've never chatted online before.

W：What? How is that possible? Why not?

M：Well，my computer is really old，so most software isn't compatible with my computer.

听第二段对话，回答 4 ~6 题。

W：Hi！Is that the new computer you bought last week? It looks very nice.

M：Yes，it is. Thanks. I'm just surfing on the Internet.

W：Here? In this café? How can you do that?

M：This café offers a wireless Internet connection. That means I can get on the net for free while I'm here. Of course，I have to buy a cup of coffee！

W：That's great. Can you do it anywhere?

M：No. You can only do it when the café offers a wireless connection. There are only about 10 or 12 places that offer it in this city.

听第三段对话，回答 7 ~ 10 题。

W：You're a big fan of Jay，aren't you?

M：Yes，I've got all his albums and most of his films on DVD. I adore him. He's my idol.

W：How come you don't have all of his films on DVD?

M：Some of his early films are hard to find nowadays, especially the ones which he only played a bit part.

W：I see. I'm sure you'll find them one day. I see you also have several posters of him.

M：Yes. These posters are new. I bought them last week and put them up on my bedroom walls yesterday.

W：Are you a member of his fan club?

M：I was, but then I discovered you can find out everything for free on the Internet, so I quit.

W：Did you see the interview with Jay in *Cosmopolitan* magazine last month?

M：Of course！ I bought two copies.

W：Two copies? One to keep and one to cut the pictures out of, right?

M：You are such a genius！

三、你将听到一段关于如何制作 popcorn 的步骤说明。根据你听到的内容，完成练习。

（一）根据你听到的内容，在做 popcorn 所需要材料的图片下打钩。

Sure, you can buy a packet of popcorn from supermarket and put it into the microwave and start it. But once you learn to make your own popcorn on the stove, you'll never want the fake-tasting kind again.

You will need 8 things：a bottle of oil, a large heavy pot with a lid, some popcorn kernels, your father or mother to help work the stove, your ears, a large bowl, salt and a chunk of butter.

（二）下面你将听到做 popcorn 的具体步骤。请根据所听到的内容，写下每个步骤的名称。每空一词。

When cooking at the stove, have an adult nearby to supervise you.

Step 1：Add oil

Take out the oil, and pour it into the pot.

Step 2：Add popcorn

Get one-third to one-half cup of popcorn, and pour that into the pot. Shake the pot gently until the kernels are evenly coated with oil, and cover the bottom of the pot in one layer.

Step 3：Heat popcorn

Place the pot on the stove, put on the lid, and turn on the burner.

Step 4：Listen

As soon as you hear the first kernels pop, shake the pot a few times so that no kernels get burned.

Step 5: Pay close attention

Keep listening. Notice when the popping slows down and finally stops. Once three seconds go by without a pop, turn off the burner.

Step 6: Let the popcorn cool

Uncover the pot and let the popcorn cool for a minute or two.

Step 7: Pour popcorn

Pour the popcorn into a large bowl.

Step 8: Add butter

If you like butter on your popcorn, put a chunk into the pot, which should still be hot. When the butter's melted, dump the popcorn back into the pot, stir it around, and pour it back into the bowl.

Step 9: Add salt

Sprinkle the still-warm popcorn with salt, if you like. Popcorn salt is very fine and clings better than table salt. But table salt tastes just as good if it's all you have.

Step 10: Enjoy

Take your bowl of popcorn and munch on it while you watch a movie. It always tastes best in front of a screen—even a little one.

Section 4

一、听寓言，并写下你所听到的故事。

As the north wind was proud of his power, he said, "Ha. Ha. Ha. No one could beat me. I am the strongest."

The sun heard that, he said, "Really? I don't think so."

"I'll show you. There is a man walking down there. Let's see who can make him take off his coat."

The sun agreed, and the north wind went first. He started to blow hard, but the man held his coat more tightly. At last, the north wind gave up.

"Watch me." The sun shone brightly on the man. At first, the man felt warm, so he didn't hold his coat. Then, the sun kept shining, the man finally felt hot and couldn't help taking off his coat.

Now, the sun smiled and said, "Well, what do you think?"

"I see. I shouldn't have bragged about myself," the north wind felt embarrassed.

二、听下面三段长对话，每段长对话后都有三至四个小题。从题中所给的 A，B，C 三个选项中选出最佳答案。

听第一段对话，回答 1 ~3 题。

W：Are you interested in history?

M：Yes，I am. I enjoyed studying it at school，though I had trouble remembering all the dates，so my teacher never gave me good marks.

W：I love history，but I've always thought that learning the reasons behind events is more important than remembering exactly when they happened.

M：I wish you had been my history teacher！I might have got better marks！

W：Some people say that history repeats itself.

M：What does that mean? The same events never happen twice，do they?

W：The idea is that the people and dates change，but the reasons why things happen stay the same.

M：I see. I think I'd agree with that statement. People often seem to make the same mistakes over and over again.

听第二段对话，回答 4 ~6 题。

W：Hi，Charlie！What are you reading?

M：Hi，Barbie. I'm reading a biography.

W：Who's it about?

M：It's about Bob Dylan.

W：Who is he?

M：He's a famous American musician.

W：Who's the author?

M：It was written by Howard Somerset.

W：What do you think about it?

M：It's great！I've learned a lot from reading it.

W：Can I read it when you're done?

M：Sure！I'm on Chapter 12 now，so I'm almost finished.

W：How many chapters does the book have?

M：There are 15 chapters in total.

W：When do you think you'll have finished reading it?

M：I should be done by Friday. I'll give it to you in class then.

W：Thanks. Charlie！

M：No problem.

听第三段对话，回答7～10题。

W：Are you a fan of art?

M：Not really. I like going to an art exhibition once or twice a year. I hardly know anything about art or sculpture. You are a true art lover, aren't you?

W：I love going to art galleries, particularly when one is holding an exhibition of abstract art.

M：I never understand the meaning of those paintings. They are too abstract for me. I didn't pay much attention in art class at school.

W：Art isn't for everyone. I'm going to an exhibition tomorrow at the National Gallery. It's an exhibition of Greek and Roman sculpture.

M：I like sculpture, especially that from ancient Rome or Greece. What time are you thinking of going? I'd love to go with you.

W：I thought I'd have an early lunch and go immediately afterwards. Does that sound OK to you? Bus 51 goes directly there.

M：That sounds fine. What time shall we meet at the bus stop?

W：Let's meet at 12:30. It will probably take us three or four hours to see all of the exhibits.

三、你将听到一段关于如何制作家庭风味 chips 的录音。

（一）听独白的前半段，选出你所需要的材料。

Satisfy your cravings by making America's favorite snack, the potato chip, at home.

You will need: four potatoes, a heavy saucepan, peanut oil, paper towels, a slotted spoon, and salt.

（二）听独白的后半段，完成制作 chips 的步骤。

Step 1: Peel the potatoes and put them into the water for at least 30 minutes.

Step 2: Fill your saucepan half full of oil and heat to 375 degrees.

Step 3: Dry the potatoes. Slice them about 1/8 of an inch thick.
Make sure your potatoes are dry or they'll splatter in the fryer.

Step 4: Add potatoes to the pan little by little.

Step 5: Fry for about 3 minutes or until golden brown.

Step 6: Remove the cooked chips with a slotted spoon and set them on paper towels to dry the oil.

Step 7: Sprinkle with salt and watch them disappear.

Section 5

一、听歌曲 *Excuse Me*，在歌曲中，表演者连续唱出了 8 个他要找的地方。请根据歌曲，依次选择 8 个你所听到地点的图片。

Excuse me

Excuse me, where is the dry cleaner's?
Excuse me, where is the university?
Excuse me, where is the post office?
Excuse me, where is the restaurant?
Excuse me, where is the gas station?
Excuse me, where is the car park?
Excuse me, where is the cinema?
Excuse me, where is the museum?

二、听下面三段长对话，每段长对话后都有三至四个小题。从题中所给的 A，B，C 三个选项中选出最佳答案。

听第一段对话，回答 1～3 题。

W: Do you always ask "Ni Chi Le Ma?" when you meet someone in China? I think it's so strange!

M: It's so common and not strange at all to me. But there are many customs in other countries that may seem strange to us. For example, in Thailand, you should never touch someone on the head.

W: Interesting. I know that in some countries, you shouldn't blow your nose in front of other people.

M: I think that's a good custom. I hate it when people do that.

W: A common habit that I hate is chewing with your mouth open. Luckily, adults rarely do it. It seems that kids grow out of it.

M: Do you often scratch your head when you are thinking?

W: Yes, I do. I wonder why people do that? Oh look, I'm doing it now!

M: I rub my chin when I'm thinking. My mother scratches her nose.

听第二段对话，回答 4～6 题。

W: When you are in a restaurant, you want the waiter to bring the bill, what do you do to attract his attention?

M: I just make eye contact with him and nod my head. Then I tell him when he comes over to the table. Why do you ask?

W: I went out with a friend to a nice restaurant last night and I noticed that many people shouted for the bill.

M: That seems a little impolite in such a restaurant.

W: That's what I thought. I just thought I'd ask you and see what you thought of it. Anyway, what did you do yesterday evening?

M: Well, it was a warm evening, so I decided to have a walk along the river. Actually, several other people had the same idea. I saw Bill.

W: Did you? How is he these days?

M: He seemed OK. We didn't stop and chat because we were on opposite banks of the river. We just waved at each other.

听第三段对话，回答7~10题。

C: How many people are there in your family, Elva?

E: As you know, China has a single-child policy. Therefore, there's just my husband, my daughter and I. What about your family, Chrisie?

C: I have a daughter and a son. Then there's my husband and I. What about your parents? Do they live with your family?

E: Not anymore. They live with my brother now. And yours?

C: My parents live by themselves now. When they get older, they'll probably go to a retirement home. Do you just have one brother?

E: No, I have two older brothers and one younger sister. What about you?

C: I also grew up in a big family. I have one older brother and three younger sisters.

E: How long have you been married?

C: About seven years now, and you?

E: I 've been married for about five years.

三、你将听到一段短文，将你听到的句子都逐一写下来。

The secret of success is not so much money as a strong will. A great man is one who has a strong will. In other words, if a man does not have a strong will to win the final victory, he will never succeed in his life. He is no more than a failure.

It is quite obvious that there is no difficult thing in the world, if you make up your mind to do it, you will certainly accomplish it in the not far future.

Unit 2

Section 1

一、听一段新闻，根据你所听到的内容填空。

The best invention of 2009 is from a light bulb that may be worth ten million dollars to an electric eye, that sees for you. The list is out; this is it right here, from *Time* magazine, *Time* website, *Time*. com, which is a partner of CNN. com. They say the best invention of the year is this NASA's Ares Rocket, we have some video for you.

"Three! Two! One! Ignition, and lift off of Ares I-X, testing concepts for the future of new rocket design."

Time calls this the best and smartest and coolest thing built in 2009, it is designed to usher in the next generation of space travel returning astronauts to the moon, and one day bringing people to Mars.

二、听下面十段对话，每段对话后有一个问题，从题中所给的 A，B，C 三个选项中选出最佳答案。听完每个问题后，你都有五秒钟的时间来作答和阅读下一小题。

1. M: Well, then, may I invite you for the next dance?
   W: Oh ... I want to dance with you. But I hurt my ankle at the last dance...
   Q: Will the woman dance with the man?
2. M: Cathy, how many people are there in your family?
   W: My family is very large. It's my mother, my father, my two older brothers, my younger sister and me.
   Q: How many members are there in Cathy's family?
3. M: Mom and I got in another fight the other day, Jennies.
   W: Oh, Iris! What was it about this time?
   M: It was over food. I simply wanted some fried chicken but she said no.
   Q: Who had another fight the other day?
4. W: My MP3 player is broken, so I want to change it for an MP4 player. Can you offer any advice about which brand to buy?
   M: An MP4 player? Why don't you buy a new cell phone? You can find an MP4

player inside any of the latest cell phones.

Q: What does the man suggest the woman to buy?

5. W: What does Micheal look like?

M: Well, he's tall and well built. He's got brown eyes and a shaved head.

Q: Which of the following is not right about Micheal?

6. M: Morning, campers!

W: Ooh, not so loud, my head's killing me.

Q: What's wrong with the woman?

7. W: What kind of films do you like, action, adventure or musicals?

M: Films about people living in the future, on other planets.

Q: What kind of films does the man like?

8. W: Ooh, what's that smell? Do I detect cheeseburger and fries?

M: Yes, I'm cooking the meal.

Q: What will the two people have for lunch?

9. M: Hurry up, Ariel!

W: I know, Justin! I'm going as fast as I can.

M: The plane's going to take off without us at this rate. You've not even finished packing yet!

Q: Who hasn't finished packing yet?

10. M: Let's sit here on the beach. What a perfect spot for an ice-cream!

W: Totally agree! I'll get two vanilla ice-creams for us!

Q: Where are they?

三、听下面一段长对话，根据对话内容填空。

W1: Hmm, what do you think, you two, how do I look?

W2: Ooh, it's a gorgeous dress, Racheal, but the other one seemed nicer.

W1: Mmm, it is lovely, isn't it? But you're right, the blue dress looks better, Joey?

M: Oh, yes, lovely, very nice. Can we go and look at the MP4 now?

W1: OK, Joey, you've been very patient. Let's just get Kate's shoes and then we can go to the electronics shop. I want to buy a camera for my brother, and then Kate wants to get a book for her Dad, don't you, Kate?

W2: Yes, and after that I expect we'll all be feeling hungry, so we'll have a quick bite to eat, and then Racheal and I both want to look at winter coats.

M: Here we go...

W1: It won't take as long as the dress, I promise!

Section 2

一、你将听到一段关于 Gorilla 的新闻，根据你所听到的内容补全所缺的词语，每空一词。

This week, we tell about a discovery of gorillas in the Republic of Congo and the loss of Bengal tigers in Nepal. We also tell about a famous heart surgeon and what you need to know about your heart.

Deep in the forests in the northern part of the Republic of Congo, scientists have made a surprising discovery. Researchers discovered more than 125 thousand critically endangered western lowland gorillas.

In the 1980s, scientists estimated that the total population of western lowland gorillas in Central Africa was fewer than 100 thousand. Since then however, the scientists believed this number had been reduced by at least half. They thought the animals were being killed off by hunters and disease, especially the deadly Ebola virus.

二、听录音，完成下列各题。

（一）听一段新闻，并根据问题做出选择。

（略）

（二）听一段歌曲，并做出正确选择。

Imagine

Imagine there's no heaven
It's easy if you try
No hell below us
Above us only sky
Imagine all the people
Living for today ...
Imagine there's no countries
It isn't hard to do
Nothing to kill or die for
And no religion too
Imagine all the people
Living life in peace ...
You may say I'm a dreamer
But I'm not the only one
I hope someday you'll join us
And the world will be as one

三、听对话，并回答下列问题。

（一）Jim 和 Kelly 正在就音乐话题进行讨论。听他们的谈话，选出最佳答案。

（二）重听对话，根据 Jim 和 Kelly 在音乐爱好方面的相同点和不同点补全内容。

K：Jim, I heard that Ben is forming his own band.

J：It will be a rock and roll band probably. Ben's a very good guitarist.

K：Jim, can you play a musical instrument? If you can, he might ask you to join the band.

J：I can play the drums, but I haven't played for a while. I'm not sure I'd be good enough to play in a band.

K：I wish I could play drum. I love music. But I can only play just a little piano.

J：That's fine, Kelly, I think you can be a DJ even if you are not good at playing the piano. You can mix dance music. You don't take a lot of practise. You know, you could probably get a computer program that would help you. You already have a computer, so you could use that to help you mix some music.

K：That's a great idea. I'll search for some information on the Internet. If it's possible to do, the Internet will have some information about it. Can I ask you a question? What kind of music do you like listening to?

J：I like music that is fast and lively, like dance music. You know, I go to a disco almost every week. Sometimes it's too loud though. You prefer classical music, don't you?

K：Yes, I do. I find it very relaxing. I often listen to Mozart or Bach in the evening after a hard day at work.

J：I must admit that I like several pieces of classical music. It's certainly more beautiful than that modern dance music.

K：Classical music is supposed to be good for your brain. Research suggests that it makes your brain more active. Students who listen to classical music while studying perform better.

J：Really? Perhaps I should listen to classical music often. I heard that listening to classical music is helpful in reducing stress.

K：Yes. That's why I listen to it in the evenings. I usually play it as background music while I'm cooking or doing other housework.

J：It must be great! I will try it.

Section 3

一、Chloe 和 Presley 正在讨论老师布置的阅读作业，根据你所听到的内容补全对话。

W：I can't believe my English teacher is making me read *Pride and Prejudice*!

M：Why not! It's a classic. In fact，it's one of my favorite novels.

W：But it's so old.

M：Don't judge a book by its cover. Do you know what it's about?

W：No，not at all.

M：First of all，it's a romance novel，setting in the early 19th century.

W：I didn't realize it was a romance novel. What's the main story about?

M：It's basically about a father who tried to marry off one of his five girls.

W：Why does he want to do that?

M：Since he doesn't have a son，he hopes that one of the girls will marry a wealthy man. In that way，all of his daughters will be cared for.

W：Won't they get his inheritance?

M：No，that's the problem. Though they are rich，once he dies，his house will go to his nephew. So，When he dies，the girls will have nothing.

W：I see. This sounds interesting! Maybe my teacher isn't so horrible after all.

M：So，are you going to read the novel or watch the movie?

W：There's a movie? My teacher didn't tell me that!

M：That's probably because she wants you to read the book first.

W：It would take a lot less time.

M：How about this? When you finish the book，I'll get the movie and watch it with you.

W：OK. That sounds like a deal.

二、听歌曲 *What Would You Do*，在歌曲中，表演者连续唱出了 8 件如果他有了 a million dollars 后将会做的事，根据歌曲，依次做出选择。

If You Had a Million Dollars

If you had a million dollars，what would you do，what would you do?
If you had a million dollars，what would you do，what would you do?
I'd buy the biggest boat，
I'd drive the fastest car，
I'd watch the biggest TV，
I'd see the greatest movies，
I'd eat the nicest food，
I'd listen to the coolest songs，
I'd party at the hippest night clubs，
I'd dance with the hottest girls.

三、听一段长对话，完成以下练习。

（一）学校举行的运动会刚刚结束，Rimy，Dorry，Dennis，Kate 的父母 Woods 夫妇正在就他们在运动会中的表现进行讨论。现在根据你听到的内容做出正确的选择。

W：How are the children doing at the sports?

M：I'm very proud of their performances. Rimy can finish the race of 50 meters in 8 seconds. That's very fast for a child at her age.

W：She's not very good at the long jump though, is she?

M：She's not bad. She can jump a distance of over 3 meters. I think she just prefers running to jumping. But Dorry's very good at the high jump. He can jump over two meters. That's fine for someone of his age, too.

W：Two meters? That means the high jump bar is above his head! Is any of our children good at long-distance running?

M：The longest race we run is the 1, 500 meters. No one but our little Dennis can finish it in less than five minutes.

W：How are they at swimming?

M：They're OK. I ask all of our children to swim 500 meters each day. That's 20 lengths of the swimming pool. They're not very fast, but that's OK. I just want them to build their strength up and keep in shape.

W：Kate is very good at diving from a height of 10 meters. And she won the competition with a very high score!

M：How great that is! I'd be afraid to jump from that height!

W：I think that these kids haven't learnt to be afraid yet. She started diving from a lower height, but she soon wanted to go higher.

M：It seems that they really enjoy to go faster, higher and further.

W：Sure they are! I'm so proud of our children!

（二）再听一遍对话，根据对话内容重现他们在运动会上的表现。

Section 4

一、你将会听到一段关于 Christmas 的广播，根据你所听到的内容，补充横线上所缺的动词。

Music fills the air. Colorful lights shine brightly in windows. Children and adults open gifts from loved ones and friends. These are all Christmas traditions.

Another tradition is snow. Christmas in the northern part of the world comes a few days after the start of winter. In many places, a blanket of clean white snow covers the ground on Christmas Day. This is what is meant by a "White Christmas."

Of course, many places do not get snow at Christmas. In fact, they may be very warm at this time of year. People who like snow, but live where it is warm, can only dream of having a white Christmas.

American songwriter Irving Berlin captured these feelings in his song, *White Christmas*. Hundreds of singers and musicians have recorded *White Christmas*. But the version most people still know best was sung by Bing Crosby.

二、听下面三段长对话，每段长对话后都有三至四个小题。从题中所给的 A，B，C 三个选项中选出最佳答案。

听第一段对话，回答 1 ~3 题。

W：We are going to the bookshop. Would you like to join us?

M：Yes, I would. I need to buy a textbook for my course and, as you know, I love browsing through the latest story books.

W：Me, too. I need some magazines to read on the flight to New York. I can never sleep on planes. And my friend Sarah wants to pick up some children's books for her daughter.

听第二段对话，回答 4 ~6 题。

W：What are you looking at?

M：I'm looking at this map of the world. Look at Russia! That's a big country.

W：Canada, China, and the USA are huge, too.

M：There are several tiny countries in the world, too. Countries like Monaco are smaller than many cities.

W：Those small countries are microscopic compared to Russia. European countries are relatively small. France looks quite big in Europe, but compared to many countries in other continents, it's not very large at all.

M：Britain is half the size of France, but Great Britain is still one of the largest islands in the world.

W：The thing with large countries is that they often have vast areas of land that are useless or hardly used. Russia and Canada have enormous areas of ice and forest.

听第三段对话，回答 7 ~10 题。

W：How long does it take us to drive to New York?

M：I think it's a distance of 190 kilometers from here to New York, so it should be a two-hour drive on the motorway.

W：If there is a traffic jam, it could take three hours.

M：You're right. We will be able to travel at high speeds for the whole journey, because we will be in built-up area.

W: So, shall we allow three hours to finish the trip?

M: OK. You haven't seen my company car, have you?

W: No. Let me take a look... it's so much longer than mine.

M: I think it's over five meters long. I can't remember exactly. It has a maximum speed of over 210 kilometers an hour.

三、White 夫妇才从国外回来，他们的冰箱已经空了，因此他们准备去超市买一些东西。

（一）听对话的前半部分，完成第一张购物清单。

W: What do we need to get from the supermarket?

M: So many things we need, we haven't been to the supermarket since our last trip to Norway, the fridge is almost empty! Now I think I'll have to make a list. We need two loaves of bread, 3 packets of sugar and a dozen of beer.

W: A dozen of beer? Why do we need that?

M: Just joking. Just two tins of beer is enough. We also need a liter of cooking oil.

W: We can buy a three-liter bottle. It works out cheaper per liter. We should buy a packet of butter and 12 bottles of milk, too.

M: I'd like to get a jar of strawberry jam and 2 bottles of tomato ketchup.

（二）听对话的后半部分，连线完成第二张购物清单。

M: Do we need any meat?

W: I think we should get half a kilo of beef.

M: OK. Let's not forget fruit and vegetables. We need a bunch of bananas, 2 kilos of tomatoes and a bag of potatoes.

W: We should also get a bar of soap. Let's get some ice cream, too. We can treat ourselves.

M: OK. We should buy half dozen of eggs. Anything else?

W: I'd like a dozen cans of coke and three dozen sausages.

M: Let's get a chunk of cheese, too. Is that everything?

W: I think so. I've got the shopping list, so let's go.

Section 5

一、听歌曲 *Have You Ever*，在歌曲中，表演者连续用歌唱的方式问了 8 个 "Have You Ever ...?" 的经历。请根据歌词，依次做出选择。

Have you ever

Have you ever eaten ice cream?

Have you ever written a song?
Have you ever been to Paris?
Have you ever seen King Kong?
Have you ever been surfing?
Have you ever flown a plane?
Have you ever forgotten a birthday?
Have you ever been in love?

二、听下面三段长对话，每段长对话后都有三至四个小题。从题中所给的 A，B，C 三个选项中选出最佳答案。

听第一段对话，回答 1 ~3 题。

M：What do you do in summer?

W：I love going out into the countryside for walks or bike ride. I love being out in the fresh summer air. How about you?

M：I don't often go for walks，but I play sports outside—you know，tennis，badminton—or just sit in the sunshine and read a good book.

W：What do you do in winter?

M：Well，I play sports indoors quite often. If I'm feeling lazy，I just watch a film at home. I prefer summer to winter.

W：I think most people do. I like wearing nice，colorful clothes in summer—you know，a nice dress or skirt. It's too cold for those kinds of clothes in winter.

M：Yes. I like wearing shorts in summer. My legs would freeze!

W：Do you think we'll have a nice summer this year?

M：Thanks to global warming，it could be hotter than ever!

听第二段对话，回答 4 ~6 题。

W：Hello! How are you today?

M：Hi. I'm feeling very nervous. I just had a test and I'm not sure how well or how badly I did.

W：It's no use worrying about it now. You've done the test and you can't change any of your answers.

M：That's true. I really should go home and prepare for the next test，but I'm feeling tired.

W：Maybe you need to relax. I'm looking forward to relaxing this coming weekend.

M：I hope that I can finally find free time，too. I've been so busy at my study recently，how might you spend the weekend?

W：I hope to do a little gardening. I find it very relaxing.

听第三段对话，回答 7 ~ 10 题。

M：I'd love to have my own farm.

W：It would be a very hard work. Are you sure?

M：I wouldn't mind getting up early in the mornings and the physical work would make me fit and healthy.

W：Running a farm would be totally different to you current job.

M：That's one reason I'd like to try it. I'd really like to get away from working from 9 to 5 in an office.

W：You'd need a lot of training before becoming a farmer. It's not something you can just walk into.

M：My uncle owns a farm and I've spent some time working with him. I love being in the countryside with farm animals and green fields.

W：Well, I'd certainly come and visit you. It would be great to take a working holiday on a farm. I'd love to get away from hustle and bustle of the city for a while.

三、你将听到一段关于冰箱的短文，将你听到的句子逐一写下来。

Before refrigerators were invented, the next best thing was an ice box. But another way to keep food fresh is to use a cooler. A common design is a tall box with several shelves inside to hold the food. The shelves are pieces of metal with many small holes through them. The sides of the box are covered with pieces of thick cloth.

Bottles of water are placed at the top and bottom of the cooler. The ends of each piece of cloth lie in the water so the cloth stays wet.

The cooler is put outdoors, but not in the sun. Air will pass through the wet cloth. The inside of the box will stay several degrees cooler than the outside. And this may be cool enough to keep foods fresh, at least for a short time.

Unit 3

Section 1

一、听歌并补全你所听到的内容。

look at me you may think you see
who I really am
but you'll never know me
every day
it's as if I play a part
now I see
if I wear a mask
I can fool the world
but I cannot fool my heart
who is that girl I see
staring straight back at me
when will my reflection show
who I am inside?
I am now
in a world where I
have to hide my heart
and what I believe in
but somehow
I will show the world
what's inside my heart
and be loved for who I am
who is that girl I see
staring straight back at me
why is my reflection
someone I don't know

二、听句子选出相应的答语。

1. Do you want to go the cinema with me?
2. What are you doing here?
3. Can you give me a hand?
4. Thank you so much!
5. How can I get to the airport?
6. Have you been taking anything for your cold?
7. Where have you been?
8. When is your train supposed to leave?
9. How much is that going to cost me?
10. How long was the flight?

三、你将听到十段对话和十个问题。请在每小题所给的A，B，C三个选项中选出最佳答案。

1. M: Where is my pen? Did you see it?
   W: I saw it on your desk a moment ago.
   Q: What is the man looking for?
2. W: We found your wallet!
   M: Really? Thank god! I thought I would never see it again.
   Q: How did the man feel now?
3. W: Shall we go fishing tomorrow?
   M: Why not? The weather report tells us that it will be a fine and clear day tomorrow.
   Q: What will the weather be like tomorrow?
4. W: Isn't it a great dinner? We had different kinds of hamburgers and cakes.
   M: Yeah, those are the most delicious cakes that I have ever had in my life!
   Q: What is not mentioned in the dialogue?
5. M: I can't imagine a world without swimming pools.
   W: Do you mean that you can't live without keeping swimming as a hobby?
   M: You are right.
   Q: What will the man probably do in his spare time?
6. W: Do you think we should go by bus or by taxi?
   M: Well, it's not difficult to choose. The bus is much slower, and sometimes it's too crowded to get on.
   Q: Which transport will they choose?
7. W: How is your weekend?

M: Boring, I just stayed at home and reviewed my lessons with my sister at weekends.

Q: What did the man do during the weekend?

8. W: Do you want to go to the seaside to spend your summer vacation?

M: No! I hate the smell of the sea water. I'd rather climb mountains.

Q: What probably will the man do during his summer vacation?

9. W: Oh! David, you are here! What did the doctor say?

M: Shhh, quiet down, can you see the sign here? "Keep your voice down, patients need rest."

Q: Where are the two people?

10. M: Hi, Jane. Look at you, did you have a late night?

W: Yeah, I got home around three in the morning.

M: How do you feel now?

W: I'm all right, thanks. Just a little tired.

Q: When did Jane get home last night?

Section 2

一、听文章，回答问题。

A guy walks into a bar with a small dog. The bartender says, "Get out of here with that dog!"

The guy says, "But this isn't just any dog... this dog can play the piano!" The bartender replies, "Well, if he can play that piano, you both can stay... and have a drink on the house!" So the guy sits the dog on the piano stool, and the dog starts playing. Ragtime, Mozart... and the bartender and patrons are enjoying the music. Suddenly a bigger dog runs in, grabs the small dog by the scruff of the neck, and drags him out. The bartender asks the guy, "What was that all about?" The guy replies, "Oh, that was his mother. She wanted him to be a doctor."

二、你将听到十段对话和十个问题，每段对话和每个问题将各读一遍。请在每小题所给的A，B，C三个选项中选出最佳答案。

1. M: Wow, you've changed so much!

W: Yeah, I used to be fat and have short hair. But now I'm thin and I have long hair.

Q: What does the girl look like now?

2. W：David! Why are you fishing here? Have you finished your homework?
M：Sorry, but I don't know what my homework is.
Q：What is the boy doing?

3. W：Tom, my bike was stolen just now.
M：Sorry to hear that. If I were a policeman, I would catch all thieves.
Q：What was stolen just now?

4. W：How do you often go to school?
M：By bike. It's cheap and convenient.
Q：How does the boy often go to school?

5. M：What does Mr. Gao teach?
W：He used to teach English, but he teaches Chinese now.
Q：What is Mr. Gao?

6. W：I like painting, singing and cooking.
M：Really? I like painting, too! Maybe we two should hang out sometime.
Q：What do they both like doing?

7. W：Can you make the breakfast, American style.
M：Of course, I just need sugar, milk, flour and eggs.
Q：What is not needed in making an American breakfast?

8. W：I think tigers are wonderful. I hate the people who kill them for their fur.
M：I agree. I'm crazy about mice. I think they're so cute!
W：Really? I don't see the attraction. I'm afraid of mice.
Q：What animal do people kill for their fur?

9. W：Your garden is looking beautiful this summer, Evans. The flowers are really colorful.
M：Thank you. I have roses, tulips, and daffodils.
Q：What will you see in Evans' garden?

10. W：Do you keep any pets?
M：I'm fairly busy, so I really need an animal that I don't need to care of very much. Actually, I'd like a pet that's a little unusual.
Q：What probably will the man choose as his pet?

三、仔细看下面的五张图片，你将会听到五段和图片有关的对话。请依次在序号后写出相应图片下的字母。

1. W：Look, what is that inside the square?
M：It's a white circle.

2. W：Is that a black circle?
M：Where?

W: Above the square!

M: Yes, it's a black circle above the square.

3. W: Is the white circle on the left of the square?

   M: No, it's on the right of the square, and there is a black circle in the middle of the square.

4. W: Is there anything at all in the square?

   M: No, it's completely empty. There is nothing in or out of the square.

5. W: Is the black circle on the left of the square?

   M: No, it isn't, the square is on the left of the black circle.

   W: Is that a white circle above the square?

   M: Yes, it is.

四、看图听句子。图中 Mr. Bean 正在桌边，按照你所听到的内容完成图画。

1. Mrs. Bean is sitting on a chair opposite Mr. Bean. PUT HER IN.
2. The door is behind Mrs. Bean's back. PUT IT IN.
3. Mr. Bean can see Mrs. Bean but he cannot see Charlie because Charlie is standing behind him. PUT HIM IN.
4. To Mr. Bean's left hand, there is a clock on the wall. PUT IT IN.
5. There is a big cup on the desk, and the cup is half full. PUT IT IN.

Section 3

一、听歌并补全歌词。

My grandfather's clock was too large for the shelf.
So it stood ninety years on the floor.
It was taller by half than the old man himself.
Thought it weighed not a penny weight more.
It was bought on the morn on the day that he was born.
And was always his treasure and pride.
But it stopped short, never to go again,
When the old man died.
Ninety years without slumbering (tick, tock, tick, tock),
His life seconds numbering (tick, tock, tick, tock).
It stopped short, never to go again, when the old man died.
In watching it's pendulum swing to and fro,

Many hours had he spent while a boy.
And in childhood and manhood the clock seemed to know.
And to share both his grief and his joy.
For it struck twenty-four when he entered at the door.
With a blooming and beautiful bride.

二、听句子，并按照每题的不同要求完成图画。

1. There are three apples in the picture, and there is an empty cup on the left of them.
   Now, please draw the apples and the cup on the paper.
2. Who is the child catching the butterflies?
   He is Jim.
   What about the girl running after him?
   That's his sister Lily.
   Now, please write down the names for the children in the right blanket.
3. What's the time now?
   It's ten to ten.
   Now, draw the time on the clock.
4. What's the weather like tonight?
   It's clear! There isn't much cloud up in the sky. We can see the moon and a few stars around it.
   Now, you can draw the things in the sky.
5. What does Leo look like?
   He is a boy with short hair and glasses.
   Now, please draw the picture of Leo.

三、听下面五个问题，每个问题后有三个答语，从题中所给的A，B，C三个选项中选出最佳答案。听完每个问题后，你都有五秒钟的时间来作答和阅读下一小题。

1. What's the matter with her?
2. What do you enjoy doing in the evening?
3. Who is the cleverest girl in your class?
4. Where does your father usually go for a walk?
5. New York City is quite busy.

四、听文章，选出正确答案并完成表格。

（一）听文章，根据问题做出正确选择。

It's Not Easy Being a Kid!

Hi! I'm Jerry. I'm in the second grade.

I have one thing to say: IT'S NOT EASY BEING A KID!

Being a kid might look like fun, but sometimes it's not.

Yesterday, I was playing outside with my friend. I was having a really good time. Then suddenly, my mother said, "Jerry, it's time to come inside now. It's getting dark." When you're an adult, no one can tell you what to do or when to do it. When you're a kid, you have to get up early in the morning and go to school. At school, you have to study math, English, science, and history. After school, you have to do your homework. When you're an adult, you do not have to go to school and you never have homework. When you're a kid, there are many things you can't watch. Last Saturday, there was a scary movie on TV. It looked really exciting. But my father would not let me watch. He said, "You're too young for this movie, Jerry." When you're an adult, you can watch anything you want. When you're a kid, the older kids sometimes pick on you. When I was walking home from school on Monday, Tom and Steve bothered me. Steve took my schoolbag and put it in a tree. It made me very mad. When you're an adult, no one can pick on you. When you're a kid, you cannot go anywhere by yourself. Last Friday, I wanted to buy a birthday gift for my friend John. But I had to wait for my Mom to return home. When I want to go somewhere, I have to ride my bike or ask my Mom for a ride. When you're an adult, you can drive a car wherever you want. When you're a kid, you have to go to bed early. On school nights, my Mom makes me go to bed at 9:00. But I do have a Mom and Dad who love me, which is really great. So I guess I like being a kid, even though IT'S NOT EASY BEING A KID!

（二）再听一遍文章，补全句子内容。

Section 4

一、听写英文诗歌。

Never Give up

Never give up,
Never lose hope.
Always have faith,
It allows you to cope.
Trying times will pass,
As they always do.
Just have patience,

Your dreams will come true.
So put on a smile,
You'll live through your pain.
Know it will pass,
And strength you will gain.

二、听电影原声回答下列问题。

（略）

三、听下面五段小对话，听完每段小对话后，你都有十秒时间来作答和阅读下一题。

1. W: David, how do you often go to school?
   M: I used to take a bus, but now I often go to school on foot.
2. W: Hi, Micheal! Over here! Don't you remember me?
   M: Wow, you are Monica, aren't you?
   W: That's right.
   M: You used to be fat, but now you are very thin and beautiful.
3. M: Would you mind my smoking here?
   W: You'd better not. Can't you see the sign "No Smoking" here?
4. W: Hi, Jack, how are you feeling today?
   M: Much better, but the doctor asked me to stay in the hospital for 2 more days.
5. M: Hi, Lucy, let's go fishing tomorrow.
   W: Well, the weather report says it will be rainy.
   M: Then what about watching a DVD at home?
   W: Good idea!

四、听两段对话，完成下列各题。

听第一段对话，回答1~3题。

M: Maggie, what's the matter with you? You look sad.
W: Yes, I feel bad. My dog, Eric, was hurt and he is in the hospital now.
M: Really? I'm sorry to hear that. What's wrong with him?
W: Last Friday morning, I took him to the park. When we were taking a walk, he was hit by a football.
M: A football? How come?
W: There were some children playing football in the park. And they were just not careful enough.
M: That's too bad. I hope he will get well soon.
W: Thanks.

听第二段对话，回答4～5题。

W：Hello. John.

M：Hello，are you in the No. 2 Middle School?

W：No，I'm in the No. 5 Middle School. Are you in the No. 3 Middle School?

M：Yes，I am. What does your father do?

W：He's a teacher. He teaches maths in the No. 4 Middle School. I know your father is a teacher，too. How old is your father?

M：He is forty-three. He is thirty years older than me. I hope you can come to visit me sometime.

W：All right. Goodbye.

M：Goodbye.

五、听文章，选出正确答案并完成表格。

（一）听文章，选出正确答案。

Most people know that chocolate is made from cocoa and that the origins of chocolate can be traced back to Central and South America. For centuries，the natives there regarded cocoa as a gift from the gods. But how did chocolate go from being the food of the gods to being the food of love?

Around A. D. 600，the Mayas were the main aboriginal group in Central America. They established the first cocoa plantations and firstly used the cocoa bean as the main ingredient in a dark，bitter drink that we would call "chocolate." The Mayas believed that chocolate had mystical properties—but cocoa also had commercial value. In fact，cocoa beans were used as a form of currency that was worth its weight in gold!

Spanish conquistador Hernando Cortez was the first European explorer to realize cocoa's commercial possibilities. When he arrived in the New World in 1519，he soon established his own cocoa plantation. In 1529，Cortez returned to Spain and introduced chocolate—as a drink mixed with sugar，vanilla，and cinnamon—to European society.

It caught on—especially with the nobility，who fancied hot chocolate as an aphrodisiac. As its popularity spread，people found new ways to make and use chocolate. These days，chocolate is enjoyed as both a tasty treat and a romantic indulgence. Whether it is in delectable desserts or crunchy candy，people over the world are still in love with chocolate.

（二）听文章，完成表格。

Section 5

一、听录音，回答下列问题。

（略）

二、听句子，选出正确答案。

1. I can't decide which book to buy.
2. What's your new teacher like?
3. Don't you think her radio is too loud?
4. Hello, Brown, it's good to see you again.
5. What about going to the park after supper?

三、听两段对话，完成下列各题。

听第一段对话，回答1～3题。

M: You've received a letter! Where is it from?

W: I don't know. I haven't seen it yet.

M: Open it!

W: Oh, it is from France. Who sent it to me? It's so strange!

M: It must be Kate. She has gone to France for a month.

W: Yeah, it's from Kate.

M: What's inside the envelop?

W: Oh, it's a Christmas card with the words "Merry Christmas" on it.

听第二段对话，回答4～5题。

W: John, could you help me with something?

M: Sure, what is it?

W: I have to be away for a couple of days. My husband and I have decided to go to England for our holiday.

M: England? It's so great. What can I do for you exactly?

W: Could you look after Polly for me? I need you to put some bird feed in its bowl once a day.

M: No problem.

四、你将听到一段独白，请把你听到的句子逐一写下来。

Millions of people all over the world use the word "OK". In fact, some people say the word is used more often than any other word in the world. "OK" means "all right" or "fine". It is used when people agree with something. You might ask your brother, "Is it okay if I borrow your car?" Or if someone asks you to do something, you might say, "Okay, I will." Still, language experts do not agree about where the word came from.

Some people say it came from the native American Indians. The Indian word "okeh" means the same as the American word "okay". Experts say early explorers in the West spoke the Choctaw language in the nineteenth century. The language spread across the country.

Unit 4

Section 1

一、你将听到几段生活中的小对话，根据你所听到的内容写下对话。

Dialogue 1

W：Hi，Herb.

M：How are you?

W：OK.

M：So you've been doing well?

W：Um，yes. I guess you're moving soon.

M：Um，to New York.

W：Oh，I just wanted to say goodbye.

Dialogue 2

M：Hello，Miss. What will you have?

W：I'll have a glass of milk.

M：Milk? OK. Why are you here alone?

W：I'm waiting for a young girl I met on the net.

M：A 16-year-old who likes computers?

W：How do you know?

M：Heh，heh. It was just a wild guess. Good luck finding your Internet friend!

二、材料中有五个句子，每个句子听一遍，然后从每小题 A，B，C 三个选项中选出能对每个句子做出适当反应的答语。

1. What would you like to drink，please?
2. How long does Rosie work in the restaurant every day?
3. Mum，I don't feel well.
4. Could you please say it again?
5. Dad，could I go to Africa next year to study Africa history?

三、材料中有五组对话，从每小题A，B，C三个选项中选出能回答每个问题的最佳答案。

1. M：Do you know the poet Byron?
   W：Yes，of course. He was a great poet in the 18th century. He wrote many famous poems during his lifetime.
2. W：What would you like to be in the future?
   M：When I was a little boy，I wanted to be a doctor. But now I want to be an astronaut. What about you?
   W：I'd like to be an artist.
3. W：Where do you work，Mr. Sheldon?
   M：I work in No. 2 Middle School. I've taught there for five years.
4. W：Shall we go to a Japanese restaurant to try Japanese food?
   M：I heard that Chinese food is much more delicious. Why not go to a Chinese restaurant?
   W：OK，let's go.
5. W：Are you a Canadian?
   M：Yes，I am.
   W：Do you speak English?
   M：Yes. I also speak French.

四、听录音，完成下列各题。

（一）你将听到一段关于西瓜冰淇淋的简易做法的独白。仔细听独白，并根据你所听到的内容，在所需要的材料下打钩。

Imagine，you can make watermelon ice cream on your own. And it's quite simple! Here are the things you will need to make it.

You Will Need：watermelon，some sugar，a little lemon juice，food processor，ice cream maker，dessert bowls.

（二）根据你所听到的内容，补全独白。

Imagine，you can make watermelon ice cream on your own. And it's quite simple!

Step 1：Cut watermelon

Cut a watermelon into small pieces and take away the seeds.

Step 2：Puree

Puree the watermelon in the food processor.

Step 3：Cook with sugar

Cook 1 cup of the puree with the sugar in a pan until the sugar has dissolved. Add the sugar gradually and taste it to make sure the mixture is sweet enough.

Step 4：Add the lemon juice into it

Mix the rest of the watermelon puree，the lemon juice and watermelon mixture.

Step 5：Cover and cool

Cover the pan and place the mixture in the refrigerator until it is cold.

Step 6：Freeze

Freeze the watermelon mixture in the ice cream maker.

Step 7：Enjoy now

Allow the mixture to freeze for at least 2 hours. When it is ready，take it out to the dessert bowls and enjoy it!

Section 2

一、听歌曲并补全所缺歌词。

Do you hear me
I'm talking to you
Across the water across the deep blue ocean
Under the open sky，oh my，baby I'm trying
Boy I hear you in my dreams
I feel your whisper across the sea
I keep you with me in my heart
You make it easier when life gets hard
I'm lucky I'm in love with my best friend
Lucky to have been where I have been
Lucky to be coming home again
Ooohh ooooh oooh oooh ooh ooh ooh ooh

二、听三段录音，完成下列各题。

请听第一段对话，回答1～3题。

W：I'm afraid there's something wrong with my car.

M：Oh，we'd better have a look at it then. Leave the car with me now.

W：Do you think it might be something serious?

M：I don't think so.

W：I hope you can mend it as soon as possible. I'm going to an important party and I want to use it this evening. Do you think it will be ready by then?

M：It might be. Could you give me a ring around five? I'll let you know.

W: All right.

请听第二段对话，回答4～7题。

M: Excuse me, is this seat free?

W: Yes. You can take it.

M: Thanks. Er... are you Korean?

W: No. I'm Chinese.

M: Did you come to England for traveling or working?

W: Well, I come to study English. I'm studying English in Brighton University.

M: You speak English very well.

W: Thank you. I've been here for just half a year, and I'll stay for another year. Then I'll go back to my hometown to be an English teacher.

M: Great! I'm sure you'll be a good teacher.

W: Thank you. Oh, I have to go now. Nice talking with you.

M: Me, too. Good luck!

请听一段独白，回答8～10题。

Today was not a good day. Everything went wrong. First, I slept late and Mom shouted at me to wake me up. When I went to the kitchen for breakfast, there was no fruit. I decided to have some toast instead, but I burned it. I had to eat it anyway because there was no more cake. There was no juice, either. I just had a glass of water.

When I was almost at the bus stop, I realized that I had forgotten my wallet, so I had to go back home and get it. Of course, I missed the bus and had to wait for the next one.

I was late for school and the teacher told me to stay in the classroom at lunchtime to catch up on (弥补) the schoolwork I had missed.

After lunch, it was the time to give the teacher our homework. I reached into my bag to get it but it wasn't there. I had left it at home. I was in trouble again.

When I got home, I went straight to my room to catch up on my homework. Mom cooked fish for dinner. She knows I don't like fish, but she thinks it is good for her son. It was a horrible day. I hope tomorrow will be better.

三、听一段独白，完成下列各题。

（一）你将听到一段关于如何照出漂亮相片的独白，根据你听到的内容，写下所需要的材料。

Sure, a beautiful photograph takes some skill behind the lens, but it takes a little skill in front of it, too.

You will need: a photographer, a camera.

（二）根据你所听到的内容，写下如何照出漂亮相片的要点。

Step 1: Choose your clothes.

When choosing your clothes, leave bright colors, crazy patterns, and horizontal stripes in the closet. Neutral colors look best.

Step 2: Check your face.

Check your face in the mirror. Could your eyes use some drop to clear up redness? Are your eyebrows just fine?

Step 3: Take pictures outside in the morning or before the sunset.

Try to have the pictures taken outside in the above time. The light is soft and flattering at these times, whereas high noon or flash photography can illuminate a little too much.

Step 4: Make sure camera is eye level.

Make sure the camera lens is at the right level or just slightly higher. Any lower and you'll look like you have a double chin.

Step 5: Lean back.

To appear more natural when standing for a photo, lean slightly back, with your weight on your rear foot, and angle one hip forward.

Keep your posture erect but not overly posed. Think "Greek Statue," not "William Shatner."

Step 6: Slightly turn your head.

Turn your head two-thirds to one side or the other for a slimming effect on your face. Avoid wide-angle lenses, which will widen the appearance of your face.

Step 7: Look at a light source.

Look at the right direction, like a lamp or light, for a few moments. It reduces the possibility of red eyes. However, never look directly at the sun.

Step 8: Keep your eyes open.

Just before the picture is taken, close your eyes and have the photographer count to three. Then open your eyes as he begins shooting. This is the best way to prevent blinking from ruining shots.

Step 9: Smile.

The last and most important part of a picture is the smile.

Section 3

一、听写。

Harry saw an ad. in a window. It said: "Wanted the best salesman in the world.

Top pay."

"I'm a great salesman," Harry told himself. "I can sell anything. I'll go in and ask for that job."

He went into the building and spoke to the manager. "I'm the best salesman in the world," he said, "give me the job."

"You must prove you're the best," the manager said.

"I'll pass every test you give me," Harry told him.

"Good."

The manager took a box of candy out of his desk.

"Last week, I bought a thousand boxes of this candy. If you can sell them all before the end of the week, you can have the job."

"That's easy," Harry said.

He took the box of candy and left the office.

Every day and night, he went from shop to shop, trying to sell the candy.

He couldn't sell one. The candy was so bad that he couldn't even give it away. At the end of the week, he went back to the manager.

"I'm sorry, sir," he said, "I was wrong about myself. I'm not the best salesman in the world, but I know who is."

"Oh," said the manager. "Who?"

"The person who sold you a thousand boxes of this candy," Harry said.

二、听录音，完成下列各题。

（一）下面你将听到一篇独白，从每小题A，B，C三个选项中选出能回答所提问题的正确答案。

There was once a large, fat woman. She had a small, thin husband. Her husband worked in a big office and got his weekly pay every Friday evening. As soon as he got home on Fridays, he had to give his wife all his money and his wife gave him back only enough to buy his lunch in the office every day.

One day the small man came home very happily. He hurried into the living room. His wife was listening to the radio and eating apples there.

"You'll never guess what happened to me today, dear," he said. He waited for a few seconds and then said again, "I won ten thousand dollars buying the lottery tickets!"

"That's wonderful!" shouted his wife happily. But then she thought for a few seconds and said angrily, "But wait a minute! How could you have enough money to buy the tickets?"

（二）下面你将听到两则广告，从每小题 A，B，C 三个选项中选出能回答所提问题的正确答案。

Four-bedroom House for Sale

This house is on a quiet street only a few meters from the beach. It has a wonderful view of the ocean and would suit a family. The location will provide a lifestyle that is very enjoyable. There are many international cafes and restaurants nearby, and it is only a short walk to the stores. It's close to public transportation. The house has two storeys. On the first floor there is a modern kitchen, a large sitting room, a dining room, and a bathroom. Upstairs you will find four bedrooms. There are also two bathrooms. There is also a swimming pool and a beautiful garden around the house. Please telephone Jim Watson at 014-735-8383.

One-bedroom Apartment for Sale

This apartment is on the top floor of a six-storey building and has a wonderful view of the city. There is a big park near the building. It is located near the centre of the city. It will be a good home for a young couple. The apartment is freshly painted. A modern kitchen and a tidy bathroom make it a very comfortable flat. The owners are eager to sell it. Call Julie Kelly at 014-735-8484 for more information.

三、你将听一段生活小趣味说明，教你如何用小写单词 boy 画出一个男孩。

（一）根据你听到的内容，写出你所需要的材料。

This is a fun trick to show the little artist in your life.

You will need: paper, a pencil or pen, crayons or colored pencils.

（二）选出你所听到的图片并排序。

Step 1: Write the word "boy".

Write the word "boy" using only simple letters. Leave some space between each letter.

Step 2: Draw the eyes.

Put dots inside both the "b" and the "o."

Step 3: Make a jawline.

Connect the tail of the letter "y" to the left end of the letter "b."

Step 4: Connect the head.

Connect the top of the letter "b" to the top right of the letter "y" in an arc.

Step 5: Draw the hairline.

Connect the top left of the "y" to the top of the "b" to form the hairline.

Step 6: Draw the face.

Fill in the features like eyebrows, nose, mouth, and ears. This is your chance to be fun. You can make him happy, sad, angry, or surprised—the choice is up to you.

（三）根据你听到的内容，补充横线上所缺的步骤。

Section 4

一、听写。

One night a hotel caught fire, and the people who were staying in it ran out in their night clothes.

Two men stood outside and looked at the fire.

"Before I came out," said one, "I ran into some of the rooms and found a lot of money. People don't think of money when they're afraid. When anyone leaves paper money in a fire, the fire burns it. So I took all the paper money that I could find. No one will be poorer because I took them."

"You don't know my work," said the other.

"What is your work?"

"I'm a policeman."

"Oh!" cried the first man. He thought quickly and said, "And do you know my work?"

"No," said the policeman.

"I'm a writer. I'm always telling stories about things that never happened."

二、下面你将听到三段录音，从每小题 A，B，C 三个选项中选出能回答所提问题的正确答案。

听第一段对话，完成 1 ~3 题。

M：Mary, would you go to the Children's Center with us this Sunday afternoon?

W：Well, I'd like to, but Dad asked me to see his nephew Jerry at No. 10 People's Hospital.

M：It doesn't matter. What's wrong with Jerry? Does he have a bad cold or have a headache?

W：I was told that he hurt his left leg in the football game.

M：I'm sorry to hear that.

W：How long has he been in the hospital?

M：Three days. He was sent to the hospital as soon as his leg was hurt.

听第二段对话，完成 4 ~5 题。

W：Excuse me. Would the train to Shanghai come soon?

M：No, it left ten minutes ago.

W: Ah... I have to wait here for 20 more minutes.

M: You can take a bus to Shanghai if you can't wait.

W: That's a good idea, but I would like to take a train instead of taking a bus. Because trains are much safer than buses or planes.

听第三篇独白，完成 6 ~10 题。

It was Mr. and Mrs. Matthew's first visit to China. They traveled to many cities, Hangzhou for 3 days, Nanjing for 2 days, Suzhou for 2 days, and Shanghai for 3 days, then they were visiting Beijing, and staying for 4 days, then they'll go to visit Guangzhou for 3 day. After that they'll go to Hong Kong by train. Today was their last day in Beijing.

Mrs. Matthew likes dogs and cats. She bought a young dog and was going to bring it to London. It's about lunch time. They were hungry and wanted to have something to eat. So they went to a small restaurant. Mrs. Matthew wanted to give the dog something to eat first, she pointed to the dog and then she pointed to her mouth, and said, "Give it something to eat, please." The waiter didn't know much English. But he said "Yes" and took the dog into the kitchen at once. About 20 minutes or so, the waiter brought the Matthews a large bowl of dog meat. After seeing this, Mrs. Matthew was very angry.

"Why did you kill my dog?"

The waiter was surprised and said, "Don't you want to eat the dog?"

"Do you know dogs are our friends? How can you kill and eat your friends?" asked Mrs. Matthew.

三、听录音，完成下列各题。

(一) Erica 和 Tony 正在讨论他们班上的同学，根据听到的内容，做出正确的回答。

W: What do you think of the people in our class? I think most of them are fine.

M: I think so. But I don't like Mark. He's so arrogant. I totally hate arrogant people.

W: Mike is smart. I like people who always have something smart to say.

M: Carol's fun to be with. I really look forward to hearing her jokes. What do you think of Tom?

W: He's all right. I don't dislike him, but I don't really like him much either. What do you think of him?

M: I think he's OK. He's very quiet, so it's hard to know what kind of person he really is.

W: I'm fond of Jane. She's a very interesting girl. She's crazy about music.

M：Really? I'm mad on music, too. I should get to know her better. Are you keen on music?

W：I think that dance music is excellent. I love going to a disco and dancing to the music. I enjoy meeting new people there.

M：I almost forget to ask, what do you think of Serina, don't you think she is the most beautiful girl in our class?

W：Sure, I agree with you, she is beautiful and good at math. As to the coolest boy, I think Dorry must be the one.

M：We have to admit that, still remember the sports meeting? He is the best on the football team! More than that, he is good at basketball, too!

W：Really? I don't know that, but wow...

（二）仿照例句写下各个同学的特点。

Section 5

一、听文章，选出正确答案并完成表格。

（一）听文章，选出正确答案。

In the UK, most children have their midday meal at school, but in many schools, parents can choose what they eat. The children can have a school dinner—a hot, cooked meal; or they can take a packed lunch with them, which usually includes cold food like sandwiches.

Often parents made the lunch decision on what their children want. Cathy, a mother of three children told us, "My children have packed lunches, because they say they hate school dinners. So I make 3 packed lunches every morning, so we're like a sandwich bar in our kitchen in the morning."

However, another mother, Susan made her choice based on the nutritious value of the food. She said, "My daughter's always had school dinners. I think she probably gets better and healthier food by having a cooked lunch at school than she would if I made a few sandwiches."

But how healthy are school dinners? Kaz, a father, wasn't impressed with them, "Very cold drinks were offered and I think there were a lot of chips."

The question of how healthy school food is, was brought to the forefront by celebrity chef Jamie Oliver, who launched a campaign to improve children's nutrition, after spending a year working in a school kitchen. The TV series about the campaign won a BAFTA award this week.

He was horrified at the junk food which he saw being served which included burgers, pizzas and chips. So he decided to ban the junk, and started cooking some good stews and curries for the children instead.

So Jamie improved the school dinners in that particular school, and trained the dinner ladies to cook healthy food. Then he put pressure on the government to improve the standards of school food across the country. And it looks like the changes have begun.

（二）听文章，完成表格。

二、你将听到三段对话或独白，根据你听到的内容回答问题。

听第一段对话，完成1~2题。

W：What's the matter? Aiden?

M：I feel tired and hungry.

W：What did you eat this morning?

M：Nothing. And I have worked here since 7 o'clock.

W：Oh, it's already 11 o'clock. No wonder you are tired and hungry.

听第二段对话，完成3~5题。

W：Good morning, officer.

M：Good morning, madam. Can I help you?

W：Yes, please. Where's the nearest police station?

M：Er, look at this map. There's a police station on 5th Street. And there's one in Isaac Street, and one in Market Street.

W：Where's the nearest one?

M：Oh, yes, the nearest police station is near Market Street.

听第三段独白，完成6~10题。

My name is Kayla. I was lucky that I went to Canada last October. I stayed there for about 70 days. I went there on October 19 and came back on December 29th. I lived with a Canadian family, the Camerons, they are very kind and friendly. Before long, we became good friends. I could practice speaking English with them every day. Sometimes, I taught them Chinese. They looked after my meals, so I have time to go to English class. The teachers there were nice. They taught us to listen, speak, read, and write in English. But it was mostly speaking I found Canadian classes are a little different from our classes here. Sometimes we can sit anywhere we like in the classroom. We can learn from each other, and we can ask our teachers questions during the class. I really like this kind of class.

三、你将听到一段独白，将你听到的句子逐一写下来。

A very special teacher in a high school had a husband who died suddenly of a heart attack. About a week after his death, she shared some of her thoughts with a classroom of students. As the late afternoon sunlight shined through the classroom windows, and when the class was nearly over, she moved a few things aside on her desk and sat down there.

With a gentle look on her face, she stopped and said, "Before class is over, I would like to share with all of you a thought which I feel is very important. Each of us is put here on earth to learn share, love and give... and none of us knows when this wonderful experience will end. It can be taken away at any moment. Perhaps this is why we must make the best of every single day."

Unit 5

Section 1

一、在横线上写出你所听到的词语。

第一组：

1. finger	2. shoulder	3. neck	4. knee	5. toe
6. arm	7. hair	8. nose	9. head	10. ankle

第二组：

11. bank	12. hospital	13. office	14. park	15. square
16. restaurant	17. station	18. factory	19. hotel	20. club

二、下面你将听到十个句子，请从 A，B，C 三个选项中选出句子中出现的词语。

1. The bag on his back is not mine.
2. She is going to go to America by sea.
3. My father works as a doctor in a hospital.
4. There is a bird flying over the building.
5. Whose is this English-Chinese dictionary?
6. You can go there by taxi.
7. I don't think he is right.
8. This is the best film I have ever seen.
9. What fine weather it is!
10. He is strong enough to carry this box.

三、你将听到五个句子，根据句子内容选择相应的图片。

1. It tells people not to go too close to it. It's dangerous.
2. We often see this sign on busy streets, so do not park your car here.
3. You should put glasses or bottles this way, or they may be broken.
4. It means that you mustn't smoke here.
5. You must put this side up.

四、听下面五段对话，根据对话内容选择相应的图片。

1. M: How many apples are there in the picture?
   W: You've made a mistake. They are not apples. They are cherries.
2. M: What is John doing?
   W: He is playing football with Sam.
3. M: Pass me the sweater.
   W: It isn't a sweater. It's a coat.
4. M: What is Billy's hobby?
   W: He likes riding a bicycle.
5. M: What's your brother like?
   W: He is a short boy with glasses.

五、听对话，选择合适的答案。

(L: little girl　　E: elder sister　　C: caller)

L: Hello.

C: He, he... hello? Uh, yeah. Is your Dad home?

L: Just a minute, please.

E: Hello.

C: Uh ... yeah ... uh hello? Yeah, um ... is ... uh ... Nick home, please?

E: Oh, he can't come to the phone right now.

C: Okay, well, I need to talk to your Dad. Um, yeah, could you ... um ... take a message?

E: Yeah.

C: Yeah. This is ... my name's Nick Johnson. And if ...

E: The phone number?

C: Yeah, if you could tell him. Yeah, the phone number is 589 [Uh-huh] 7248.

E: 589-7248?

C: Yeah, right and if you could tell him to call me tonight between 7:00 and 8:30?

E: Okay.

C: Alright, and uh. Now, I think ... are you his daughter?

E: Yeah.

C: Yeah, now what's your name?

E: I ... I'm not supposed to tell that.

C: Ah, that's really smart. Alright, well, just tell him I called.

E: Okay.

C: Okay, bye.

E: Bye.

Section 2

一、请根据要求写出你在句子中所听到的词语。

第一组:写出你所听到的职业名称。

1. Don't you think that the police might be the best people to ask for help?
2. The young driver died in the car accident.
3. I am going to have a shave at the barber's.
4. A cook cannot work without a cooker.
5. To be a scientist is my dream.
6. Do we have to leave some tips to the waiter?

第二组:写出你所听到的时间或数字。

7. There are more than one thousand languages in the world.
8. Let's make it to the tennis court at a quarter to nine.
9. About one-fifth of the world's population speaks Chinese.
10. I have studied English for twelve years.
11. Stephen Hawking was born on January 8, 1942.
12. My telephone number is 84695007.

二、听下面的句子，并根据句子内容在横线上写出正确的日期或星期。

1. The school begins on March 7th.
2. My sister will travel to France on January 19th.
3. We'll take the test on November 22nd.
4. On June 18th, the store will have a big sale.
5. Can you send me an email by September 30th?
6. My grandparents will come to see me next Saturday.
7. Thanksgiving Day falls on the fourth Thursday in November.
8. Do you know that next Wednesday is my birthday?
9. Will you be free this Tuesday?
10. Is Sunday or Monday the first day of a week?

三、听下面五段对话，根据对话内容选择相应的图片，并将代表该答案的字母填在题前的括号内。

1. M: Is it raining?

W：Yes，it is. It's raining very hard.

2. M：Nice and bright this morning.

W：Yes. Much better than yesterday.

3. M：It's freezing today. How cold is it?

W：It's ten below.

4. M：Do you have any brothers or sisters?

W：No，I don't have any brothers or sisters.

5. M：Where is the girl?

W：She is behind the monster.

四、听下面的对话，并根据对话内容选择正确的答案。

M：Hey，young lady. May I help you?

W：Well，yeah，I'm looking for a Father's Day gift.

M：OK. How about getting your father a new wallet?

W：Umm. How much is that wallet?

M：Err，which one?

W：The black one.

M：Oh，it's only $40.95.

W：That's too expensive for me. Do you have a cheaper one?

M：How about this brown leather one?

W：I don't think my father would like the design on the outside. And it doesn't have a place to put pictures. How much is it，anyway?

M：It's $25.99.

W：I don't have that much money.

M：OK. How much money do you have to spend?

W：I'm not sure.（The sound of counting the coins.）Probably about ten dollars. I've been helping my Mum around the house for the past week to earn some money. This is all I have.

M：Umm. How about this tie?

W：That's really pretty. But the price tag says $13.99. And I know that I don't have that much money.

M：Well. Let's just say that the tie would be on sale. How about five dollars? What do you say?

W：Oh，thanks. I'll take it.

五、听下面这段文章，选图填空。

My alarm clock rings at 7:00. I jump out of bed and do some exercises. I have a big breakfast every day. At 7:30 I put on my school uniform and go to school. I go to school by bus. I usually arrive at school at about 8:00. Class begins at 8:10. I attend four classes in the morning and two in the afternoon. After class I always go to the library. I do my homework there. I usually go home at five. After supper I watch TV news for half an hour. Sometimes I read newspapers or novels. I go to bed at 10:00.

Section 3

一、听写句子。

1. I hardly eat any fruit and vegetables.
2. Tom is the tallest boy in his class.
3. I didn't finish my homework until 10 o'clock last night.
4. Are you strong enough to lift this box?
5. Mary is good at writing funny stories.
6. The women doctors are from France.
7. Did you enjoy your birthday party yesterday?
8. How long has your brother been on the farm?
9. It is hotter today than yesterday.
10. The Greens usually spend their vacation in some foreign countries.

二、根据你所听到的歌曲内容完成下面的练习。

I'm riding on a horse. I'm riding on a horse. I'm riding on a horse. I'm riding on a horse.

I'm riding on a horse. I'm travelling on a train. I'm sailing on a ship. I'm driving in a car.

Over the mountains. Through the trees. Travel the world and seven seas.

Over the mountains. Through the trees. Travel the world and seven seas.

三、听一段独白，根据下面这幅图判断句子的正误并做出相应的选择。

The hotel is next to the bank. The bowling alley is on East Street. The library is between the post office and the supermarket. The zoo is behind the post office. The bowling alley is behind the bookstore. The bar is on the corner of West Street and South Street. The city hall is in front of the library. The hospital is near the bus station. The zoo is opposite the police station.

四、你将听到两段独白，请根据独白内容完成下面的练习，每空填一个词。

第一段：The United Kingdom is a small country. It's in Europe. Germany is in Europe, too. Your Teacher is an English teacher in Germany. She's British. She's from Derby. Derby is a big city in England. Mr. Smith is an English teacher, too, but he's not English. He's an American. He's from Washington.

第二段：Mr. Bean is going to go on holiday this year. What do you think he's going to do? He's not going to rest and relax. He's going to learn how to swim. He's going to write everyone a postcard.

Section 4

一、你将听到几段广播录音片段，请根据内容完成下面的练习。

听第一段录音，完成 1 ~2 题。

This is a download from BBC. Hi, there. I'm Senali with the BBC world news for children. It's Friday, the 29th of January. Coming up...

听第二段录音，完成 3 ~4 题。

This is IN THE NEWS in VOA Special English.

President Barack Obama has begun his second year in office. The forty-fourth president, and first African-American president, was inaugurated last January twentieth.

BARACK OBAMA: "Today I say to you that the challenges we face are real, they are serious and they are many. They will not be met easily or in a short span of time. But know this, America, they will be met."

Those challenges included an economic downturn, wars in Afghanistan and Iraq and a promise to reform the health care system.

二、下面你将看到一些同音异形词，请听句子并判断出句子中出现的那个单词。如果表格中的词语是正确的就打"√"，错误的打"×"。

1. It's important to weigh yourself every few months.
2. In some pubs in England you are not allowed to smoke.
3. I knew him before he was famous.
4. There isn't any flour on the floor now.
5. He was able to sit, but was too weak to stand.
6. He didn't begin to write until he was five years old.
7. I can arrive at the airport by six o'clock.

8. Don't read in the sun. It's bad for our eyes.

三、请听句子，并在横线上写出句子中出现的动词词组（写动词的原形）。

1. Don't forget to take off your shoes before you enter the room.
2. May I come in?
3. What are you looking for?
4. When do you get up every day?
5. Don't turn off the TV.
6. Parents often worry about their children.
7. Hurry up, children. It's time for class.
8. You can look up the new words in the dictionary.
9. Do you often go over the lessons?
10. I've been waiting for the bus for half an hour.
11. The earthquake took place ten days ago.
12. It's impolite to laugh at the others.

四、根据你所听到的句子选择合适的图片。

1. M: Where are you going?
   W: I'm going to buy some flowers for my teachers.
2. M: What do you usually eat on the Lantern Festival?
   W: We usually eat sweet dumplings with our family members.
3. M: Come on, Jenny.
   W: Don't make so much noise. We are in the hospital.
4. M: Where can we park our car?
   W: Look, there is a parking lot over there.

五、请听五个句子，并完成下面的五个小题。

1. The bus to Reno, Nevada, leaves at 9:50 am.
2. The bus to Boise, Idaho, arrives at 9:35 pm.
3. The bus fare to Seattle, Washington, is 112 dollars.
4. The bus bound from Fresno, California, leaves at 11:00 sharp.
5. The bus heading to Reno is scheduled to arrive at 4:30 pm.

六、你将听到一篇文章，请根据文章内容完成下面的练习。

You probably think that the hamburger is a typical American food. Americans often have a hamburger for a quick lunch or snack. But do you know that the favorite American "fast food" actually comes from many different countries?

The hamburger is made of beef, not ham. The idea of chopping meat into very small pieces comes from Turkey. The name "hamburger" comes from the town of Hamburg in Germany.

The pickle, or pickled cucumber, comes from Eastern Europe. It is popular in Poland and Russia.

The word "ketchup" comes from China. "Ke-tsiap" is the Chinese name for a sauce made of pickled fish and spices. The first recipe for tomato ketchup is in a 1792 American cookbook.

Mayonnaise, sometimes called "mayo", is a yellow-white sauce made of eggs, oil, and lemon juice. It comes from the Spanish island of Minorca, but its name is French. Mayonnaise is also used as a dressing for salads.

The bun is a kind of bread. It comes from an English recipe, and the sesame seeds on top come from the Middle East. So, the "American" hamburger is a truly international meal.

Section 5

一、下面你将听到一些电影片段，请根据片段内容完成下面的题目。

听第一段录音，完成1～2题。

Hello. My name's Forrest. Forrest Gump. Do you want a chocolate? I could eat about a million and a half of these. My Mama always said, "Life was like a box of chocolates. You never know what you're going to get." Those must be comfortable shoes. I bet you could walk all day in shoes like that and not feel a thing. I wish I had shoes like that.

听第二段录音，完成3～4题。

Nemo: Wake up, wake up! First day of school.

Marlin: I don't want to go to school—five more minutes.

Nemo: Not you. Dad, me.

Marlin: OK.

Nemo: Get up, get up. It's time for school, time for school.

Marlin: All right, I'm up.

Nemo: Whoa!

Marlin: Nemo!

Nemo: First day of school!

Marlin: Nemo, don't move! You'll never get out of there yourself. I'll do it. Unh!

You feel a break?

Nemo: No!

Marlin: Sometimes you can't tell 'cause fluid rushes to the area. Are you woozy?

Nemo: No!

Marlin: How many strips do I have?

Nemo: I am fine.

Marlin: Answer the stripe question.

Nemo: Three.

Marlin: No! See? Something's wrong with you. I have one, two, three—that's all I have? You are OK. How's the lucky fin?

Nemo: Lucky.

Marlin: Let's see. Are you sure you want to go to school this year? There's no problem if you don't. You can wait 5 or 6 years.

Nemo: Come on, Dad, it's time for school.

二、听下面的句子，并根据句子内容选择相应的图片。

1. I like to walk in the mountains with my dog.
2. My Dad goes to the city pool twice a week.
3. He rides his bike to work because it is a good way to exercise.
4. She usually uses her watercolor in the art work.
5. They are the most suitable presents on Valentine's Day.

三、听下面几段对话，根据题中的问题选择合适的答案。

1. M: Hi, Susan.

   W: Hi, Michael. How are you feeling today?

   M: Very well. How about you?

   W: So-so.

   M: What's wrong?

   W: I have a sore throat.

2. M: Good evening, sir, madam.

   W: Good evening. We have a reservation for a table for two in the name of Smith.

   M: Yes, madam. This way, please.

3. M: Where are your uncle and aunt?

   W: They are at the parking lot.

   M: What are they doing?

   W: They are washing their car.

4. M：Did you like the film?

W：Not particularly. I was rather disappointed. I'd expected it to be much more exciting.

5. W：Hey, Mike, can you give me some suggestions? I'm going to write an article on geography.

M：Why don't you go to the school library? There may be some good books.

W：Oh, that's right. I didn't think of that. Thank you very much.

M：You're welcome.

四、请听一段对话，并完成下面的练习。

W：So, what's your usual day like? You always seem so busy.

M：Well, I usually get up around 5：00 am and work on the computer until 6：00 am.

W：Why do you get up so early?

M：Well, I have to leave home at twenty to seven, so I can catch a bus at 7：00 o'clock . It takes me about twenty minutes to walk to the bus stop from my house.

W：And what time do you get to work?

M：Uh, my bus takes about an hour to get there, but it stops right in front of my office.

W：That's nice. And what time do you get off work?

M：Uh, around 5 o'clock. Then, we eat dinner around 6：30, and my wife and I read and play with the kids until 8：00 or so.

W：So, when do you work on your website? You said one time that you create it at home?

M：Well, my wife and I often watch TV or talk until 10 o'clock. She then often reads while I work on my site, and I sometimes stay up until the early hours of the morning, but I try to finish everything by one or two.

W：And then you get up at 5：00 am?

M：Well, yeah, but it's important to live a balanced life. I enjoy what I do, but you have to set aside time for the family and yourself.

W：I agree.

M：But I think my wife has the toughest job. She spends her whole day taking care of our family ... taking the kids to school, working in the garden, buying groceries, taking the kids to piano lessons ... Wow! It's a full-time job, but she enjoys what she does.

W：Well, it sounds like you're a busy, but lucky man.

M：I think so，too.

五、你将听到一段短文，请将短文内容写在下面的横线上。

Our food is very important. We like eating it，and it makes us strong and healthy. In most countries，people have three or four meals every day. Having a good meal is like filling a car with petrol. It gives us fuel for the work we do. The most important meal is breakfast. Doctors say that if you don't have a good breakfast，you can't work well. Vegetables and fruit are also very important. Our bodies need them to stay healthy. We enjoy sweet food，but we don't need it.

Unit 6

Section 1

一、写出你所听到的词语，并找出与其他三个不同类的一项，并将代表该选项的字母填在题前的括号内。

1. A. cow	B. chicken	C. beef	D. pork
2. A. cup	B. knife	C. fork	D. spoon
3. A. violin	B. piano	C. drum	D. band
4. A. bus	B. taxi	C. lorry	D. bicycle
5. A. television	B. refrigerator	C. sofa	D. oven

二、下面你将听到一些电影或歌曲片段，请根据片段内容完成下面的题目。

听第一段录音，完成 1 ~2 题。

Mufasa: Simba, I am very disappointed in you.

Simba: I know.

Mufasa: You could've been killed. You deliberately disobeyed me. And what's worse, you put Nala in danger.

Simba: I was just trying to be brave like you.

Mufasa: I am only brave when I have to be. Simba, being brave doesn't mean you go looking for trouble.

Simba: But you are not scared of anything.

Mufasa: I was today.

Simba: You were?

Mufasa: Yes. I thought I might lose you.

Simba: Oh, I guess even kings get scared, huh? But you know what?

Mufasa: What?

Simba: I think those hyenas were even scareder.

Mufasa: 'Cause nobody messes with your Dad. Come here, you.

Simba: Oh, no! No!

听第二段录音，请填出空格中所缺的英文歌词。

Moon river, wider than a mile;
I'm crossing you in style some day;
Oh, dream maker, you heart breaker;
Wherever you're going, I'm going your way.

三、你将听到一段对话，请根据对话内容找出下面这段对话中的错误。在错误的地方画上横线，并将正确的内容填在后面的括号内。第一个错误已经给出。

W: I had a terrible morning, John!

M: Oh, Rita. What happened?

W: Well, I went to the bus stop as usual. I waited for twenty minutes but the bus didn't come.

M: So, what did you do?

W: I ran to the station. I decided to take the eight o'clock train. But I was too late. I missed the train.

M: Oh, no!

W: So, I went outside and found a taxi. But the taxi driver went the wrong way. He got lost! I was late for school again! I got there at nine thirty!

四、听一篇文章，完成下面的练习。

Paragraph 1: Sadie and Bessie Delany are sisters who live in Mount Vernon, New York. Sadie is 104 years old, and Besie is 102. They tell their life story in a book called *Having Our Say: The Delany Sisters' First Hundred Years*. Here is some of their advice for living a long, healthy life.

Paragraph 2: Get up early. The Delany sisters get up at 6:30 or 7:00 am. Have a good breakfast. The sisters eat oatmeal, half a banana, bran, and eggs with a little cheese. Exercise every day. The Delany sisters like to do yoga. They also walk every day. Eat lots of vegetables, specially garlic. Garlic is good for your health, even if it's not good for your breath!

Paragraph 3: Don't eat a lot of salt and fat. These things are bad for you. Don't get married! The sisters say, "We are still alive because we don't have husbands who worry us." Don't listen to the doctor. "Most doctors don't know what to do with us," Sadie says. When something's wrong, they say, "You're still living, what do you expect?"

Section 2

一、请在左边的横线上写出你所听到的国家名称，在右边的横线上写出你所听到的首都名称，然后将对应的国家和首都连线。

1. Japan 2. Germany 3. France 4. America 5. Russia

A. Washington D. C. B. Tokyo C. Berlin D. Paris E. Moscow

二、请听一段对话，并根据对话内容填出句子中所缺的词语。

Amy: Hi, Victor. How are you?

Victor: Oh, I'm fine.

Amy: So, are you going to the class tonight?

Victor: Maybe ... But I don't think so.

Amy: Really? What's the matter?

Victor: I don't know. I'm just feeling a little sad.

Amy: Listen. Come with me to class, and after class we can go out for dinner.

Victor: Now that's a good idea. Thanks a lot, Amy. I'm feeling better already.

三、你将听到一些关于英文名著的介绍，请根据介绍将它们与右边的作者连线。

Welcome to our school library. Today I'll introduce some English masterpieces to you. The first one I'll introduce is *Pride and Prejudice*. This is a novel written by a female writer, Jane Austen. The second one is a comedy called *A Midsummer Night's Dream*, which is written by William Shakespeare. If you are interested in travelling and adventure, I highly recommend Jules Verne's novel *Around the World in 80 Days*. And the next writer I want to introduce to you is an American writer, Mark Twain. Twain is most noted for his novels *Adventures of Huckleberry Finn* and *The Adventures of Tom Sawyer*. And the last novel is *A Tale of Two Cities* written by Charles Dickens.

四、请根据你所听到的句子选择合适的图片。

1. There are different kinds of trees in the forest.
2. I don't like ball games. I like boxing best.
3. My car is out of petrol. Let's go and get some.
4. I like this season, for I can step on the fallen leaves.
5. Congratulations! You've graduated from the university.

五、请听下面关于教室的介绍，根据你所听到的内容选出你所听到的物品。

This is my classroom. There is a sign on the door. It says: Welcome to our classroom! There are many desks. This is my desk. My name is on it. This is my teacher's desk. There are many interesting things. There is a fish bowl on the cabinet. His name is Goldy. Her name is Swimmy. There is a large blackboard on the front wall. My teacher writes our homework on it. There is a birthday chart on the back wall. My teacher puts our names and birthdays on it. There is a round clock above the door. It tells us what time it is. There are our drawings on the side wall. There is a reading couch in the corner. This is my favorite place.

六、你将听到一段对话，请根据对话内容完成下面的练习。

M: Let me see now. Which train do I need to get on?

W: Excuse me. Do you need any help?

M: Yes, I want to go to Tokyo Tower, but I'm really lost. This is my first visit to Japan, so I have no idea on how to ride the trains.

W: First, you need to buy a ticket to your destination.

M: Um...

W: From here, it's a hundred and thirty yen.

M: A hundred thirty yen. Okay.

W: Then, get on the Hibiya Subway Line at platform number 4.

M: Number 4, alright. Oh, and how often do the trains come around this time of day?

W: Usually, they come about every six minutes or so.

M: Alright. And where do I get off the train?

W: Get off at Kamiyacho Station, three stops from here. The sign at the station is written in English, so you'll be able to read it.

M: Three stops. Got it. Thanks for your help.

W: No problem. Good luck.

Section 3

一、在横线上写出你所听到的句子。

1. Can I leave a message?
2. How many pounds of potatoes do you want?

3. I'm going to catch the ten o'clock train.
4. Would you like anything to drink?
5. I'll pick you up around seven thirty.
6. What language did the musician learn to speak?
7. He is one of the most famous singers.
8. Nobody can do it like this.
9. It's easy enough for me to answer the question.
10. How beautiful these flowers are!

二、听下面十个句子，根据所听内容选出相应的答语，并将代表该答案的字母填在题前的括号内。

1. Can I help you?
2. Hello, may I speak to Anna?
3. Why don't you have a picnic?
4. Your English is very good.
5. I think it will be windy tomorrow.
6. How do you usually come to school?
7. Could you help me to put the bag in the car?
8. What's wrong with your watch?
9. Who is on duty today?
10. I don't know how to repair this bicycle.

三、你将听到几段小对话，请根据对话内容完成下面的练习。

听第一段对话，完成1～3题。

M: Excuse me. I'm your new neighbor, Jack. I just moved in.
W: Oh. Yes?
M: I'm looking for a grocery store. Are there any around here?
W: Yes, there are some on Pine Street.
M: OK. And is there a laundry near here?
W: Well, I think there's one across from the shopping center.
M: Thank you.
W: By the way, there's a barber shop in the shopping center, too.
M: A barber shop?!

听第二段对话，完成4～6题。

W: Tom, I'm so excited! We have two weeks off! What are you going to do?
M: I'm not sure. I guess I'll just stay at home. Maybe I'll catch up on my reading. What about you? Any plans?

W: Well, my parents have rented a house in Florida. I'm going to take long walks along the beach every day and do lots of swimming.

M: Sounds great!

W: Say, why don't you come with us? We have plenty of rooms.

M: Do you mean it? I'd love to.

听第三段对话，完成7 ~8 题。

M: Say, Anna, what are you doing tonight? Would you like to go out?

W: Oh, sorry, I can't. I'm going to work late tonight. I have to finish this report.

M: Well, how about tomorrow night? Are you doing anything then?

W: No, I'm not. What are you planning to do?

M: I'm going to see a film. Would you like to come?

W: Sure, I'd love to! But let me pay for the tickets this time. It's my turn.

M: All right! Thanks!

四、你将听到一段对话，请根据对话内容完成下面的练习。

Son: Dad!

Father: Yeah, Mickey.

Son: Can I have a really good snack?

Father: Uh, I don't know. I think it's... Uh... What time is it? I think it's going on dinner.

Son: Uh, it's three thirty.

Father: Three thirty. Uh... We'd better wait.

Son: Why, Dad?

Father: Well, what kind of snack do you want?

Son: Candy?

Father: No, candy is out. Oh, how about some donuts?

Son: No!

Father: Uh, carrots?

Son: No!

Father: Well, what else can you suggest?

Son: Candy.

Father: Candy. No, I don't think... I think you'd better wait.

Son: A sandwich? A spinach sandwich?

Father: Spinach sandwich? Spinach sandwich! When did you start liking spinach?

Son: Uh, today.

Father: Well, what about a small sandwich?

Son: Okay.

Father: Okay, I'll whip it up in a minute. Play with your computer while you're waiting for it.

Section 4

一、听句子，选出与你所听到的意思相近的句子。

1. Susan walks to school every day.
2. Lily will leave for Paris tomorrow.
3. Will you go to see the film tonight instead of tomorrow night?
4. This dress is as expensive as that one.
5. What does your father do?

二、你将听到几段广播录音片段，请根据你所听到的内容完成下面的练习。

听第一段录音，完成1~2题。

VOICE ONE:

Welcome to THIS IS AMERICA in VOA Special English. I'm Shirley Griffith.

VOICE TWO:

And I'm Steve Ember. Lomax is a name well-known to historians of American musical culture. Today we have the first of two programs about how the Lomax family helped keep American folk music from being lost.

听第二段录音，完成3~4题。

John Avery Lomax was born in eighteen sixty-seven. He came from the state of Mississippi but grew up in Texas. His interest in cowboy music led him to research and collect examples of cowboy songs.

In nineteen ten he published a book called *Cowboy Songs and Other Frontier Ballads*. It contained not only the words to songs but some of the music as well. It began with an introduction by President Theodore Roosevelt.

Cowboy Songs and Other Frontier Ballads was an important research achievement. And it started John Lomax on his lifelong work.

The book included classics like *Sweet Betsy from Pike*, *Git Along*, *Little Dogies* and *Home on the Range*. Gene Autry was a singing cowboy in old films. Here he is singing *Home on the Range*.

三、请听问句，并标出问句的顺序，然后把问句与相应的答句连线。

1. Does Dad enjoy dancing?

2. Is Sam's father reading a book?
3. Do you like swimming?
4. What are you doing?
5. What's he doing?

四、你将听到几段小对话，请根据对话内容完成下面的练习。

1. M: Hey, Jane. Did you post the letter for me on your way home yesterday?
   W: Oh! Gosh! I forgot it.
   M: And did you remember to bring me your book?
   W: Oh, sorry. It seems that I have a very bad memory. I think I need to buy a notebook to take down all the things.
2. W: May I help you, sir?
   M: Err... Yes. I just want to know how much this wallet is. I can't find a price tag on it.
   W: Let me help you. It's 21 dollars, sir.
   M: Well, thank you. That's not expensive.
3. W: Happy birthday, Bobby! Here is a present for you.
   M: Thank you. Is it a model plane?
   W: Open it and see.
   M: Goodness! What a beautiful skateboard! This is my dream present. Thank you, Mum.
   W: Then you can learn how to skate.
4. M: We'll move to our new house next week. Is there anything else we should buy?
   W: We've already bought a bed, a TV set, a sofa...
   M: Yeah, wait a moment. Have we got a bedside table yet?
   W: Yes, of course. We bought it last week.
   M: Well, I think I'll buy a comfortable armchair. Then I can sit in it with a good book every night.

五、你将听到一篇文章，请根据文章内容回答下面的问题。

听第一篇短文，回答 1 ~4 题。

Once I was visiting an English friend in London. Since he was busy for the time being, I drove his car along the streets. I felt lucky because I had my driving license with me. But suddenly a policeman stopped me and said that I was not driving on the right side. I was puzzled because I was indeed driving on the right side. But the policeman said that I was driving on the right side, but the right side was the wrong side.

听第二篇短文，回答5～8题。

I go to work by bus every day. Last Friday I got on the bus as usual and sat next to a "Mrs. Dumpling". The bus was very crowded. She had several shopping bags, so I had little room on the seat. I didn't feel comfortable. When the bus got to the station, all the passengers started to get off. I was very polite, so I stood up to let the fat lady get off before me. She said "Thank you", and tried to get out of the seat with all her bags. But she couldn't move because she was stuck.

I had to push her. The conductor pulled her. Finally we got her free, but she wasn't pleased. "I'll write to the bus company!" she said. "I'll tell them not to make buses with such small seats!"

Section 5

一、你将听到几段广播录音片段，请根据你所听到的内容完成下面的练习。

听第一段录音，完成1～2题。

Welcome to THIS IS AMERICA. I'm Faith Lapidus. This Thursday is a day for families and friends to share a special holiday meal and think about what they are thankful for. This week on our program, we ask some people to share their favorite memories of Thanksgiving Day.

听第二段录音，根据歌曲内容在空格处填上合适的词语。

From this valley they say you are going,
I will miss your bright eyes and sweet smile.
For I know you are taking the sunshine.
That has lighten my pathway a while.
Come and sit by my side if you love me,
Don't hasten to bid me do,
But remember the Red River Valley,
And the one that has loved you so true.
Just remember the Red River Valley,
And the one who has loved you so true.

二、你将听到一些广告语，根据广告内容选择相应的产品。

1. We lead. Others copy.
2. All you need is a taste for adventure.
3. Give a Timex to all, to all a good time.

4. The world's coolest CDs aren't made in New York, London or L. A. They are made in my apartment.
5. Give your hair a touch of Spring.

三、你将听到几段小对话，请根据对话内容完成下面的练习。

听第一段对话，完成1~3题。

W: Please close the window, Mike. It's a little chilly here.
M: Okay. Is there anything else I can do for you before I leave?
W: Could you turn off the light in the kitchen?
M: No problem. Anything else?
W: Umm, please hand me the remote control for the TV. It's over there.
M: Sure. Here.
W: Thanks.
M: I'll stop by again tomorrow. Take care of yourself. Take good care of that broken leg. Don't trip over anything.
W: Don't worry, I'll be careful. Thanks again.

听第二段对话，完成4~6题。

M: Diane Grant? I haven't seen you for ages!
W: Brian! How have you been?
M: Pretty good. Say, you've really changed!
W: Oh, well, I've lost some weight. And my hair is longer than before.
M: Well, you look great! How are you?
W: I'm doing really well. I got married about three years ago. I have two kids now.
M: That's terrific!

听第三段对话，完成7~9题。

M: Hi, Stephanie. I hear you have a new job.
W: Yes, I'm teaching math at Lincoln High School.
M: So how do you like it?
W: Well, the salary is a little low, but the students are nice. How are things with you?
M: Not bad. You know I'm an air traffic controller now.
W: Now that's an exciting job!
M: Yes, but it's very stressful.

四、你将听到一篇短文，请将短文内容写在下面的横线上。

Do you know anything about the moon? The moon is smaller than the earth, but the sun is much bigger than the earth. The moon is far from the earth. It's 380, 000 kilometers away. On the earth we see that the moon looks like a cake. There is no air on the moon, so there are no living things there. The side of the moon towards the sun is very hot, while the other side is very cold. People can jump higher on the moon than on the earth and walk more easily there. People can't live on the moon. They have been to the moon. It takes more than three days to get to the moon by spaceship.

Unit 7

Section 1

一、请写出你所听到的词语，并在后面的括号内写出它们所属的种类名称。

1．pear，watermelon，grapes
2．sunflower，bamboo，grass
3．shoulder，arm，knee
4．coffee，wine，orange juice
5．pants，blouse，gloves

二、听句子，并从选项中选出你所听到的句子。

1．Mum baked some cakes a little while ago.
2．I hope you don't mind my smoking.
3．Asia is four times larger than Europe.
4．He is too weak to carry this refrigerator.
5．What's happened in the bank?

三、听下面的歌曲，按要求完成以下练习。

The stars are out，the moon is up. It's time to go to bed.
I'm so glad you have a place to lay your little head.
Have a deep and peaceful sleep. Dream away the hours.
When you wake the sun will come，to smile upon the flowers.
Go to sleep my little friend，beneath the evening star.
You will always have a friend，no matter where you are.

四、你将听到五个句子，根据句子内容选择相应的图片。

1．She is teaching me to skate.
2．My sister Jenny likes singing very much.
3．Mum always told me stories when I was young.
4．I work as a secretary in a big company.

5. The young lady is drawing a beautiful picture over there.

五、你将听到几段对话，请根据对话内容完成下面的练习。

听第一段对话，完成1~3题。

M：Do you want to watch television tonight?

W：Well, there's nothing interesting, but turn it on if you want to.

M：I want to see the program Changjiang Travel.

W：Is there any other exciting program?

M：Yes. I remember there's an NBA match on CCTV5.

W：Oh, great! Let's watch it.

M：Let me see. Hmm. The paper says it starts at one o'clock tomorrow morning.

W：One o'clock tomorrow? Then I prefer to sleep.

听第二段对话，完成4~6题。

M：I give up. I simply can't learn Chinese.

W：Why do you say that? I think you are making a lot of progress.

M：No, I'm not. I try and try and I still can't speak it very well.

W：Please don't give up. Why don't we practice those dialogues together?

M：Good idea. That just might help.

W：Let's sit down and have some tea.

M：I'd like to have some.

W：By the way, what's your mother tongue?

M：French. I did not learn to speak English until I was seven.

W：But your English is quite good.

M：Better than my Chinese.

听第三段对话，完成7~8题。

W：Excuse me. Am I on the right way to the Concert Hall?

M：Sorry, I'm afraid you're going in the opposite direction.

W：You mean I have to turn back and...

M：Yes. Turn back and go straight along the street. You'll see the hall after two blocks.

W：Thank you very much.

M：Not at all.

Section 2

一、在横线上写出你所听到的词组或短语。

1. look out　　2. hurry up　　3. have a rest　　4. all the time

5. have a cold　6. at the weekend　7. go for a walk　8. on duty
9. by taxi　10. make friends　11. high jump　12. turn off

二、听下面的句子，并根据句子的内容选择合适的答语。

1. What would you like to have, tea or juice?
2. Have a good weekend, Mary.
3. I don't feel well.
4. What's your mother like?
5. Hello, may I speak to Jenny?
6. Why don't you have a picnic?
7. How often do you write to your pen pal?
8. I think it will be windy tomorrow.
9. What are you going to do this summer?
10. Give me your book.

三、你将听到一段歌曲，请根据歌曲内容填上合适的词语。

I'm a policeman dressed in blue, here are some things I like to do.
Direct the traffic in your town, help to keep you safe and sound.
It's my job and I like it fine. No one has a better job than mine.
I'm a policeman dressed in blue, I want to be a friend to you.
You can see me every day, I will wave my hand and say.
It's my job and I like it fine. No one has a better job than mine.

四、你将听到一段天气预报，请根据天气预报的内容将下面代表国家的国旗与相应的天气连线。

W: Now it's time for the world weather with Peter. Hello, Peter!

M: Hello, Amy. There's a lot of different weather around the world today. In England it is raining. In Portugal it is sunny. In Japan it is foggy. In Australia it is very hot. In Sweden it is snowing. In China it is windy. In Egypt it will be cloudy. In India there will be storms.

五、你将听到一篇短文，请根据对话内容将下面的事件按发生的顺序排序。

A rich American went into a shop in London. He wanted very much to buy a nice looking watch. He saw a watch and liked it very much. But the owner of the shop asked five hundred dollars for it. Suddenly, a young man came into the shop, took the watch out of the owner's hands and ran out with it. It all happened in a few seconds. When the owner ran out into the street, the young man had already been lost among the people. The American went on. At the next corner, he saw the young man with the stolen watch in his hand. "Do you want to buy a fine watch, sir?" He said in a low voice. "It's only a hundred dollars." The young man doesn't know the rich American saw him stealing the watch. So the American paid at once, and went back to his room with the watch. He told his friend about the fine watch. His friend took a look at the watch and started laughing. He said, "You are a fool. This watch isn't worth even ten dollars. I'm sure that the shop owner and young man planned this together."

六、请听下面的一段独白，完成下面的表格。

Hi. My name's David, and I'm originally from New York, but my family moved to Los Angeles when I was about 3, so I grew up there. I graduated from high school about three years ago when I was fifteen years old, and I am now attending a university in my city. I'm a junior, and I am majoring in science. I also work part time as a waiter in a local restaurant. Life is really busy, but I enjoy hiking, reading, and hanging out with friends in my free time. When I graduate, I want to work for a company in this area.

Section 3

一、听下面的句子，并写出横线上所缺的词语或者是完整的句子。

1. That's why a lot of people are swimming in the river.
2. It's going to be warmer later on.
3. Everyone is here except him.
4. Thousands of people are learning foreign languages in our country.
5. I can see a cat running across the street.
6. Is the museum far from here?
7. Nobody knows what to do next.
8. We will go sailing together next Saturday.
9. There will be more and more deserts in the world.
10. Sometimes young people visit their parents once a year.

二、听下面一段话，补全横线中所缺的词语。

Mr. and Mrs. Brown live in a small town in the south of England. Mr. Brown is a dentist. His wife works in a school. She teaches history. Mr. and Mrs. Brown go to work together by car. Mr. Brown always drives. Mrs. Brown never drives. The Browns have a boy and a girl. Peter is fourteen and Ann is nineteen. Ann doesn't live with her family. She lives in London and works as a nurse in a hospital.

三、听下面的对话，根据对话内容回答相应的问题。

1. W: What can I do for you?
   M: Can you show me a dress?
2. W: What's the time, please?
   M: It's a quarter to two.
3. W: Excuse me, where does Jane live?
   M: She lives in Room 1044.
   W: And what about her sister?
   M: She lives next door to Jane, in Room 1046.
4. M: I don't think it's a nice day, is it?
   W: No, it isn't.
5. W: Excuse me, could you tell me the way to the post office, please?
   M: Sure. Walk along this road, and take the first turning on the right. You'll find the post office.
   W: Thanks a lot.
6. M: Does the play start at 7:00 or 7:15?
   W: Neither. It starts at 7:30 and ends at 10:00.
7. W: Have you finished reading the book, Mike?
   M: Not yet. I've been very busy these days.
8. M: Has Jack returned from Sydney?
   W: Yes, but he was at home for only a week. Then he was sent to work in Tokyo.
9. M: I want to send this letter to America, please.
   W: That will be forty cents.
10. W: Morning, Peter! Did you have a good Sunday?
    M: Yes, Miss Williams. I went to the zoo yesterday and I saw lions and tigers.

四、你将听到几段对话，请根据对话内容选择合适的图片。

1. M: Oh, Jane. You're getting fat. Are you still on a diet?
   W: Yeah, right. But it doesn't work. I need to weigh myself now.
2. W: What a wonderful house! Did you build it by yourself?
   M: Yes, and next I should paint it.
3. M: Hey, honey. Why don't you sit down and have a rest?
   W: I'll be right there after cleaning the toilet.
4. W: Clean up your room, Billy! And throw away the waste paper.
   M: OK, Mum. But the dustbin is full.

W：All right. Put it in that box.

5. W：Look at your beard. Go and have a shave.

M：I want to, but I can't find my electric shaver.

五、你将听到一段对话，请根据对话内容完成下面的练习。

(I'm going to tell you about an interesting thing that happened the other day. The day before yesterday, about eight o'clock at night, a young woman went to the box office of the best movie theater in the city. Her big dog went with her as well. She bought two tickets and went toward the door, followed by her dog. The manager of the theater spoke to her, saying...)

Manager：I'm sorry, miss, but dogs aren't allowed in this theater.

Woman：But I have a ticket for him.

Manager：I'm very sorry, but animals aren't permitted.

Woman：You don't understand. This is a special case. My dog is so well trained and so intelligent that he's almost human.

Manager：I see that you have an exceptional animal, but ...

Woman：I promise you that if there is any problem we'll leave the theater immediately. I assure you that this dog isn't like any other dog you've ever seen.

Manager：Well... all right. I'll let you go in, since the theater is almost empty tonight. Nevertheless, your dog will have to behave himself, or you will have to leave.

(Several hours go by, and the people are leaving. The manager sees the girl with her dog.)

Manager：I congratulate you. You were right; your dog behaved very well. I've been watching him, and it's amazing how quiet he was.

Woman：I told you that he's well trained and very intelligent.

Manager：He certainly is. It even seemed as if he was enjoying the movie.

Woman：Oh, he did enjoy it. He liked the film very much. However, he liked the book much better.

Section 4

一、请在左边的横线上写出你所听到的词语，并根据你所听到的词语选出它们的反义词。

1. clean　2. empty　3. heavy　4. wet　5. expensive

二、你将听到一些关于名人的介绍，请根据内容完成下面的练习。

AMELIA EARHEART

In 1928 this pilot became the first woman to fly across the Atlantic Ocean as a passenger. In 1932 she completed a solo transatlantic flight. She also tried to fly around the world, but she disappeared over the Pacific in 1937.

WALT DISNEY

This artist and film producer was the creator of Mickey Mouse. Mickey Mouse's first animated cartoon appeared in 1928. Mickey Mouse soon became the world's most popular animated cartoon character, and he received over 2,000 letters a day.

LEONARDO DA VINCI

This Italian painter lived from 1452 to 1519. In about 1504 he painted the *Mona Lisa*, the most famous painting in the world. The *Mona Lisa* is now in the Louvre Museum in Paris. It was stolen in 1911, but it was found again two years later.

NEIL ARMSTRONG

This astronaut was the first human to walk on the moon. He stepped onto the moon on July 20, 1969. He said, "That's one small step for man, one giant leap for mankind."

三、你将听到一些录音片段，请根据所听内容完成下面的练习。

听第一段录音，完成 1 ~3 题。

This is the VOA Special English Education Report.

March Madness is the name for the busy championship season in American college basketball. But March also means another kind of madness—the nervous wait for admissions letters from colleges and universities.

This week in our Foreign Student Series, we jump ahead to the subject of where to live. Housing policies differ from school to school. Some schools have limited housing or none at all.

Dormitory buildings might house a small number of students or many hundreds. Some dorms have suites. A suite has several bedrooms, a common area and a bathroom. Other dorms have rooms along a common hallway. Two, three or four students might share a room.

听第二段录音，完成 4 ~5 题。

Cinderella: Remember, you'll catch more flies with honey than with vinegar.

Anastasia: What does that mean? Who'd want to catch flies?

Cinderella: I mean the best way to impress the baker is just to be nice to him.

Anastasia: How do I do that?

Cinderella: You could start with a smile.

Anastasia: Better get me a bigger necklace.

Cinderella: Come on.

Anastasia: I make babies cry, too.

Cinderella: Here. He'll never be able to resist.

Anastasia: You think so? But what if mother catches me? She told me never to speak to the baker again.

Cinderella: Maybe it's time to stop following someone else's orders and start following your heart.

Anastasia: It's late. I have to go.

Cinderella: But what about the baker? I could walk you to his shop. Meet you in the market at noon tomorrow?

Anastasia: I can hardly wait.

四、下面你将听到一段文章，请根据文章内容分别写出下面各个人物和“我”的关系以及他们的名字。

It is Sunday today, and all my family members are staying at home. That's my grandfather John. He is in the kitchen, and he is washing the dishes. My father is in the living room. He is watching TV. He is interested in the news and politics. His name is Bill. Where is my Mum Sally? She is in the yard, and she is washing the car. My grandmother likes playing games. She is doing a puzzle in the dining room. Her name is Susan. Who is beside her? That's my brother Jim. He has to practice playing the piano two hours a day. How poor he is! And do I have a sister, too? Yes. She is Lily. She is playing a computer game upstairs. Oh, I forgot to tell you something about me. My name is Lucy. I am doing my homework in my bedroom.

五、你将听到一段短文，根据短文内容判断下列句子的正误。正确的在括号内写“T”，错误的在括号内写“F”。

The most common disease in the world is the cold. It often starts with a sore throat. You sneeze and your nose runs. You usually have a headache, too. Often you have a cough afterwards. It's not a serious disease, but you can feel quite ill. There isn't a cure for a cold, but you can take aspirin to get rid of your headache. It is good to rest, and to drink a lot of water, too. A doctor once told me, "With the right medicine, a cold will last for seven days. With no medicine, it will go on for a whole week!"

Section 5

一、根据你所听到的内容，将下面电影票的内容填满。下面已经给出一个例子。

1. The first movie is *Ice Age*. It will be shown at the Green Theater. And you can watch this movie on January 12th. This movie is a famous cartoon. And for children, the price is only 5. 5 pounds.
2. Let's look at the Blue Theater. The movie *Shrek* is going to be shown here on May 23rd. The ticket for adults is 20 pounds. But for students it is only half price.
3. Do you like fiction movies? Then I think you should go to the Magic Theater. There you can watch the most popular film *Harry Potter*. If you are a student, that's great. The price is 8. 25 pounds. And don't forget the date is August 5th.
4. This is a movie about a fat cat, whose name is *Garfield*. If you like it, you can go to the Sky Theater on July 30th. The ticket price for kids is only 3 pounds.
5. Let's go to the Garden Theater in America. You can enjoy the movie *High School Musical*. The ticket for adults is 15. 99 dollars. And it will be shown on October 21st.

二、你将听到几段对话，请根据对话内容选择合适的答案。

1. W：Who is the best at drawing in your class, Mike?
   M：Lucy. Bill is not good at drawing, and I'm the best at singing.
   Q：Who is the best at singing?
2. M：Hello, Mrs. Smart. I want to know how my daughter Amy is getting on at school.
   W：Well, Amy is doing better this year. But she still finds it difficult to make friends.
   Q：Who is the man speaking to?
3. M：Oh. The No. 3 bus is coming.
   W：The No. 3 bus? No, it's No. 8. The No. 3 bus passed by only three minutes ago.
   M：Oh. We'll have to wait seven minutes. Can I take the No. 8 bus to get there?
   W：I think so.
   Q：How often does the No. 8 bus come?

4. W: Please turn down the radio a little.
M: Why, I thought you like the music.
W: Yes. But not when I am writing a novel.
M: Oh, sorry.
Q: What's the woman doing now?

5. M: Another piece of apple pie?
W: No, thanks. I'm on a diet.
M: But you've hardly eaten anything.
W: It's delicious, but I don't think I should eat it.
Q: Why won't the woman eat any more?

三、你将听到两段对话，根据对话内容完成下面的练习。

听第一段对话，完成1~5题。

M: Hey, Kathy. I'm thinking about renting a movie for tonight's party, and I want to know what kind of movies you like.
W: Okay. What kind of movies do you have in mind?
M: Well, what about action movies?
W: Ah, I don't really like action movies. Too much violence.
M: Okay, do you like comedies?
W: Now, I do enjoy comedies.
M: Fine. Well, what do you think of horror movies or love stories?
W: Uh ... I'm not really crazy about horror movies, but love stories are often fun to watch. Oh, and I really like foreign films, too.
M: Okay. I'll go to the video store and see what I can find. Thanks.

听第二段对话，完成6~10题。

Girl: Dad, will you read to me?
Dad: Uh, let me finish the newspaper first?
Girl: You've been saying that forever!
Dad: Well, how about reading the business section of the newspaper together?
Girl: That's boring. Let's read this book. It's about a bear and a cat that become friends. And these books, too.
Dad: Whoa. I thought you said one book. There must be ten here.
Girl: My teacher, Mrs. Green, says you have to read to me every night, and the newspaper doesn't count. And let's eat some popcorn and cookies while we're reading.
Dad: Well, it's bedtime right now. So, okay, here we go. Once upon a time in a deep, dark forest, lived a brown bear ...

四、你将听到一段短文，请将短文内容写在下面这张明信片里面。

Dear Tom,

We're having a wonderful time here. When we arrive in New York, it was rainy, but it's fine now. New York is a beautiful city and people here are very kind. The famous Statue of Liberty is here and we will visit it tomorrow. It was built a hundred years ago and it was really very magnificent. I can't wait to go and see it.

I have bought some souvenirs for you and Bob. I do hope you can come here one day.

Hope to see you soon!

Love,

Sara

Unit 8

Section 1

一、在横线上写出你所听到的词语。

1. ticket	2. gift	3. match	4. forest	5. hotel
6. model	7. postbox	8. lake	9. factory	10. question
11. sugar	12. pork	13. tomato	14. delicious	15. soup
16. beef	17. sandwich	18. vegetable	19. sausage	20. pizza

二、你将听到十个句子，请选出你所听到的词语。

1. I don't believe that he can pass the exam.
2. The bread would taste better with some butter.
3. The post office is at the corner of King Street and Palm Street.
4. The bus is very crowded.
5. Please dial 110 when you are in danger.
6. You know a lot about J. K. Rowling.
7. There is something bad on today's news.
8. The rich man founded this hospital in 1998.
9. The man doesn't like this pair of shoes.
10. This blouse doesn't suit me.

三、请听下面的人物介绍，并为他们的职业选择合适的工具。

1. My name is Mike. I am a cook in a three-star hotel.
2. I'm Alice. I'm a journalist working for the newspaper *China Daily*.
3. My name is John Carpenter, and I am a carpenter, too.
4. I'm a tailor. My name is Lisa, and I like making clothes.
5. I'm Roy, and I am a mechanic. I often fix some machines.

四、听下面两段独白，根据独白的内容完成下面的练习。

听第一段独白，完成1 ~5 题。

"Hello and thank you for calling American Vision, this area's finest store in eyeglasses for you and your family. Our store hours are Monday to Friday, 8:00 am to 5:30 pm. We're open on Saturdays until six. Closed on Sundays.

Please visit our store on Saturday for an additional 20% off on our already low prices on all brands of eyewear. And remember: Eye exams are free."

听第二段独白，完成6~10题。

"Hello, Shoppers. We have a lost boy named Martin who was found in the sporting goods section of our store, and he's looking for his Mom. He's five years old, and he's wearing a blue and white sweat shirt, tan pants, and a black and white baseball cap. You can find him at the check-out counter at the main exit. Thank you."

Section 2

一、请根据你所听到的句子写出句子中所缺的部分。

1. This is the teachers' reading room.
2. The Summer Palace is one of Beijing's finest parks.
3. It's made from cow's milk.
4. I have just received a present.
5. None of the students knew the answer.
6. You'll leave for Beijing next week, won't you?
7. What is your favourite festival?
8. There is a swimming pool near our house.
9. I was listening to a tape at 9 last night.
10. She invited us to go with her.

二、听下面十个句子，选出与你所听到的句子意思相同或最相近的句子。

1. What nice pictures they are!
2. I hope that I can go abroad one day.
3. What size are these shoes?
4. How far away is the hospital from here?
5. Did you have a good time at the seaside?
6. I prefer tea to coffee.
7. I seldom go on a business trip.
8. May I borrow your dictionary?
9. Liz is cleverer than any other girl in her class.
10. Miss Green left an hour ago.

三、请看下面这幅地图，并根据你所听到的句子判断出以下五个地点，并在横线上填入表示该地点的词语。

1. “A” is a shop where you can buy things like beds, chairs and tables.
2. You can drink coffee with your friends near “A” in Green Street.
3. You can buy some medicine behind “A”.
4. You can buy some books opposite “A”.
5. If you want to save your money in a safe place, you can go to the corner of Green Street and Brown Street.

四、听下面的对话，并根据对话的内容将下面的句子补充完整。

W: Do you come from a big family, Peter?

M: Yes, I do. When I was young, there was a new baby every year! Both my Mum and Dad love children. When number five was born, we had to move to a bigger house. We all had a good time together.

W: How about your parents? Are they from big families, too?

M: My mother has three brothers and two sisters, so she grew up in a big family, too. She often helped her parents look after the little ones.

W: And your father?

M: No, my father doesn't have any brothers or sisters. As a kid, he got a lot of presents, but he always wanted children to play with.

W: Now he has seven children.

五、你将听到一篇文章，请根据所听内容判断正误。正确的用“T”表示，错误的用“F”表示。

Once there was an old farmer, with a horse which was almost as old as himself. He set out one morning with his young son, to sell the horse before it died. Father and son walked, because the farmer did not want the horse to be too tired.

They met two men on the road. They said, “Why are you walking, farmer? You have a horse. It's a long way to the market.” The farmer knew that this was true, so he rode on the horse, while his son walked.

Then they met two old ladies. “What are you doing up there, farmer? Can't you see how tired your boy is?” So the farmer got down, and his son rode instead.

Next, three old men stopped them. One said, “Why are you walking, farmer? Get up. It's too hot for an old man like you to walk today.” So the farmer got up behind his son, and they rode on.

Some time later, a young woman passed them. “Why aren't you walking?” she asked. "It isn't far to the market. Give your poor old horse a rest."

So the farmer and his son got down once again. It is a fact that you cannot please all the people all the time.

Section 3

一、听写句子。

1. For thousands of years men couldn't fly.
2. I wonder what's wrong with the animal.
3. Let's hurry so that we can get there before supper.
4. He walked such a long way that he felt pretty tired.
5. They made it clear that they didn't agree with you.
6. It's impossible for him to work out this maths problem.
7. It's best for people to wear silk clothes in summer.
8. A third of the land is covered with snow.
9. There is no need to have a further discussion.
10. Thanks to your help, I finished the work on time.

二、根据你所听到的歌曲内容完成下面的练习。

When you mail a letter, you can send it anywhere.
On foot; by truck; by aeroplane. The postman gets it there.
So write a letter to a friend, maybe she'll write you.
No matter what you always know. The mail must go through.
Well, the mail must go through. The mail must go through.
No matter if it rains or snows. The mail must go through.
The mail must go through. The mail must go through.
No matter if it rains or snows. The mail must go through.
Some folks live in a city, some live in a little town.
Even if you live out on a farm. There's a postman making his rounds.
So mail someone a letter, even just a card will do.
You know it's nice when the postman has a letter in his sack for you.

三、根据你所听到的问句，挑出你所需要的物品。

1. How do we celebrate the new year?
2. What do you need if you want to exercise?

3. What do you need to enter a theater?
4. What do you need to look far away?
5. What do you need if you want to relax?

四、听下面十个句子，并选择相应的答语。

1. Have you seen this movie before?
2. When do you want to see the show?
3. Don't forget to turn off your cell phone before the movie starts.
4. How long is the movie?
5. May I take your order, please?
6. How would you like your steak?
7. Is everything OK with your meal?
8. Do you offer classes in the evening?
9. How often does the class meet?
10. Where can I buy the textbook for the class?

五、你将听到一篇短文，请根据短文内容为下面的事件排序。

One night Mr. Smith parked his car outside his house as usual, but when he came downstairs the next morning to go to his office, he found that the car was not there. He called the police and told them what had happened. The policeman said he would try to find it.

When Mr. Smith came home from his office that evening, the car was again in its usual place in front of his house. He checked it carefully and found two movie tickets on one of the seats and a letter which said, "We're sorry. We took your car because of a sick boy." So Mr. and Mrs. Smith went to the cinema with the two tickets the next night and of course they enjoyed themselves very much. But when they came back home, they found that the thieves had stolen everything they had in their house.

Section 4

一、你将听到一段录音片段，请根据所听内容完成下面的练习。

Part One Life at Gateshead

Chapter One The Fight

We couldn't go outside at all on that cold, rainy afternoon. The rain was pouring down, and the wind was blowing hard. I didn't care, I was happy to stay indoors.

Trying to take long walks in the winter was terrible! It was supposed to be healthy for our bodies, but I hated coming home in the dark with my feet and hands as cold as ice. And I was always unhappy because Bessie, one of the servants, was always scolding me. I had always known that I was different from my cousins, John, Eliza, and Georgiana Reed. They were prettier and taller than I, and everyone loved them.

These three children were not very nice to other people or to each other. Usually they spent their time fighting and crying with each other. However, today they were with their mother in the sitting room, sitting quietly and talking in front of the warm fire. I wanted to join them but Mrs. Reed, my aunt, said I could not. She was angry with me because Bessie had told her I was being troublesome.

二、请根据你所听到的对话，选择最佳的答案。

1. W: Would you like beer or wine?
   M: Neither, thanks. I think I'd rather take a cup of tea.
2. W: What can I do for you?
   M: I need some oranges. Are they fresh?
   W: Of course, these oranges are just from Taiwan. But they cost 12 yuan per kilo.
3. W: What do you want to be when you grow up?
   M: I want to be an engineer. What about you?
   W: I want to be a woman football player. I am keen on sports.
4. W: What's your hobby, Bob?
   M: I like fishing. I'm going fishing this weekend. What about you, Mary?
   W: I like swimming very much.
5. M: Shall we go to the theater this Saturday afternoon?
   W: Well, what I really like is to see a film, but I have to go to a lecture.
   M: Never mind.
6. M: Kathy, are there enough chairs for the meeting this afternoon?
   W: Oh, yes. There're thirty.
   M: I'm afraid we need five more.
7. W: When is the library open on weekdays?
   M: From 9:00 am to 8:00 pm.
   W: What about weekends?
   M: On Saturdays it is open from 10:00 am to 5:00 pm. It is usually closed on Sundays.
8. M: How did you like the movie yesterday?
   W: It was so moving that I couldn't help crying. How about you?

M: I'm not interested in this kind of movie.

9. W: Excuse me, would you please tell me where the Hubei Museum is?
   M: Oh, it's in downtown, far from here.
   W: How can I get there? I mean the quickest way.
   M: Well, you may take Underground Line 1. It's much quicker than bus or taxi.
   W: Thanks a lot.
   M: My pleasure.

10. M: Mary, you didn't come to school yesterday. Was there anything wrong?
    W: Yes. I had a bad cold. The doctor asked me to stay in bed for a day.
    M: I'm sorry to hear that. Are you better now?
    W: Yes, much better, thank you. The headmaster told me that you gave lessons instead of me yesterday. Thank you very much.
    M: It's a pleasure.

三、听句子，根据下面这幅图判断句子的正误并做出相应的选择。

1. The dry cleaners is between the museum and the supermarket.
2. The mall is next to the supermarket.
3. The park is to the east of the river.
4. The art gallery is in front of the cafe.
5. The pharmacy is on the corner of Sun Street and 3rd Street.

四、你将听到一家宾馆对 Tom 电话的回复。请根据所听内容完成下面的表格。

Hi, Tom. Thank you for your telephone call. I'm glad to tell you that we have two double rooms ready for you now. The two rooms are on the fifth floor. They face the Red Sea, so you can see it well. The price for each room is \$115 per night. Every morning from 6:30 to 9:00, we offer free breakfast, but you have to pay if you have lunch and supper in our hotel. Don't forget to bring your ID card with you. If you have any more questions, please let us know and we shall be pleased to help you. We are looking forward to welcoming you to our hotel on August 18th. We hope you will enjoy your stay with us. Thanks again for choosing our hotel.

五、你将听到一段长对话，请根据对话内容完成下面的练习。

Interviewer: Today, I'm interviewing nine-year-old Alice about her feelings on how people can help save the environment. So, Alice, how can we save the environment?

Alice: By saving water.

Interviewer: Well, how can we do that?

Alice: By not using too much water when we wash dishes, take a bath, and when we do other things, like watering the plants outside.

Interviewer: Oh, I think I can do that. What else?

Alice: When drinking or eating something outside, you should keep the garbage until you find a trashcan to put it in because littering makes our planet dirty. Do you like seeing trash all over the ground?

Interviewer: No, I don't. Do you have any final suggestions?

Alice: Yes. We shouldn't waste paper because trees are being cut down to make the paper. By recycling paper, we save the forests where animals live.

Interviewer: So, how can children recycle paper, I mean, everyday?

Alice: Well, for example, when I was in kindergarten, I used to save the newspapers so that I could make things out of them, like paper trees, instead of just throwing them away. Now, the children in our neighborhood collect newspapers once a month to take them to a recycling center.

Interviewer: That's great. Well, thank you for your ideas.

Section 5

一、你将听到一段对话，请根据对话内容找出下面这段对话中的错误。在错误的地方画上横线，并将正确的内容填在后面的横线上。

M: Mary, have I shown you my pictures?

W: No, you haven't. Are these your pictures of New York?

M: Yes, they are. I took them last month.

W: Did you take any pictures of the tall buildings there?

M: Yes, I took some. Here they are.

W: You took wonderful pictures! Did you have a good time in New York?

M: Yes, I did. Have you ever been there?

W: No, I haven't. I've never been anywhere!

M: Don't you want to visit New York sometime?

W: Yes, I do. I'll go there someday.

二、听句子，根据下面这幅图判断句子的正误并做出相应的选择。

1. First, walk down Green Street for two blocks. Then, turn right and the bank is

the third building on the left side.

2. Go straight down Yellow Street until Blue Street. The school is on the corner of Yellow Street and Blue Street.
3. Drive along Green Street to White Street and turn right. Next, go straight one block, cross Brown Street, and the library is the first building on the right corner.
4. First, go down Yellow Street for one block, turn right, and then go to the first intersection. Then, keep going straight, and the hotel is the second building on the left.
5. Walk along Green Street until Black Street. Then, turn right and go straight, and the church is the last building at the end of the street on the left.

三、听下面几段对话，根据题中的问题选择合适的答案。

听第一段对话，回答 1 ~3 题。

W：Hi, Sam. I have a problem.

M：What's wrong with you, Linda?

W：I have a terrible headache. I need to go to the doctor's. But my car doesn't work. Could I borrow yours, please?

M：Of course you can.

W：Thank you.

M：Do you want me to drive you there?

W：Oh, yes, please. That would be very nice. Thank you very much.

M：Not at all. Shall we leave now?

W：All right. I was told to get to the doctor's at a quarter to nine.

听第二段对话，回答 4 ~5 题。

W：What's your trouble, young man?

M：I've got a headache and a bad cough. I feel terrible.

W：How long have you been like this?

M：Ever since last Friday.

W：Have you taken your temperature?

M：Yes, it's a bit higher.

W：Oh, I see. Just a little cold. Don't worry. Nothing serious. You'd better stay in bed. Take this medicine and you will soon be better.

听第三段对话，回答 6 ~7 题。

W：Hello! English Help Center. Can I help you?

M：Yes. I have some problems with English.

W：Well, what are they?

M: First, I can't understand what the teacher says in class.

W: Why not listen to more English tapes?

M: OK. I'll try. But I can't speak English well, either. What should I do?

W: Don't worry. You should join an English club to practice speaking English.

M: Thank you very much. I'll do as much as I can.

W: You're welcome. I hope your English will be better soon.

四、请看下面的图表，根据你所听到的问题选出合适的答案。

We surveyed 300 young people on what they like to do at weekends. One hundred people are from the ages of 11-18, one hundred 19-26 and one hundred 27-35. The following chart shows their answers:

Question One: How many people enjoy playing computer games in the 11-18 group?

Question Two: How many people enjoy taking a walk in the 19-26 group?

Question Three: What do the people of 27-35 enjoy most?

Question Four: Which group of people don't like taking a walk most?

Question Five: Which two activities do most people enjoy doing?

五、你将听到一篇短文，请将短文的内容写在下面的横线上。

We can see walls everywhere in the world. But the Great Wall of China is the longest of all. It is more than 6, 000 kilometers long. It was really very difficult to build such a great wall without any modern machines long ago. People had to do all the work by hand. It took many men hundreds of years to build it. The Great Wall has a history of over two thousand years. The men began to build the first part of it about 2, 700 years ago. Today it has become a place of interests. Both the Chinese people and foreigners come to visit it.

Unit 9

Section 1

一、听写单词。

1. visit	2. cinema	3. ticket	4. read	5. novel
6. watching	7. holiday	8. beach	9. swimming	10. sunglasses
11. garden	12. plant	13. chatting	14. cooking	15. dish
16. football	17. basketball	18. baseball	19. volleyball	20. golf

二、听下面的十个句子，选出与句子内容相关的图片。

1. How is your father doing?
2. He likes playing football better than playing volleyball.
3. These days, many teenagers enjoy their evenings by chatting with net-friends.
4. Do you know when the film will be on?
5. These sneakers are too small for me, I'd like to try another pair.
6. I often drink coffee without milk. What about you?
7. I'm leaving for Japan on a business trip tomorrow.
8. There's a cafe near the movie theater. How about meeting there at 7:30?
9. Can I make a right turn on red here?
10. What a vast sea! The water extends as far as the eyes can reach.

三、听下面的六段对话，根据对话的内容选出最佳答案。

1. M: Clear... Blue... Good day to fly.
   W: Yes. Would you like to have a try?
   M: Sure. You want to go, too?
   W: I'll get my sunglasses.
2. M: So what happened next?
   W: Then I stopped near the bus stop and got my clothes changed.
   M: Did somebody see you?
   W: I don't think so.

3. M: Look at the clouds. It's going to snow.
   W: Well, I suppose there will just be an icy sleet.
   M: Anyway, let's go home quickly. It's so cold here in the classroom.
   W: OK.
4. M: Excuse me, may I use your English-Chinese dictionary?
   W: Sorry. But I'm using it now. What about this E-dictionary?
   M: Oh, thanks!
   W: My pleasure.
5. M: Is everyone in the classroom?
   W: Billy is absent, sir.
   M: What's the matter with him?
   W: He has a serious headache and is in the hospital.
6. M: When did you come home?
   W: I guess we got home at about 3:00. We spent a good 6 hours there.
   M: That's a long time! Did Ann get burnt?
   W: No, unlike me. She didn't even turn brown.

四、听短文，完成下面两组练习。

Frank and Alice are husband and wife. They are busy every week. In the morning Frank cooks breakfast. Alice cleans the house. In the evening, they cook together. After supper, Alice goes out to walk the dog, Coddy. Coddy loves this. Frank watches TV at home. On Saturday morning, Alice goes to visit her friends. Frank stays at home and reads the newspaper. On Saturday afternoon, they go shopping together. On Sunday, they go to church together. On Sunday afternoon, Alice stays at home and takes care of the garden. Frank goes to play baseball with his friends. On Sunday evening they stay at home together, talking or playing cards.

Section 2

一、听一段英文歌，填补所缺的内容。

Hold me like a friend
Kiss me like a friend
Say we'll never end
Searching for the colors of the rainbow
Melody, never say goodbye

I'll be near you
Some people handle love in and never try
I can almost fly with your wings to set me higher
Some day we'll see the world
And through the grey have faith in our hands
Hold me like a friend
Kiss me like a friend
Say we'll never end
Searching for the colors of the rainbow
Melody, never say goodbye
We'll always be forever friends

二、听下面的十个句子，选出对应的答语。

1. Could you tell me the way to the hospital?
2. Is your uncle at home?
3. Where do you want to visit this summer?
4. How do you usually go to school?
5. When is Children's Day?
6. How soon can I get my suit back?
7. Thanks again for inviting us. We've had such a good time.
8. You did a good job on this.
9. What's the price for these long necklaces?
10. Hello. Could I speak to Jennifer, please?

三、听下面的六段对话，选出与对话内容相关的图片。

1. M: Which sport are you good at?
   W: I swim well, but I'm not good at playing tennis. What about you?
   M: I'm good at playing basketball. I'm on the school team.
   Q: Which sport is the woman good at?
2. M: Are you doing anything this weekend?
   W: Yes. We're going to the park to take photos of the beautiful flowers. Would you like to join us?
   Q: What are they going to do this weekend?
3. M: Sally, dear. Do you know where my shirt and tie are?
   W: They are in the second drawer on the left. Would you like me to get them for you?
   M: Thanks, dear.

Q: What is the the man looking for?

4. M: Where are we going for dinner?

W: What about KFC? I want to try the new cheeseburger there.

M: But KFC may make me get fat. I'd rather have Chinese noodles.

Q: What is the man probably going to have for dinner?

5. M: Are you going to the EXPO in Shanghai this summer?

W: Sure. And I will be a volunteer there. I worked as a volunteer for the Olympics in Beijing last summer.

M: Wow. That sounds like quite an experience.

Q: Which event will the woman work for?

6. W: I'm going shopping now. Would you like me to bring you something?

M: That's really nice of you. I want some chocolates. And there aren't any vegetables left in the fridge. Would you please buy some, too?

W: OK.

Q: Where is the woman going?

四、听短文，按照你所听到的顺序给句子编号。

I saw Mark yesterday morning. He was walking very quickly in the street. I called him, but he didn't hear me. Maybe he was listening to his MP3 player.

I met Mrs. Jenkins in the park yesterday afternoon. She was walking her dog. I went to talk with her. While we were talking, her dog ran away. Later we looked for the dog and found it. It was playing with another dog.

Yesterday after school, I was walking home by myself, when suddenly a bike knocked me down. Luckily, nobody was hurt. The bike-boy said sorry to me, and I told him to ride more slowly and carefully next time.

五、听对话，回答问题。

W: Tim, you look so excited. Any good news?

M: I just received a letter from one of my old middle school classmates.

W: That's nice!

M: Well, in fact, I haven't heard from him for ages.

W: To be frank with you, I've been out of touch with most of my old friends. Only one or two still keep me posted about what they are doing.

M: I know. It's really hard to maintain contact when people move around so much.

W: That's right. People just drift apart! But you're lucky to be back in touch with your friend again.

Section 3

一、听写词组。

1. go away	2. go over	3. give up	4. give in
5. give away	6. take on	7. take off	8. look after
9. look out	10. look for	11. turn on	12. turn off

二、听短文，判断下列句子是否正确，正确用 T（True）表示，错误用 F（False）表示。

How wonderful! Today is Friday. We're free after this evening. All the students in my class are going somewhere this weekend. Sky is going to his grandpa's this evening. Bob is going to his dentist tomorrow. Poor Bob. Angela is going to her piano class on Saturday and Sunday evening. Judy and Emily are going to the beach on Saturday morning. Grace and Karen are going to see a movie on Saturday afternoon. Timmy is going to the park with Tom and Mike on Sunday afternoon. And the students in Jennifer's class are going to have a party this weekend. What about me? I have no idea now. I may go to the party or stay at home.

三、听六段独白，完成连线。

My name's Robin. I come from Canada. I'm a fireman and I speak English.

I'm Ester. I am a cook. I come from France and I speak French and English.

I'm Bill. I'm an English teacher. China is where I come from and I can speak Chinese and English.

My name is Albert. I'm an Australian. I'm a worker. I speak English.

My name's Kyo. I'm from Japan. I work in a company as a manager. I speak Japanese and a little Chinese.

I'm Bruce and I'm an American. English is my native language and I can speak German. I'm a doctor.

四、听英文歌，根据歌词内容选择最佳答案。

（略）

五、听对话，填补所缺的内容。

(telephone ringing)

W: Directory Assistance.

M: Good morning. I'd like to have the telephone number of Mr. William Abel, please.

W: Yes, sir. How do you spell his last name?

M: It's A-B-E-L.

W: Thank you. And could you tell me his address?

M: It's 6418 Green Street.

W: The number is 586-3208.

M: 586-3208. Thank you very much.

W: You are welcome. Have a good day.

(telephone ringing)

W: Directory Assistance.

M: Good morning. I'd like to have the telephone number of Thomas Eakins, please.

W: Yes, sir. How do you spell his last name?

M: It's E-A-K-I-N-S.

W: Thank you. And his address?

M: It's 75 Pine Avenue.

W: Yes. The number is 926-6832.

M: 926-6832. Thanks.

W: You are welcome. Have a good day.

(telephone ringing)

W: Directory Assistance.

M: Good morning. I'd like to have the telephone number of Miss Alice Moore, please.

W: Yes, sir. How do you spell her last name?

M: It's M-O-O-R-E.

W: Thank you. And could you tell me her address?

M: It's 279 Woodland Drive.

W: The number is 789-5430.

M: 789-5430. Thank you.

W: You are welcome. Have a good day.

(telephone ringing)

W: Directory Assistance.

M: Good morning. I'd like to have the telephone number of Mrs. Diana Paxon, please.

W: Yes, sir. How do you spell her last name?

M: It's P-A-X-O-N.

W: Thank you. And her address?

M: It's 12-C Lincoln Lane.

W: The number is 287-3952.

M: 287-3952. Thank you very much.

W: You are welcome. Have a good day.

(telephone ringing)

W: Directory Assistance.

M: Good morning. I'd like to have the telephone number of Mr. James Bingham, please.

W: Yes, sir. How do you spell his last name?

M: It's B-I-N-G-H-A-M.

W: Thank you. And could you tell me his address?

M: It's 5213 Rose Road.

W: Yes. The number is 654-8358.

M: 654-8358. Thank you.

W: You are welcome. Have a good day.

Section 4

一、听写单句。

1. Where are you from?
2. What's wrong with Peter?
3. Do you want to have a job there?
4. We'll meet here tomorrow afternoon.
5. How often does his mother water the flowers?
6. How are you doing today?
7. How many days are there in a week?
8. Which country are you from?
9. Thank you very much for helping me.
10. Excuse me. What is this in English?

二、听下面六段对话，每段对话后有一个问题，仔细听这个问题，并根据对话内容选出最佳答案。

1. M：Which would you like to have，tea or milk?

   W：Milk，please.

   M：Just a minute.

   Q：What does the woman want?

2. M：Do you know Miley Cyrus?

   W：Yes. She's a famous singer. She also acted in a movie called *Hannah Montana*.

   M：I'd like to see this film.

   Q：What does Miley Cyrus do?

3. M：What's the address of Shangri-La Hotel?

   W：It's 129 Central Street.

   M：Mmm，it's a little far. Are there any buses?

   Q：Where is Shangri-La Hotel?

4. M：Why are you so late，Lily?

   W：Sorry，Billy. My bike was broken on the way.

   M：I see. Come in，please.

   Q：Who is late?

5. M：Who does the housework in your house?

   W：My mother washes our clothes and my fathers cooks our meals.

   M：What about you?

   Q：What are they talking about?

6. M：Operator，this is an emergency！Get me the Fire Department.

   W：Your address，please.

   M：Just in front of the Children's Hospital.

   Q：Where are they talking?

三、听一段电影评论，根据你所听到的内容选出最佳答案。

（略）

四、听独白，完成相应的练习。

My name is Lee. I'm interested in music，art and the theater. I would like to go to New York. I don't care much for sports；I can't ski and I can't swim. I hate hot weather.

My name is Sarah. I enjoy the peace and quietness of the mountains. I love to ski and I want to get away from big cities. I think Acapulco is too expensive and besides I can't speak Spanish.

I'm Jewel. I want to go to Acapulco. I love Mexican food, and I can speak Spanish. I want to relax, swim, fish, and go to discos in the evening. I don't like to ski much; I've only done it once. I think New York is dirty, dangerous and expensive.

Section 5

一、听独白，根据所听内容给每个人物写上名字。

Hello. My name is David. I'm an office clerk. You can always see me wearing a shirt and tie. I work in my office all day and seldom go out. This is my twin brother Tom. We don't look much alike but we both wear glasses. Tom works in a big hospital. He is a doctor. This is my college classmate Steve. He works in the same hospital with Tom. He is a nurse there. The man with a big brush and some paint is Billy. Billy liked painting when he was a child, so I guess that's why he's become a house painter. You might have met my cousin Henry before. Henry works as a policeman in our neighbourhood. He's very energetic and hardworking. Who's that strong guy with a helmet and an axe? That's Michael, the lumberjack. I'm now standing between Michael and Robert. Robert began to learn to cook when he was 11 years old and now he is a famous cook in a Chinese restaurant. Everyone enjoys the dishes he cooks. Did I miss anybody? Oh, this is Robin. He works as a plumber. He can fix your toilet within only a few minutes.

二、听四段电影片段，根据你所听到的内容选出最佳答案。

(略)

三、听对话，填补所缺的内容。

W: Can you tell me something about your life experience?

M: I began school in Wilmette.

W: Did you? And when was that?

M: Let's see now. That was in 1960. And then I moved to LA and started high school there.

W: Which high school did you go to?

M: Lincoln High. After I graduated from that school, I went to Europe in 1972.

W: So that was when you were 18 years old, right?

M: Yes. I got an apartment in Munich a year later and lived there for a while, and then I came back to America and went to UCLA.

W：Which year was that?

M：Er, in 1975.

W：What did you do after finishing college?

M：After I finished my four-year college life, I went to the law school of USC and continued my study.

W：I see. And you got your first job with Smith and Jones here after graduating.

四、听写篇章。

Dear Peter,

How are you? I'm fine. Spring Festival is coming. As you know, it is the most important festival in China. My family are going to get together during the holiday season. My family and I want to invite you to come.

We are going to have a lot of food on Chinese New Year's Eve. And we are going to watch the Festival program on CCTV. Then as usual we are going to set off fireworks. On the morning of New Year's Day, my classmates and I are going to visit some old people in the nursing home. We are going to sing songs for them. I hope you can play the violin. We're going to have a good time.

Write back soon.

Yours,

May

Unit 10

Section 1

一、听写单词。

1. street	2. road	3. avenue	4. boulevard	5. corner
6. center	7. block	8. village	9. city	10. town
11. English	12. American	13. Germany	14. Swiss	15. French
16. Japanese	17. Korean	18. Indian	19. Mexican	20. Chinese

二、听下面的十个时间，根据你听到的顺序给表盘排序。

9:00	1:25	7:30	11:15	12:30
4:40	9:25	3:00	8:55	6:10

三、听下面的六段对话，选出与所提问题相关的最佳图片。

1. W: Excuse me, young man?
   M: Yes, ma'am?
   W: Could you tell me where the bank is? I've lost my way.
   M: Certainly, ma'am. Just take the escalator to the first floor and turn left. You can't miss it.
2. W: Scofield, do you have the number for that McDonald's on the corner?
   M: Yeah, just a second. I've got it in my drawer. Here it is. 4008517517.
   W: 4008517517. Great, thanks.
   M: My pleasure. Pick me up something to eat, too, please.
3. W: Sam? Are you finished with that grammar book I lent you?
   M: Oh, yeah, I don't need it anymore.
   W: Great. Could you bring it here tomorrow morning? I will have a test this Friday.
   M: Sure. Sorry for keeping it for so long.
4. W: Are you going anywhere this summer holiday?
   M: I'm thinking of visiting the Eiffel Tower, but I might go to Egypt instead.

What about you?

W: My brother wants to go to Sydney, but I would like to stay here in Beijing.

M: We just have so many choices but so little time for holiday.

5. M: What a nice park! Look at these flowers!

W: That would be a good shot. Can you take my picture here, dear? Please try to get the flowers in the frame as well.

M: All right. Would you please stand closer to the flower bed? Good. Smile. Say "cheese". OK, got you. That's terrific.

W: Thanks.

6. M: What do you usually do on the Internet?

W: Well, there are a lot of things, like reading news, email, shopping, etc. But mostly I chat online.

M: I never chatted online before. What's it like?

W: Well, it's similar to the face-to-face chat, but you type instead of talking. You should try it at least once.

四、听对话，填补所缺内容。

(telephone ringing)

W: Hello.

M: Hello. Could I speak to Kelly?

W: Speaking.

M: Oh, hi, Kelly. This is Edward. I just call to ask if you feel like going to see the movie *Detective Conan* with me on Saturday night.

W: I'd love to, Edward. But I'm afraid I can't this Saturday. I'm going to Wesley's party at 7:00. It's his birthday.

M: Oh, I understand. Could we make it on Thursday night?

W: Sorry, but I have to go to an important lecture at 8 pm on Thursday. And I will be tested on that in the final examination.

M: Well, of course, work is more important. Then what about Wednesday?

W: On Wednesday I will have a meeting with my English teacher and group members at 8:30. We will talk about the duty report next week.

M: It seems that you're quite busy these days, Kelly. Say, are you doing anything on Monday or Tuesday?

W: I've got to go to a yoga class at 7:30 on Tuesday and I promised to have dinner with Jennifer on Monday. It's at 7 pm.

M: Mmm, I guess I should have invited you earlier. How about this Friday night?

W: Friday would be fine. What time does the movie start?

M: At 8 sharp, but I think we can have dinner first.

W: Oh, that sounds very nice.

五、听短文，完成下面两组练习。

"How are you" is a nice question. It's a friendly way to greet each other. But when a person says "how are you", he wants to hear an answer like "fine" or "quite well", even if his friend isn't really fine. In fact, "how are you" isn't really a question, and "fine" isn't really an answer. They are just common ways of saying "hello" or "hi".

Sometimes people don't say exactly what they mean. For example, when a friend asks you "do you think so", maybe you don't really agree with him. But it sounds very rude to say "no, I think you are wrong." So, you may say, "I'm not sure." This is a polite way to say that you have a different idea.

People don't say exactly what they are thinking about, either. For example, when someone wants to finish a chat, he may say "I have to go now" and sometimes gives an excuse like "I have too much homework today." Does he really have too much homework? It may be real, or it may be not. It is just a polite way to stop a conversation.

Whether they are greeting each other, talking about an idea, or ending a conversation, people often don't say directly what they are thinking about. By doing so, people try to be friendly to each other. It is a part of the game of language.

Section 2

一、听句子，填补所缺的单词。

1. Western people don't like to tell people their age.
2. They are very tired and hungry now.
3. Tony is born into a driver's family.
4. He turns around the boat and runs after the hat.
5. We can't buy anything because we don't have enough money.
6. George Washington was the first president of the United States.
7. I walked for two days and came to a village.
8. He is now looking after some sheep at the top of a small hill.
9. Every day he carried water from down the hill and cooked for himself.
10. By this time, the bears were on their way back home.

二、听下面的六段对话，选出与所提问题相关的最佳图片。

1. W：Terry. You look different today.
 M：Oh. I've had a haircut. Do you like my new hairstyle?
 Q：What has Terry done?
2. W：Look. There're so many people crowding there. What's happened?
 M：There must be an traffic accident. Someone might have got hurt. Let's call 120 for help.
 Q：Which service do they need?
3. W：The plate was so hot. It nearly burned my fingers.
 M：If I were you，I would wear a pair of gloves before taking the plate out of the microwave oven.
 Q：What does the man advise the woman to wear?
4. W：The movie is about to start. Would you like to have some popcorn?
 M：No，thanks. I want to have some coke.
 Q：What does the man want?
5. W：Excuse me. What's wrong with my boy?
 M：Nothing serious. Just a cold. He needs to take this medicine twice a day and have a good sleep.
 Q：Where are they talking?
6. W：Hey，Timmy. I've got something to tell you. I won the fist prize in the speech contest.
 M：Congratulations！I knew you were to win. You're always working hark on that.
 Q：What happened to the woman?

三、听下面的五段对话，填补所缺的内容。

(telephone ringing)
W：Post office.
M：Hello. Could you tell me when the post office opens?
W：It opens at 9：00.
M：And when does it close?
W：It closes at 5：00.
M：Thank you.

(telephone ringing)
W：Citibank.
M：Hello. Could you tell me when the Citibank opens?

W：It opens at 9：00.

M：And when does it close?

W：It closes at 3：00.

M：Thanks a lot.

(telephone ringing)

W：Museum of Modern Art.

M：Hello. Could you tell me when the museum opens?

W：It opens at 11：00.

M：And when does it close?

W：It closes at 6：00.

M：Thank you very much.

(telephone ringing)

W：Macy's Department Store.

M：Hello. Could you tell me when the Macy's opens?

W：It opens at 9：00.

M：And when does it close?

W：It closes at 6：45.

M：Thank you.

(telephone ringing)

W：Raxall Drugstore.

M：Hello. Could you tell me when the drugstore opens?

W：It opens at 8：00.

M：And when does it close?

W：It closes at 7：30.

M：Thanks.

四、听下面的五段对话，根据对话内容选出最佳答案。

听第一段对话，回答1～2题。

M：Say, what do you think you're going to do tomorrow evening?

W：I was thinking of going shopping. But I guess I'd better wash the car instead.

M：Why? You just did it the day before yesterday.

W：Well, there's going to be a party in town on Saturday night. And I need to get prepared.

M：Get the car prepared? Why? Are you going there with someone?

W：It's a secret.

听第二段对话，回答 3 ~4 题。

M：Nice picnic, isn't it?

W：Yeah, really. The hamburgers and the homemade salad are wonderful.

M：My name's Mike Bradley, by the way.

W：Nice to meet you. I'm Susan Taylor.

M：What do you do, Susan?

W：Well, I work as a history teacher. What about you?

M：I work at P&G. I'm a salesman.

听第三段对话，回答 5 ~6 题。

M：Excuse me. Could you tell me where Cinema One is?

W：The movie theater? Uh, I think it's on Pine Street, just before you come to Macy's.

M：Right or left on Pine?

W：Left.

M：Is it far?

W：About 600 meters from here.

M：OK, thanks.

W：You're welcome.

听第四段对话，回答 7 ~8 题。

M：May, you played the violin quite beautifully.

W：Thank you. I enjoy playing the violin very much. Do you have any hobbies, Ben?

M：I'm interested in taking photos. I find it great fun.

W：Photography is an interesting hobby though it's a little expensive. Have you taken lots of pictures in Beijing?

M：Not many. Ricky suggests I take pictures here when leaves turn color in October.

W：That's a good idea. Shall we have a photographic journey then?

M：Yes, I'd love to.

听第五段对话，回答 9 ~10 题。

M：Hey, Angela, great to see you here!

W：Hey, Larry, what a pleasant surprise! I see you're walking your dog?

M：Yes, her name is Lizzy, isn't she a cutie?

W：Yes, she looks so energetic and lovely. How old is she?

M：I don't know, really. She's a present from one of my friends. She's just been to my place for about 2 months. Do you have any pets?

W：Yes，in fact I have 2 dogs，a cat and a parrot.

M：Wow，I see you are a fan of pets!

W：More than that，I also work for an animal hospital now.

五、听短文，完成下面的两组练习。

（略）

Section 3

一、听下面的一段英文歌，填补所缺的内容。

Caterpillar in the tree
How you wonder who you'll be
Can't go far but you can always dream
Wish you may and wish you might
Don't you worry，hold on tight
I promise you there will come a day
Butterfly，fly away
Butterfly，fly away，butterfly，fly away
Flap your wing now you can't stay
Take those dreams and make them all come true
Butterfly，fly away，butterfly，fly away
We've been waiting for this day
All along and knowing just what to do
Butterfly，butterfly，butterfly，butterfly，fly away

二、数字游戏。回答你听到的每个问题并将答案写在相应的图形内，然后按照要求计算。

（一）What's my seat number?

1. What's three and eight? Write your answer in the triangle.
2. How many legs does a dog have? Write your answer in the square.
3. What time is it in the middle of the day? Write your answer in the star.
4. How many stars are there on our national flag? Write your answer in the circle.
5. How many days are there in August? Write your answer in the rectangle.
   Then add all the numbers. Write the results in the small circles and add them. The final result is my seat number.

（二）When is the meeting?

1. How many is a dozen of eggs? Write your number in the cloud.
2. What is ten minus two? Write your number in the circle.
3. How many meals do you have every day? Write your number in the square.
4. In which month is the Children's Day? Write your number in the star.
5. How many eyes do you have? Write your number in the triangle.

Now you can write your answer in the rectangle.

三、听下面的几段对话或短文，完成相应的练习。

（一）听一段短文，完成连线。

Jimmy's International Restaurant is a special place. Every day Jimmy cooks a different kind of food. On Monday he cooks Chinese food. On Tuesday he cooks Italian food. On Wednesday he cooks American food. On Thursday he cooks Japanese food. On Friday he cooks French food. On Saturday he cooks Mexican food. And on Sunday he cooks Indian food.

（二）听下面的几段对话，根据对话和上一篇短文的内容选出最佳答案。

1. M：Are you doing anything after work this Thursday?
   W：Nothing much. Why?
   M：What about having a dinner in Jimmy's Restaurant?
   W：Well, I'm not very interested in Japanese food. I like Italian food better.
2. M：What kind of food do you like?
   W：I like English food.
   M：When do you go to Jimmy's Restaurant?
   W：I don't go there.
3. M：Do you often go to Jimmy's Restaurant?
   W：Yes. I go there on Monday, Tuesday and Saturday.
   M：How do you like the food there?
   W：I think they taste very nice.
4. M：Hello. Jimmy's Restaurant.
   W：Hi. I want to know if you cook Korean food today.
   M：Sorry, but we don't cook Korean food. Our food today is Mexican food.
   W：OK, I guess I'd like to give it a try.

四、听下面的一段短文，回答问题。

The Clarks will move to a new house in another city. They decide to go on March 29th. However, all the family members have something important to do, so they are going to start on different dates. Mr. Clark will go there two days later and his wife will go there six days later, or four days after Mr. Clark starts his journey. Their son, Sandy, will go there thirty-three days after Mr. Clark leaves. Sandy's sister, Sue, is studying in China. She hears about the news twenty days after Mr. Clark starts to go and promises to come home three weeks later.

Question: When does each person of the family go to the new house?

Section 4

一、听写单句。

1. Thank you for your present.
2. I want to make friends with you.
3. Could you say something about yourself?
4. He likes sports, so he is healthy and strong.
5. How do you spell the word?
6. Always do as the teacher tells you to do in the lab.
7. Sorry, I can't go swimming with you this afternoon.
8. How often do you go to the cinema with your parents?
9. Who's on duty today?
10. She's busy reading the book.

二、听下面的几段对话，根据所听到的内容连线。

1. M: Emily, do you know where the TV guide is?
   W: Isn't it on the television?
   M: No, it's not there.
   W: Well. Maybe it's on the table next to the sofa.
   M: Oh, yeah, I got it. Thanks.
2. M: Excuse me, Miss Williams. Do you know where our reading report is?
   W: Isn't it on your desk?
   M: No, it isn't there.
   W: Well, then it must be back in the file. I'll get it for you.
3. M: Alice, I can't find any aspirin. Do you know where it is?
   W: Isn't it in the medicine cabinet?
   M: No. I just looked. It's not here.
   W: Well, I think I've got some in my purse.
   M: And where's that?

W: On the dresser in the bedroom.

4. M: Bella, honey, where is my new shirt?

W: In the drawer, on the right.

M: I've checked, but it isn't there.

W: Oh, I remember. I haven't ironed it yet. So it must be on the ironing board.

5. M: Excuse me, I wonder if you know where the best-selling CDs are.

W: Sure, they are on the shelf to the right of the door.

M: Thank you very much.

三、听下面的三段对话，根据对话内容选出最佳答案。

听第一段对话，回答 1 ~3 题。

W: Nice day, isn't it? What about an outdoor exercise?

M: Good idea. The air is so fresh and the sunshine is so joyful.

W: By the way. Which exercise do you usually do?

M: I'm fond of playing basketball, and I like jogging and dancing as well. How about you?

W: I like doing yoga, swimming and so on.

M: Which one do you like best?

W: I think there is nothing better than swimming for exercise.

M: How do you like doing yoga?

W: Well, doing yoga helps form the balance of one's life. I learn how to find peace in my heart by doing yoga.

听第二段对话，回答 4 ~6 题。

(telephone ringing)

M: Hello?

W: Hello. May I speak to Steve, please?

M: Speaking.

W: Hi, this is Tracy. I'm Mike's friend.

M: Hi, Tracy. Mike has told me about you. What's up?

W: Today is Mike's birthday and we're having a party for him this evening. Would you like to come?

M: Oh, I didn't know it was his birthday today. Sure. I'd love to come. When and where?

W: Well, we're all meeting at Mike's neighbor's house at about 6:30. It's at 249 Joy Street.

M: I'll be there. Do you want me to bring something?

W: Bring some chocolates if you can.

M: No problem. See you then.

听第三段对话，回答7~9题。

M: I'm going to fly to Beijing this Sunday. This is going to be the first time for me to take a plane.

W: You must be very excited.

M: Yes, and a little bit nervous.

W: I understand. I used to take the overnight train to Beijing. It was nice.

M: I took the train, too. But this time I want to try something new. Flying is quick, isn't it?

W: No doubt. But don't forget to get to the airport 90 minutes before take-off.

M: I will. Thank you. I'll call you up when I arrive.

W: OK. Good luck on your first flight.

四、听短文，完成下面两组练习。

（略）

Section 5

一、听五段对话，在地图中按顺序用数字在方框内标明所找的地点。

1. You are now standing at A.

   M: Excuse me. Do you know where Macy's is?

   W: Macy's. Yes. It's down 15th Street on the right... At the end of the next block.

   M: The end of the next block, on the right. Thanks a lot.

2. You are now standing at B.

   M: I wonder if you could help me? I'm looking for Jimmy's Restaurant.

   W: Jimmy's. That famous international restaurant? It's around the corner of Baker Street. On the corner of 16th.

   M: OK. Thank you very much.

3. You are now standing at C.

   M: Excuse me. Could you tell me where the No. 1 Middle School is?

   W: It's next to the post office. You can't miss it.

   M: Thanks.

4. You are now standing at D.

   M: Sorry to bother you. But would you know where the train station is?

W: Yeah. It's on Ash Street opposite the Sun Hotel.

M: On Ash opposite the Sun. Would you happen to know the cross street?

W: I think it's 15th.

M: Ash and 15th. OK, Thanks a lot.

5. You are now standing at E.

M: Pardon me. Could you tell me where Lily's lady's shop is?

W: I think it's on Palm Street, just after you go past the Green Hotel.

M: On Palm behind the Green Hotel. Thanks.

二、听下面的四段电影片段，根据你所听到的内容选出最佳答案。

(略)

三、听短文，填补所缺的内容。

My name is Vivian. I'm a news reporter. I have a lot of friends.

My friend Ronan is a writer. He likes fishing and playing golf. We see each other when he isn't writing his book. When we meet, he always tells me about his new ideas for stories.

My friend Sophie is a pop singer. She likes going shopping. We see each other when she isn't having a concert. When we meet, she always tells me about her life as a pop star.

My friend Harry is a scientist. He likes reading and playing golf. We see each other when he isn't busy in his lab. When we meet, he always tells me about his new experiments.

My friend Jennifer is a teacher. She likes watching movies and taking photos. We see each other when she is on holiday. When we meet, she always tells me about her students.

四、听写。

Welcome to our school.

Our school has a long history. Three years ago, there was only a teaching building and a playground. Now we have three teaching buildings, a library, an office building, two dorm buildings and five labs. Last year, we built an indoor gym. There are also many trees and flowers in and around our school.

Our school is one of the key schools in Hubei. The students come from different cities. Both teachers and students are working very hard here.

Now I'd like to show you around the school. Thank you.

Unit 11

Section 1

一、听写单词。

1. tiger	2. lion	3. puma	4. wolf	5. elephant
6. panda	7. bear	8. deer	9. monkey	10. snake
11. horse	12. cow	13. sheep	14. chicken	15. dog
16. pig	17. cat	18. mouse	19. rabbit	20. fish

二、听下面的十个谜语，选出代表谜底的图片。

1. Give me food and I live. Give me water and I die. What am I?
2. I'm green and yellow, like a little boat. Everyone likes to eat me, but never eats my coat.
3. Look at my back, but you can only see me. Look at my face, and you can see yourself.
4. What goes up when the rain comes down?
5. Which animal wears big black glasses?
6. I have a face and two hands. I have no feet but I can go. I can wake you up though I can't talk. What am I?
7. I look like a tiger, but I'm smaller. I like to eat fish.
8. Which fruit is round and green outside and yellow or red inside?
9. Little fellow stands in the middle. Without it, you can't smell.
10. Thousands in one big family are busy every day, making sweets for others and giving them away.

三、听下面的四段对话，根据对话内容选出最佳答案。

听第一段对话，回答 1 ~3 题。

M: Hi, Anna. This is Frank. I'm calling from Tahiti.

W: From Tahiti? What are you doing in Tahiti?

M: I'm on holiday.

W：How's the weather in Tahiti? Is it sunny?

M：Not, it isn't. It's raining.

W：Is it hot?

M：No, it isn't. It's cold.

W：Are you enjoying yourself there?

M：No, I'm not. I'm having an awful time. The weather is terrible here.

W：I'm sorry to hear that.

听第二段对话，回答 4 ~6 题。

M：Good afternoon, Helen.

W：Good afternoon. It's really nice to see you again.

M：How are you feeling today?

W：Much better. The stomachache is gone, and the doctor says I can go home three days later.

M：That's great. Well, these are for you. I hope you will like them.

W：What beautiful flowers! Thank you, Kevin.

M：And here are some story books for you. I hope they'll keep you from getting bored in hospital.

W：You're so sweet. Thanks.

听第三段对话，回答 7 ~9 题。

M：How do you like this blue dress?

W：Well, I don't think blue is my color.

M：What about the pink one?

W：The color is OK, but I think it is a bit too long.

M：How do you like this white dress?

W：I like it, but it's too expensive. Do you have some cheaper ones?

M：Yes, ma'am. Do you like this red one? It's less expensive, but still fashionable.

W：OK, I think I'll take it.

听第四段对话，回答 10 ~12 题。

M：Do you know what comes next?

W：I think there's a 007 movie on.

M：Let me look in the *CCTV News* first.

W：What's on CCTV 6 at eight o'clock?

M：A quiz show, I guess.

W：Would you mind if I watch it?

M：Of course not. I'm looking forward to it myself.

四、听短文，填补所缺内容。

Linton Zoo is the largest zoo in our city. The ticket for an adult is 12 dollars.

Children over 1.20 m in height can pay only half of the price, and those under 1.20 m can enter the zoo for free. The zoo opens from 9:00 am to 4:00 pm, from Monday to Friday. It opens from 8:30 am to 5:30 pm on weekends.

By the way, you'd better not give the food you take to the animals while visiting the zoo. And don't get too close to or touch the animals. That would be dangerous. Please keep the zoo clean as well.

Wish you a good time here.

Section 2

一、听下面的一段英文歌，填补所缺的内容。

I don't want a lot for Christmas
there is just one thing I need
I don't care about presents
underneath the Christmas tree
I don't need to hang my stocking
there upon the fireplace
Santa Claus won't make me happy
with a toy on Christmas day
I just want you for my own
more than you could ever know
make my wish come true
all I want for Christmas is you... you baby
I won't ask for much this Christmas
I won't even wish for snow
I'm just gonna keep on waiting
underneath the mistletoe
I won't make a list and send it
to the North Pole for Saint Nick
I won't even stay awake to
hear those magic reindeer click
'cause I just want you here tonight
holding on to me so tight
what more can I do
baby all I want for Christmas is you

二、听下面的六段对话，选出与所提问题相关的最佳图片。

1. M：What's wrong with our aunt?
   W：She's going to have a baby.
   M：Good news! I'm so glad to hear that.
   Q：What's the matter with their aunt?
2. M：What does your mother do?
   W：She's a gardener. She plants lots of beautiful flowers.
   M：Can I see her flowers some day?
   Q：What is her mother?
3. M：Can I help you，Miss?
   W：Yes. I'm going to England. I want to exchange some money.
   M：How many pounds would you like to exchange for?
   Q：Which money does she need?
4. M：I'm going camping this weekend. Would you like to come?
   W：Sure. Have you checked the weather?
   M：Yes. The weather report says it will clear up during the weekend though it's raining now.
   Q：What will the weather be like this weekend?
5. M：Hurry up，Sue. We'll be late for class.
   W：Don't worry，Sandy. It's 7：15. We still have 30 minutes to go.
   M：OK，then.
   Q：What time does the class begin?
6. M：Sally. You've got so much lucky money for the Chinese New Year. How are you going to spend it?
   W：Well，I'm going to save it.
   M：Why don't you buy yourself some presents?
   Q：What is Sally going to do with the money?

三、听对话，在图书馆里允许做的事情前画圈（○），否则画叉（×）。

M：Excuse me. I'm a new student here. I have some questions about the library rules.

W：Sure. Glad to help.

M：Can we eat or drink in the library or take my dog there?

W：No，you can't.

M：Are we allowed to smoke in the reading room?

W：No，they won't let you. Smoking is not good for people's health.

M：I see. Can I take the magazines home if I don't finish reading it there?
W：I'm afraid you can't. Magazines and reserved books may not be borrowed.
M：What about CDs and tapes? Can I borrow them?
W：Yes, it's permitted.
M：Thanks. By the way, how many books can I borrow at one time?
W：Well. No more than four.
M：May I copy the articles in the books? I might need them for my reading report.
W：Yes. You can do that, but only for personal use.
M：My last question. Is it OK if I wear T-shirt or shorts in the library?
W：Yes, it's allowed, but only in summer.
M：Thank you very much.
W：You're welcome. Have a nice time here.

四、听对话，根据对话内容选出最佳答案。

M：Hey, Susie. Good to see you come back. Did you have a nice trip?
W：Hi, Brad. Yes, I had a great time.
M：Tell me about your trip to Switzerland. How was the weather there?
W：It was kind of cool. So I took some warm sweaters and coats.
M：Uh huh. What about the hotels?
W：The hotels were excellent, but a little expensive. I could see the beautiful mountains just from my hotel room window.
M：That was great. By the way, did you have trouble speaking to the people there? I mean, do they speak English?
W：I'm afraid not. There are hardly anyone speaks English except for the people in the hotels. But the staff of the hotels were really helpful and friendly.
M：Well. That's good. Did you buy much while you were there?
W：Just small gifts. Things are much more expensive than in the United States.

五、听短文，填补所缺内容。

Welcome to 2010 Summer Camp!

2010 Summer Camp opens between 9：30 am and 11：30 am from July 10th to July 30th. All children aged 7-14 are welcome. Each child can take part in only one of the following activities and needs to pay 200 yuan for it.

1. Sports. You can play basketball, volleyball, or table tennis here.

2. Hobby groups. We have organized groups for painting, singing, dancing, piano, and computer. There will be a teacher with each group to help.

3. English world. Learn to sing songs, watch films, play games or act in plays in

English with us. If you want to improve your spoken English, this is a good choice.

Some English children are coming to the camp, too. If you really want to have an interesting summer holiday, please join us for learning with fun. Act now! Book your ticket as soon as possible either by phone or by email. Our telephone number is 84857319 and our email address is labc2010@yahoo.com. Pay before July 8th, and the first 10 members can have a Mickey T-shirt for free. Come on, we are here waiting for you.

Section 3

一、听对话，填补所缺的内容。

M: Excuse me, may I borrow your bike, please?

W: OK.

M: Where is it?

W: Over there, under the tall tree.

M: Oh, I see it.

W: Where are you going, may I ask?

M: I'm going shopping. I need to buy some vegetables.

W: Is that so? Can you bring some tomatoes for me?

M: Sure.

W: Here is the key. Thanks.

M: Well, I must go now. See you later.

W: See you.

二、听对话，完成地图并画好路线图。

M: Excuse me.

W: Yes.

M: Can you tell me the way to the post office?

W: Certainly. Walk out of the cafe, turn right and go along Downing Street.

M: Along Downing Street.

W: Yes, you can see a cinema along the street on your left and a bookstore on your right. Walk along and then turn left at the second corner.

M: I see. And ...

W: Then go along Main Street. It's straight ahead, on your right. Just past the hotel. You can't miss it.

三、听下面的十个句子，选出与所听到的句子意思相同或最相近的句子。

1. Whose pencil is this?
2. What is his father's job?
3. It's a pleasure.
4. How interesting the game is!
5. Would you like a glass of water?
6. Please write me a letter.
7. Where do you come from?
8. Have you any brothers or sisters?
9. I don't feel like eating now.
10. What's the matter with you?

四、听下面的三段对话，根据对话内容选出最佳答案。

听第一段对话，回答1 ~3 题。

W: Hey, Jack. What are you looking for?

M: I'm picking up the wasted plastic bags. You see, there are wasted plastic bags here and there.

W: Yes. I'll join you.

M: Thank you. The workers of the park should put up a notice telling people not to throw waste paper and waste plastic bags anywhere.

W: After picking up the waste plastic bags, let's go and give a suggestion to the office of the park.

M: Good idea! We'd better write a report to the Mayor and let all people keep our city clean.

听第二段对话，回答4 ~6 题。

M: What do you like best about London?

W: The British Museum and the Tower of London.

M: I know the British Museum is one of the largest museums in the world.

W: Yes. And I especially enjoy talking with the Beefeaters at the Tower of London. In fact, they are the guards of the tower.

M: Tell me why they are called Beefeaters.

W: One old story is that they used to have beef as part of their salary.

听第三段对话，回答7 ~10 题。

M: Why do you want to go to the US?

W: I want to learn more things about making films. Since Hollywood is there, the US is a great place for me.

M: What will you do when you come home?

W: I'd like to be a director like Lee An and Zhang Yimou.

M: Do you feel your English is good enough for the study?

W: Yes. I scored very high in GRE and TOEFL.

M: Who will support you during your stay in the US?

W: Myself. I have saved enough money for my study by doing part-time jobs these years.

M: How long do you think you will stay there?

W: I will be there for two years.

五、听短文，完成下面两组练习。

（略）

Section 4

一、听写单句。

1. On Sunday we are going to see Miss Wang.
2. The house is just on the other side of the road.
3. I think people get old because they give up things.
4. My friends and I often sing pop songs together.
5. It's about five minutes' walk from here.
6. How much shall I pay for it?
7. There is a phone call for Alice.
8. What can you see in the picture?
9. He likes reading books about history.
10. Don't be late for class.

二、听下面的五段对话，填补所缺内容。

1. M: Good morning, ma'am. What can I do for you?

   W: Could you tell me when the plane for Amsterdam leaves?

   M: What's the name of the airline, please?

   W: It's Pan Am. Flight PA726.

   M: Just a moment. Ah, yes. It leaves at 7:10 pm.

   W: At 7:10 pm. Thanks. And when does it arrive in Amsterdam?

   M: It arrives at 10:15 am.

2. M: Good morning. Can I help you?
W: Yes. I want to know when the plane for Sydney leaves.
M: What's the name of the airline, please?
W: It's Quantas. Flight QU411.
M: Just a minute, please. The plane leaves at 9:00 pm.
W: At 9:00 pm. Fine. And when does it arrive in Sydney?
M: It arrives at 6:05 am.

3. M: Good morning, ma'am. What can I do for you?
W: Could you tell me when the plane for Frankfurt leaves?
M: What's the name of the airline, please?
W: It's Lufthansa. Flight LH634.
M: Just a moment. Yes. It leaves at 8:25 pm.
W: At 8:25 pm. OK. And when does it arrive in Frankfurt?
M: It arrives at 9:50 am.

4. M: Good morning, ma'am. Is there anything I can do to help?
W: Yes. Could you tell me when the plane for Paris leaves?
M: What's the name of the airline, please?
W: It's Air France. Flight AF942.
M: Just a moment. Yes. The plane leaves at 7:30 pm.
W: At 7:30 pm. Fine. And when does it arrive in Paris?
M: It arrives at 8:35 pm.

5. M: Good morning, ma'am. What can I do for you?
W: Could you tell me when the plane for Tokyo leaves?
M: What's the name of the airline, please?
W: It's Japan Air Lines. Flight JAL27.
M: One minute, please. The plane leaves at 12:40 pm.
W: At 12:40 pm. Thank you. And when does it arrive in Tokyo?
M: It arrives at 5:20 pm.

三、拼写游戏。你将听到一些单词，这些单词都是由图片上物品的拼写加上或者减去一些字母组成的。先在横线上写下你所听到的单词，然后选出算式中问号所代表的图片。

1. teach 2. sleep 3. I 4. free
5. sunday 6. six 7. on 8. come

四、听短文，完成下面的两组练习。

（略）

Section 5

一、听下面的五段对话，根据所听到的内容连线。

1. M：Excuse me. Is there a place near here where I can buy a newspaper?
   W：Yes. There's a magazine shop at the end of the hall.
   M：Thank you.
2. M：Excuse me. Is there a place where I can mail these letters?
   W：Yes. I think there's a mail box next to the coffee shop.
   M：Thanks a lot.
3. M：Excuse me. Is there a place where I can change some money?
   W：Yes. There's a bank next to the elevator.
   M：Thank you very much.
4. M：Excuse me. Is there a place where I can get something to eat?
   W：Yes. There's a restaurant opposite the souvenir shop.
   M：Thank you.
5. M：Excuse me. Is there a place where I can find about city tours?
   W：Yes. I think there's a tour desk near the entrance.

二、听下面的四段电影片段，根据你所听到的内容选出最佳答案。

（略）

三、听下面的一段短文，填补所缺的内容。

Hello！I'm a Chinese girl. My name is Xiao Wei. I'm 14 years old. There are four people in my family，my father，my mother，my grandmother and I. We live in Wuhan. Do you know Wuhan? It is one of the largest cities in China.

I'm in No. 109 Middle School. It is a big and nice school. My favourite subject is Chinese，and I like music and computer games very much. We have very nice teachers in our school，especially my English teacher，Susan. She told me that you wanted to make pen-friends from China. I like making friends. So I write you this letter.

OK. That's all. Please write to me soon.

四、听写。

Jack Smith is an American boy. He is 15 years old. He lives in New York with his father and mother. His father is a painter and his mother is a nurse. Now, Jack studies at Apple Tree School. Maths and English are his favourite subjects. He loves studying. He likes doing sports in his free time. He usually plays football with friends after school, and he often goes swimming in summer. Jack has a dog. The dog's name is Adam. On Saturdays, Jack helps in the local animal hospital. On Sundays, he stays at home playing with Adam or watching TV.

Unit 12

Section 1

一、听写单词。

1. bottle 2. cup 3. tea-pot 4. glass 5. bowl
6. plate 7. knife 8. fork 9. pan 10. kitchen
11. river 12. sea 13. stream 14. ocean 15. hill
16. mountain 17. grassland 18. travel 19. trip 20. journey

二、听下面的八个句子，选出与句子内容相关的图片。

1. This is my teacher, Miss Zhao.
2. Are you from England?
3. What time is it by your watch?
4. Sometimes Judy flies a kite with me.
5. Hello, 65613799.
6. Who is singing in the next room?
7. Sue, may I borrow your pencil sharpener?
8. He has egg and bread as his breakfast.

三、听下面的六段对话，根据对话内容选出最佳答案。

1. M: Is this ruler yours?
   W: No. It looks like mine, but it's Angela's.
2. M: Where are your group members?
   W: Three of them are here with me, and the other four are in the school library.
3. M: Is your email address WFLS@126. com?
   W: No. It is WEFLS@163. com.
4. M: Look! There is a map of the world on the wall in the classroom.
   W: Cool. Then we can go on with the game.
5. M: Hello, is that 87365127?
   W: Sorry. I'm afraid you have the wrong number. It's 87425127.

6. M：Excuse me，is this seat taken?

W：I don't think so. That boy got his schoolbag and left a few minutes ago.

四、听短文，判断下列句子是否正确，正确用 T（True）表示，错误用 F（False）表示。

Many years ago two men were traveling together. They were walking along a road in the wood. Then they found a beautiful gold stick on the ground. One of them picked it up and said，" Look here. I have found a gold stick. "

"Don't say 'I'，but 'we' have found the gold stick，" said the other. "We are friends. We ought to share it between us. "

"No，" said the first man，"I found the gold stick，so it is mine. "

Soon after they heard someone running after them. They looked back and found a very strong man. The man called out，" Stop，thieves! Stop，thieves!" The first traveler asked，" What shall we do? He is running after us. We shall be caught by him. "

"Don't say 'we'，but 'I' shall be caught. You found the gold stick，and you say it is yours，" said the other，and left him alone.

The first traveler tried to hide the gold stick，but he did not know where to hide it. And at last he was caught by the owner of the gold stick.

五、听短文，填补所缺的内容。

Emily works in a company about ten kilometers from her home. She loves her job and works very hard. Every day，Emily leaves her home early and walks to a bus stop. The bus stop is in front of a radio station. It's about 250 meters from her home. She often catches the Number 46 bus to work，but sometimes she goes by bike. Her work starts at half past eight，and finishes at a quarter to six. So Emily gets back home at ten past six. She does the same thing every weekday.

Section 2

一、听下面的一段英文歌，填补所缺的内容。

I was a quick wet boy，diving too deep for coins
All of your street light eyes wide on my plastic toys
Then when the cops closed the fair，I cut my long baby hair
Stole me a dog-eared map and called for you everywhere
Have I found you
Flightless bird，jealous，weeping or lost you，American mouth

Big pill looming
Now I'm a fat house cat
Nursing my sore blunt tongue
Watching the warm poison rats curl through the wide fence cracks
Pissing on magazine photos
Those fishing lures thrown in the cold
And clean blood of Christ mountain stream

二、听下面的十段对话，选出与所提问题相关的最佳图片。

1. M: Rosemary, why are you in such a hurry?
   W: I must be home soon. I forgot to water the flowers this morning.
2. M: You don't look well, Mandy. What's wrong with you?
   W: I have a terrible stomachache and I need some medicine.
3. M: What date is it today?
   W: It's December 7th. Anything special?
4. M: Good morning. Can I help you?
   W: I want two tickets for the play, please.
5. M: How did you know there would be an art exhibition?
   W: Well, the TV news program said so.
6. M: Would you like a hamburger and some chips for lunch?
   W: Yes, and a coke, please.
7. M: Look at the wall. Wow, Mary, you are so good at painting.
   W: Thanks, John. Do you like the picture I drew?
8. M: Mom, have you seen my key? I can't find it.
   W: Is it in your schoolbag?
9. M: Glad to see you back. How was your trip to Nanjing?
   W: Great. I especially enjoy the service on the plane.
10. M: Do you want to be a nurse when you grow up?
    W: No. I'd like to be an airhostess.

三、听下面的十个句子，选出与你所听到的句子意思相同或最相近的句子。

1. There isn't any milk in the glass.
2. The schoolbag under the desk is his.
3. How many kites are there in the sky?
4. I want a shirt like this.
5. My father usually gets home at 6:50.
6. Mr. Lee is my next door neighbour.
7. What do you think of the coffee?
8. Thank you for sending me the email.

9. They often play football after school.

10. Do you enjoy playing computer games?

四、听对话，选出表格内所缺的内容。

W：Good morning. May I help you?

M：Yes. I'm looking for a flat. With three bedrooms and a big kitchen.

W：All right. Have a seat, please. We need to fill in some forms and I'll ask you a few questions. First, what is your name, please?

M：My name is Albert Enakei.

W：Could you spell your last name, Mr. Enakei?

M：E-N-A-K-E-I.

W：And what is your present address, Mr. Enakei?

M：It's 1267 Lindon Street.

W：1267 Lindon. That is in San Francisco, isn't it?

M：Yes, it is.

W：Do you have a telephone?

M：Yes. It's 285-9841.

W：285-9841. And could you tell me your job, please?

M：I'm an engineer. I work for Apple Computer.

W：Thank you, Mr. Enakei. You are looking for a flat with three bedrooms and a big kitchen.

M：That's right.

W：Could you wait just a minute, please? I'll take a look in our files.

五、听短文，填补所缺的内容。

Linda is an American doctor. She is now in China. She works in a children's hospital in Wuhan. She is also learning Chinese medicine there. Linda loves to work for children, and she works hard during the day. She wants to know Chinese medicine well so she often reads English books about it at night. She says the Chinese people are friendly and helpful. She learns Chinese from the Chinese doctors and her Chinese friends. Now Linda can speak some Chinese and even read some Chinese, too.

Section 3

一、听句子，填补所缺的单词。

1. He often walks home after school.

2. I can see some flowers on the table.
3. There aren't any students in the classroom.
4. Look at the map on the wall.
5. Is it OK to call you at 9:00 pm?
6. How many pairs of shoes does Timmy have?
7. Today is Wednesday, and it is windy.
8. Everyone in my family is happy at this time.
9. What do you want to have for supper?
10. Who's that girl in the teachers' office?

二、听下面的六个句子，选出最佳答语。

1. Mom, could you come here, please?
2. Where is your pencil?
3. Would you like some more soup?
4. When is Lily's birthday?
5. Don't cross the street when the traffic lights are red.
6. What's wrong with the clock?

三、听下面的四段对话，根据对话内容选出最佳答案。

听第一段对话，回答 1 ~2 题。

M: I'm sorry, Miss Chen. I think I have to go home. I feel awful.
W: What's the trouble?
M: I have a terrible headache and I feel faint.
W: Go home and take a good rest.
M: Thanks. I'll do that.

听第二段对话，回答 3 ~4 题。

M: I'll give you some medicine to take. By the way, are you here for the Olympic Games?
W: Yes. I'm a tennis player.
M: Oh, I'm a tennis fan. I wish you good luck.
W: Thank you very much, doctor.

听第三段对话，回答 5 ~6 题。

M: Hello. I'm here to check in.
W: Good morning. You must be Mr. Jenkins.
M: Yes, I am.
W: Welcome to Planet Hotel. Would you please fill out this form?

听第四段对话，回答7～8题。

M：May I come in?

W：Yes，please.

M：How are you doing，madam? My name is Wu Zhe. I'm coming for an interview as required.

W：Fine，thank you for coming，Mr. Wu. Please take a seat. I'm Carol Blair，the assistant manager.

四、听英文歌，完成下面两组练习。

One day when I came home at lunch time，
I heard a funny noise.
Went out to the back yard to find out if it was，
One of those rowdy boys.
Stood there with my neighbor called Peter，
And a Flux Capacitor.
He told me he built a time machine.
Like one in a film I've seen，
Yeah yeah... he said...
I've been to the year 3000
Not much has changed but they lived under water.
And your great great great grand daughter，
Is doing fine (is doing fine).
He took me to the future in the flux thing，and I saw everything.
Boy bands，and another one and another one ... and another one!
Girls there with round hair like Star Wars float above the floor
We drove around in a time machine，
Like the one in the film I've seen.
Yeah yeah... he said...
He said，I've been to the year 3000.
Not much has changed but they lived under water，
And your great great great grand daughter，
Is doing fine (is doing fine).

五、听一段天气预报，给图片排序并写出相应的天气和温度。

Welcome to obama-weather. com. Let's take a look at the weather in some cities in China.

It will be snowy in Harbin，and the temperature will be 0℃-2℃，so people there need to wear overcoats and jeans. A scarf also helps to keep people warm.

The weather in Haikou will be sunny and a little hot with a temperature between 27℃ and 33℃. People there had better wear T-shirts, shorts and havaianas.

The sky above Wuhan will be covered with thick cloud. The temperature will be 19℃-24℃. People there wear jackets and pants.

There will be showers in Beijing. The lowest temperature will fall to 10℃, and the highest, 15℃. It's better to wear jumpers, jeans and sneakers. And don't forget to take your umbrella when you go out.

It will be cloudy in Zhengzhou with a temperature between 12℃ and 18℃. A jacket and jeans are enough for a man.

Shanghai is going to be really wet. The temperature will be 13℃-18℃. It's better to wear jackets and jeans, and always remember your umbrellas.

The weather in Qingdao will be fine. The temperature will go from 21℃ to 27℃. People there wear shirts and pants.

Section 4

一、听写单句。

1. We have seven English classes every week.
2. Let me help you clean the bedroom.
3. We have a walk after supper every Sunday.
4. Is there a computer in your office?
5. How many oranges does the woman want?
6. What color is your coat?
7. School begins at 9 am and ends at 3 pm.
8. They must go home now because it's going to rain.
9. These are his books and those are hers.
10. Where can I get some stamps, please?

二、听下面的六段对话和问题，根据你所听到的内容选出与所提问题相关的最佳图片。

1. W: Which season do you like better, summer or winter?

   M: I like swimming in summer and I also like skating in winter. Mmm... summer, I think. It is too cold in the winter.

   Q: What does the boy like to do in summer?
2. W: Do you like watching TV, Jerry?

M：Yes, I like it very much.

W：Which games would you like to watch in 2012?

M：Football games.

Q：Which game would Jerry like to watch?

3. W：Can I help you?

M：I want some peaches, please.

W：How much do you want, sir?

M：Half a pound, please.

Q：What does the man want to buy?

4. W：Is there any orange in the bag?

M：No, I'm afraid not.

W：Is there any bread, then?

M：Yes, there is plenty of bread.

Q：What is in the bag?

5. W：I'm going to the supermarket now. Would you like me to get you some bananas?

M：Please get me 1 kilo of grapes. I like grapes better.

W：OK.

Q：What does the man want?

6. W：Are you going to listen to the radio this evening?

M：I wish I could. But I have to read my textbook. The final exam is coming.

Q：What is the boy going to do this evening?

三、听短文，填补所缺的内容。

Good morning, every one. Welcome to Tony's tour. We are going to take the No. 77 tour bus and take a look around the city on the first day. The bus leaves the terminal at 8:30 in the morning. So please get there on time. Our first stop is City Hall, and we will be there at about 8:45. The bus will arrive at Shopping Center at 9 am. You can buy souvenirs there on the last day of your trip. We will go past Swimming Pool at about 9:20, and No. 2 Middle School 15 minutes later. Then the bus will stop at Sports Stadium at 9:40. The new stadium was built half a year ago. After a short rest, we will go on our trip on the bus and arrive at Zhongshan Park at about 10:30. This is one of the most popular places in the city and it is free. The most famous hospital, People's Hospital, is only 10 minutes' bus ride from Zhongshan Park. Our last stop in the morning is May's Garden. We will get there at about 11:30 and have lunch in a nearby restaurant.

四、听下面的五段对话，根据对话内容选出最佳答案。

1. W：Did Steven say who broke the window?
M：Yeah，he said it was his sister Cissy.
W：Do you believe that?
M：Of course not. This naughty boy always gets into trouble.
W：And he never admit it by himself at first every time.
M：Right. Just now he was playing baseball. So I think it was him who did so.

2. W：Ted is back from his holiday.
M：Oh，I know but I still haven't the chance to see him. Is he OK?
W：Yes，as soon as he stepped off the plane，he began to tell me a lot about his life in Osaka.
M：It seems that he had a great time in Japan. He enjoyed it very much.
W：Of course.

3. W：What are you doing right now?
M：I'm trying to get these things back to order. It's so untidy in my room.
W：I see. Well，I'm wondering if you'd like to go to the cinema with me.
M：I'd like to，but I don't think I can today. How about tomorrow?
W：That sounds fine.

4. W：What is your present for Father's Day?
M：A shirt. A very famous brand. Do you think it's nice?
W：Yeah，the color and the style are so in fashion.
M：Thank you. I went shopping for four days and buy this one at last.
W：It must be a pleasant surprise for your Dad.

5. W：What do you do for exercise every day?
M：I go on the treadmill for half an hour each morning. How about you?
W：I play tennis every day after work.
M：I would love to join you sometime. It should be more fun.
W：Sure.

五、听短文，完成下面两组练习。

（略）

Section 5

一、听对话，在 Laura 和 Allen 要买的东西图片下画○，否则画×。

W：Allen，what do you feel like having tonight?

M: Well, just not pizza, everything else is fine.

W: Wow, the roasted chicken smells great! Should we get some?

M: Sure, and maybe we should pick up some vegetables for salad?

W: Yeah, let me see... Here, we can buy some tomatoes and carrots. And will you help me cut it up, dear?

M: OK. Let's go and get some bread and milk for this week's breakfast.

W: Err... Can we get some cereal instead of bread? I think cereal is more healthy.

M: Of course.

W: So, are these all we need?

M: Yes! Oh, hold on, we forgot salad dressing.

W: You can go to wait at the cashier. I'll run to grab a dressing. French is OK?

M: Yeah!

二、听下面的四段电影片段，根据你所听到的内容选出最佳答案。

（略）

三、听下面的一段短文，填补所缺的内容。

My name is Fiona. I get up at 6:00 every morning. I make the bed quickly. Then I take a shower, washing my face and my hair. Breakfast is ready at about 7:15. After breakfast, I ride my bicycle to school and have four classes. I have lunch with my friends at school at 12:10. At about 4:00 in the afternoon, I come back home. I do my homework first, and then I play the piano. Sometimes I help in the kitchen. I have dinner at 7:00. After dinner I play computer games for an hour. Then it's about 9:00 and it is time for bed.

四、听写。

Jane likes English very much. She works hard. She reads English in the morning every day. She likes speaking English and she often speaks English with her classmates in school. When Jane is free, she often listens to some English radio programs. She watches TV only on Friday evening. Does she like dancing? No, she doesn't. But she likes drawing and playing the piano. Her parents like her very much. And all the teachers and her friends like her, too.

Unit 13

Section 1

一、听词组，把你所听到的词组写在下面的横线上。

1. give up 2. dress up 3. turn up 4. care for 5. call for
6. look for 7. get in 8. break into 9. slow down 10. throw away

二、听下面的十句话，选出与你所听到的句子一致的答案，并将代表该答案的字母填在题前的括号内。

1. My parents are planning their vacation.
2. We live near the bus stop.
3. Don't forget to bring your books.
4. Let's work on our project tomorrow.
5. Is the girl a new student?
6. Write your name at the top of the page.
7. I'm not interested in going to the concert.
8. Paul is older than Simon but younger than Tom.
9. Has the gym opened yet today?
10. The teacher's students use the school library.

三、听下面的三段材料，在你所听到的物品下面的方框内打钩。

1. I like to wear casual clothes at home, a sweater and pants, but for work I always wear more formal things, like a dress and a jacket or a top and a skirt.
2. Different cultures have different ways to celebrate the New Year. Many cultures celebrate with special dishes and objects. In China, people prepare traditional food to share with friends and family. On New Year's Day, Chinese families eat a kind of food called dumplings. It is made of flour, meat, and vegetables. The Chinese also traditionally celebrate the New Year with fireworks.
3. M: Hey, look what it says here—Jonas Hanway began to use the umbrella

in 1756.

W: You're kidding me! People used umbrellas around 250 years ago? What else does it say? Let me see.

M: Look. Joseph Merlin invented roller skates in 1759.

W: And people in Europe and America rode roller coasters in amusement parks in the mid-1800s.

M: Wow! That is such a long time ago. What about this—sneakers! They were invented in 1917 by the US Rubber Company. Hey, I like this one—in 1967, Mary Quant created the miniskirt.

W: That's a long time ago, too. But get this—Farnsworth invented the television in 1928.

M: I didn't know that.

四、听下面的一段材料，根据内容判断下列句子的正误，将T（正确）或F（错误）填入题前的括号内。

This is the largest sports center of the city. Every citizen is welcome. In order to help people build up their health and young people to develop their skills, we have a lot of arrangements for them. We have several ball classes. Tennis is open all day long. Basketball is provided from 10 o'clock in the morning till 5 in the afternoon. Volleyball is arranged in the evenings. Football is at weekends. But we don't have baseball classes because very few people like it, though it is exciting. Besides ball games, we have many other kinds of sports. You are always welcome at any time.

Section 2

一、听下面的一首歌，根据歌词填空。

Almost heaven west Virginia
Blue ridge mountains Shenandoah River
Life is old there older than the trees
Younger than the mountains
Growing like a breeze
Country roads take me home
To the place I belong
West Virginia mountain momma
Take me home country roads

All my memories gather around her
Miners lady stranger to blue water
Dark and dusty painted on the sky
Misty taste of moon shine
Tear drops in my eyes
Country roads take me home
To the place I belong
West Virginia mountain momma
Take me home country roads

二、看下面的十五幅图，每幅图你都会听到三个描述此图的句子 A，B 和 C，请选出正确描述此图的句子。

1. A. This is a two-story building.
   B. This building has many windows.
   C. This building has no roof.
2. A. There are some children in the playground.
   B. There are not any boys in the playground.
   C. There are not any girls in the playground.
3. A. The chair is on the desk.
   B. There is no chair in the picture.
   C. The chair is next to the desk.
4. A. There are three TV sets in the picture.
   B. There are four TV sets in the picture.
   C. There are two TV sets in the picture.
5. A. The father is crying.
   B. The mother is standing.
   C. They are both laughing.
6. A. The person on the left is taller than the one on the right.
   B. The person on the right is taller than the one on the left.
   C. They are of the same height.
7. A. There are some vegetables in the picture.
   B. This is a nice birthday cake.
   C. This is a small piece of cake.
8. A. The bear is catching a fish.
   B. The bear is swimming.
   C. The bear is far away from the river.

9. A. The girl has short hair.
   B. The girl has long hair.
   C. The girl wears trousers.
10. A. This is a Japanese cartoon.
    B. This is an American cartoon.
    C. This is a German cartoon.
11. A. They are walking with their dog.
    B. They are playing roller skating.
    C. They are skiing.
12. A. The girl is on the floor.
    B. The girl is on a desk.
    C. The girl is in a bed.
13. A. A boy and two girls are dancing.
    B. Three girls are dancing.
    C. Three boys are fighting.
14. A. They are riding a horse.
    B. They are riding a camel.
    C. They are riding an elephant.
15. A. The two girls are playing basketball.
    B. The two girls are playing badminton.
    C. The two girls are playing golf.

三、听短文，根据所听内容填写下列表格。

And now here's today's weather report for some big cities in the world. In London it will be sunny with the temperature 6℃ to 15℃. In Paris you'll have heavy rain during the day-time. The lowest temperature will be 3℃ and the highest will be 11℃. Washington will have a rainy day. The temperature will be 18℃ to 28℃. If you live in New York, you'll have beautiful sunshine. It will be sunny with a low of 21℃ and a high of 32℃. If you live in Wuhan, you will meet a strong wind and the temperature will be 15℃ to 26℃.

Section 3

一、听下面的十个句子，把你所听到的句子写在下面的横线上。

1. What's wrong with you?

2. How are you recently?
3. What is your favourite fruit?
4. How can I get there?
5. Which do you prefer?
6. I will go shopping next week.
7. She gets on well with her classmates.
8. My father is an engineer.
9. I like playing the piano.
10. My best friend is a basketball fan.

二、听下面的十个问题，根据问题选出最佳答语，并将答语排序。将代表答语的序号写在横线上。

1. Why don't we go for a walk?
2. Why don't you eat more vegetables?
3. Why don't we have fish for lunch?
4. Why don't we play basketball?
5. Why don't you ever go swimming?
6. What are you doing?
7. What's the date today?
8. What can we do this weekend?
9. What can you see from the picture?
10. What's your favourite colour?

三、听下面的十段小独白，根据独白内容选择相应的图片，并将代表该图片的字母填在题前的括号内。

1. I have a big fur tail and I like living in a tree. Who am I?
2. I have a long neck and I like eating leaves. Who am I?
3. I live in Arctic and I'm not afraid of cold. Who am I?
4. No child likes me because I like drinking their blood. Who am I?
5. I like summer best and I have a big pair of eyes. Who am I?
6. I'm black and most of people don't like me. They say I'm unlucky. Who am I?
7. I have a beautiful tail. It looks like a colourful fan. Who am I?
8. I'm black and white. I like eating bamboo. Most of people think I'm lovely. Who am I?
9. I have a little bag for my babies. I can jump with my two strong legs. Who am I?
10. I like living in a group and I like having a shower by my trunk. Who am I?

四、听下面的一段独白，根据独白内容完成下列各小题。

My sister and I are very different. I'm a teacher. She is a doctor. I live in New York. She lives in London. I have a large house in the suburbs. She has a small apartment in the city. I'm married. She's single. I play golf. She plays tennis. I play the piano. She doesn't play a musical instrument. On the weekend I usually watch videos and rarely go out. She never watches videos and always goes to parties. As you can see, we are very different. But we're sisters and we are friends.

Section 4

一、听下面的一段对话，用你所听到的单词或句子补全对话。

Sindy: How far is it to the National Park?
Guide: It is about 50 miles.
Sindy: How long will it take to get there?
Guide: About an hour.
Sindy: Look at that high mountain! How high is it?
Guide: It's a volcano. It's about 2, 500 meters.
Sindy: How many feet is that?
Guide: It's about 8, 200 feet.
Sindy: How deep is the hole?
Guide: It's about 350 feet deep.
Sindy: Oh! There is a temple. How old is this temple?
Guide: It's about 400 years old.
Sindy: Is that the beach? How long is it?
Guide: I'm not sure, but it's probably 10 miles long.

二、听下面的一段独白，根据独白内容完成下列表格。

Sally's International Restaurant is a very special place. Every day Sally cooks a different kind of food. On Monday he cooks Italian food. On Tuesday he cooks Greek food. On Wednesday he cooks Chinese food. On Thursday he cooks Indian food. On Friday he cooks Japanese food. On Saturday he cooks Mexican food. And on Sunday he cooks American food.

三、听下面的一段长对话，根据对话内容选择最佳答案。并将代表该答案的字母写在题前的括号内。

Jimmy：Hi，Linda. Are you going home? Can I help you with those bags?
Linda：Thanks. That would be great. You're the best neighbour.
Jimmy：How is your holiday shopping going?
Linda：Fine. I bought the most beautiful necklace for my mother.
Jimmy：What's it made of?
Linda：Silver. It's from Mexico. You know Mother's Day is coming.
Jimmy：What else did you buy? Something for your brother?
Linda：No. I didn't buy anything for my brother，but I bought a pair of sneakers for my father. He likes playing tennis. His old pair isn't good enough.
Jimmy：Why don't you buy something for yourself? Your birthday is coming.
Linda：I didn't buy anything as my birthday gift，but I want to have a party. So I bought so many kinds of snacks，some drinks and a birthday cake. Would you like to come?
Jimmy：Sure，I'd love to.

四、听下面的一段独白，根据要求完成各个小题。

Mann's Chinese Theater is a movie theater that was built in 1927. In the courtyard，160 movie stars have set their handprints and footprints in the path.

Beverly Hills is an extremely wealthy area. There are so many expensive shops here. The famous shopping street，Rodeo Drive，is here.

Universal Studios is a film studio where visitors can see how movies are filmed and special effects are created. They will see dinosaurs from the movie *Jurassic Park*，and the shark from *Jaws*.

The Walk of Fame is a 1.6 km road. Where the names of over 2，000 actors and actresses are written in the stars in the sidewalk. This practice started in 1960，and new stars are still being added.

The Hollywood Bowl is a huge outdoor concert hall that opened in 1922. It's one of the largest outdoor theaters in the world. Because Los Angeles has a desert climate，concerts are seldom cancelled.

Section 5

一、听下面的五段对话，根据对话内容判断其发生地点，并与相应的图片连线。

1. M：Excuse me. How do I get to the City Center Mall from here?

W: Pardon?

M: Can you tell me how to get to the City Center Mall?

W: Go east on Holbrook Road. Go to Vine Street. Turn left on Vine. The City Center Mall is right there.

M: Thanks.

2. W: Here you are. They are on sale.

M: Thank you. Do you have a pair in green, too?

W: I'm sorry. We don't have that color in your size.

3. M: Could I have a window seat?

W: All right, sir. Your seat number is 30A. Your flight begins boarding at Gate 18 at 2:30. Here is your boarding pass.

M: Thank you.

4. M: What's wrong with you?

W: Oh, I've got a pain in my ear. It hurts a lot.

M: How long has it lasted?

W: For nearly two days.

M: Let me see.

5. M: What do you want to have today?

W: I'm not hungry. Just a salad and a cup of coffee. How about you?

M: I prefer spaghetti. This is my favourite. And I like the music here.

二、听下面的一段独白，根据独白内容完成下列表格。

Jessie is a very athletic girl. She does a different kind of exercise or sport every day. On Monday she jogs. On Tuesday she plays tennis. On Wednesday she does yoga. On Thursday she swims. On Friday she goes to a health club. On Saturday she plays basketball. And on Sunday she rides her bike.

三、听下面的两段材料，根据所听内容完成各个小题，并将代表最佳答案的字母填在题前的括号内。

听下面的录音，回答1~3题。

(略)

听下面的一段歌曲，回答4~6题。

(略)

四、听下面的一段独白，请把独白中的每一句话完整地记录下来。

Peter works in a bank, and he works 40 hours a week. He begins working at half past eight in the morning and stops at half past five in the afternoon. At half past five the bank closes. Everybody goes home. Some people drive home. Some people take the train and other people take the bus.

Unit 14

Section 1

一、听下面的十个句子，用英语写出句子中所提到的日期。

1. This year the Spring Festival is on January the twenty-first.
2. St. Valentine's Day is on February the fourteenth.
3. My birthday is on September the nineteenth.
4. Tree Planting Day is on March the twelfth.
5. The final examination of this term will be held on June the twenty-ninth.
6. Halloween Eve is on October the thirty-first.
7. Labour Day is on May the first.
8. Christmas Day is on December the twenty-fifth.
9. This year Thanksgiving Day is on November the twenty-fourth.
10. April Fools' Day is on April the first.

二、听下面的十个问句，根据所听到的内容选出相应的答语，并将代表该答案的字母填在题前的括号内。

1. What does your sister do?
2. Whose computer is that over there?
3. How long will you stay here?
4. May I speak to John?
5. How is the weather?
6. Where does your father work?
7. How often do you exercise?
8. Which season is your favourite?
9. Why don't you like English?
10. What day is it today?

三、听下面的一段独白，根据独白的内容将以下人物的名称写在相应图片下的横线上。

Thanks for the message. I am always very happy to receive your emails.

You can see some photos of my friends. They are at my birthday party. I like the photos very much. Can you see a girl in a pink dress? She is putting some glue on the chair. Her name is Mary. Luckily, no one is sitting on the glue. In another picture, Betty is dancing on the table. My best friend, Peter, is a greedy boy. He likes sweets very much. He is hiding some sweets. Can you also see Ben, a boy in blue jeans? He is cutting Helen's hair. Her hair is very long.

My friend are too naughty. Do you have naughty friend, too? Can you see me in the photo? Of course you can't. I always take photos at parties.

I must do my homework now. I'll email you again soon.

四、听下面的一段独白，根据独白内容完成下列各题。

My name is Peter and I'm thirteen years old. I live in Washington and I go to St. Mary's School. I get up at half past seven in the morning and I have breakfast at eight o'clock. For school I wear school uniform. I go to school by school bus. School starts at half past nine and we have six lessons a day. We learn English, math, geography, history, science, French and art. I like math and art, but I don't like French. Lunch is at one o'clock in the afternoon. I have lunch at school. In the afternoons we have lessons or sports. They begin at two o'clock. School finishes at a quarter to four and I go home. Before supper I read or play with my friends. We have supper at six o'clock and then I do my homework at half past seven. After homework I usually watch television. I go to bed at ten o'clock.

Section 2

一、听下面的一首诗，请将诗中所缺的内容补充完整。

I listen to the trees, and they say:
"Be true to yourself.
Stand alone, and stand together.
Be brave.
Be patient.
With time, you will grow."

I listen to the wind, and it says:
"Breathe.
Take care of yourself — body, mind, and spirit.
Take time.
Be quiet.
Listen from your heart.
Forgive."

I listen to the mountains, and they say:
"Be there.
Be honest.
Be trustworthy.
Do what you say you're going to do.
Be true, genuine, and real.
Speak from the heart.
Don't cheat."

I listen to the flowers and small plants, and they say:
"Be humble.
Be simple.
Respect the beauty of small things.
Respect the beauty of humility and truth.
Let go of perfectionism.
Love yourself as you are; it opens the door to change.
Practice acceptance."

I listen to the moon, and it says:
"Love.
Share love.
Make love.
Be romantic — touch and caress.
Allow yourself to be loved.
Be gentle, kind, and understanding."

I listen to the earth, and it says:
"I am your mother.
I give you life.

Respect all that is around you. "

二、听句子，然后从 A，B，C 三个选项中选出一个与你所听到的句子意思一致或最接近的选项。

1. I'm not sure of his coming.
2. What fine weather it is!
3. Tom sent his classmate a card to wish him a happy birthday.
4. John doesn't look like his father.
5. Robert has fifteen books and fifteen pencils.

三、听下面的一段对话，根据对话内容选择最佳答案，并将代表该答案的字母填在题前的括号内。

W: Oh, Jack. When did you get back from China? How was your tour?

M: Last week. I visited Shanghai and Guilin.

W: Which city did you like better?

M: Well, it's hard to say. Shanghai is much bigger than Guilin. It's the biggest city in China. There's a great variety of goods in the stores and the downtown area is always crowded.

W: What's Guilin like?

M: Guilin is much prettier than Shanghai. The city is famous for its green hills, clear water, fantastic caves and rocks.

W: It seems you had a wonderful trip. I'm thinking of visiting these two cities sometime next year.

四、听下面的一段材料，完成各个小题。

Our world is getting smaller and smaller. We can fly around the world in less than 50 hours. The newest plane can fly at 600 miles an hour. You can have breakfast in Tokyo and supper in Paris.

But hundreds of years ago, it took people a long time to go around the world. Magellan's men were the first to make that trip. They went by ship and it took them more than two years. On September 20, 1510, he left Spain with five ships and 240 men. He was killed in the Philippines. More than two years later, on December 21, 1512, only one of the five ships with just 31 men returned to Spain.

Magellan's trip taught us that the world is round and that people can go around the world.

Section 3

一、听下面的一篇短文，按要求完成各个小题。

The best way of learning a language is by using it. The best way of learning English is to talk in English as much as possible. There may be times when people will speak too quickly and you cannot understand them, and you may get your words mixed up in answering them and they might not understand you. Don't be unhappy if people seem to laugh at your mistakes. If you keep your sense of humor, you can always have a good laugh over the mistakes you make. It's much better for people to laugh at your mistakes than to be angry because they don't understand what you are saying. The most important rule for learning English is "Don't be afraid of making mistakes". Everyone makes mistakes.

二、听下面五段对话，根据对话内容选择相应的图片，并将代表该答案的字母填在题前的括号内。

1. M: The summer holiday is coming! Where should I go?
   W: How about Japan?
   M: I want to go to some place which has a long history.
   W: Egypt is a good choice.
   M: That sounds great.
2. W: Wow! Isn't it hot today?
   M: Yes, very hot.
   W: And look at those clouds, big black clouds over there.
   M: Yes, there are some big clouds. I hope it rains.
3. W: Are you free tomorrow morning? I want to talk with you.
   M: Sorry, I will have a meeting at noon so I will prepare for it at that time.
   W: How about tomorrow night? I will phone you. We can talk through the line.
   M: OK, that's good.
4. M: I'm going to Beijing next week.
   W: What for?
   M: Go on a business trip.
   W: How do you go there? By train or by plane?
   M: I prefer by train. It is cheaper, safer and more comfortable.
5. M: Do you keep any pets?

W: Yes, I have a parrot.

M: Why don't you keep a rabbit? It's lovely and smart.

W: My mother says that rabbits, cats and dogs are very dirty.

三、听下面一篇短文，按要求完成各个小题。

Do you know how to grow pumpkins? Farmers plant the seeds of pumpkins in a greenhouse in spring. The ground is dark and wet in the greenhouse. Then farmers wait for three weeks. The seeds grow into little plants. The plants have roots under the ground. They have leaves above the ground. Farmers take the plants to the field and plant them in the ground on little hills. They water the pumpkin plants. The plants grow bigger and bigger. The leaves are heart-shaped. Yellow bell-shaped flowers grow into little pumpkins. The pumpkin plants need water and sunlight. Pumpkins grow very quickly. In autumn the pumpkins become big enough for the farmers to pick and sell at the market.

Section 4

一、听下面十个句子，把所听到的句子写在下面的横线上。

1. Jack can play basketball very well.
2. Watching TV is my favourite hobby.
3. She plays the piano three times a week.
4. It is relaxing to climb the mountains and ride a horse.
5. How does the mother go to the shop?
6. Jerry is reading under an umbrella on the beach.
7. The girl in a blue dress is my sister.
8. Sandy needs 40 minutes to go to school on foot.
9. Does the woman try the sweater on?
10. The children in England are very lucky for they don't have many classes and much homework.

二、听下面五段对话，根据对话内容选择相应的图片，并将代表该对话的序号写在图片下的括号内。

1. M: This is a nice card, Jenny. Whom are you going to send it to?

   W: I'm going to send it to my sister. It is for her favourite festival. She likes this festival a lot because she likes the colorful eggs. I will send this card to my sister in spring.

2. M: Do you like Halloween?

W: Yes, I like this festival very much. Every October I usually knock on neighbours' doors and say "Trick or Treat" for candies. And I also like jack-o'-lanterns.

3. M: It's the most important traditional Chinese festival, isn't it?

W: Certainly, all the relatives will sit together to have a big meal. The children can play fireworks and receive lucky money.

4. M: Did you buy presents for your friends?

W: Not yet. Tomorrow I will buy all the presents and a tree for my family. And then I will put these presents under the beautiful tree.

5. M: Do you like moon-cakes? I think they are delicious.

W: No, I don't like sweet food. But I like enjoying the full moon. And I like the weather in Autumn.

三、听下面一段短文，根据短文内容选择最佳答案。

Scientists are trying to make deserts into useful land once again. They want to bring water to deserts, so people can live and grow food. They are learning a lot about deserts but more and more of the earth is becoming deserts. Scientists may not be able to change deserts. They think that people make deserts by doing bad things to the earth.

Some places on the earth don't get much rain but they don't become deserts. This is because plants are still growing there. Small green plants and grass are very important to dry places. Plants don't let the hot sun make the earth become even drier. Plants don't let the wind blow the dirt away. When a little bit of rain falls, the plants hold the water. Without plants, it will be easier for land to become a desert.

四、听下面一段电影录音，完成下列各题。

(略)

Section 5

一、听下面一段对话，根据对话内容选择最佳答案，并将代表该答案的字母填在题前的括号内。

W: Can you imagine the home in the future?

M: Fascinating! It'll be computerized.

W: Computerized?

M：Yes. You needn't always bring your keys.

W：Yes? You mean that we'll not need to close our door when we go out?

M：No. Your door will read only the fingerprints of your own family members and open when you put your fingers on the button. Besides, all the housework will be controlled and done by the computer.

W：Then we'll have more time to study and enjoy ourselves.

M：And more time to join the community activities.

二、听下面一段短文，根据短文内容选出最佳答案。

I go in for a lot of sports in my spare time, among them are running, swimming and some ball games. Because of my heavy schedule, I can hardly go to play ball games very often. So most of the time I like going to swim with my friends.

Swimming is considered as one of the most popular sports in the world. Many people like it because it is not so exhausting as running or playing basketball. But it can make people cool, relaxed and comfortable, especially in summer. Swimming in the cool water, taking deep breath, people may have a sense of refreshment. Besides, it can also make people energetic by providing an opportunity for people to get enough exercise. The last but not the least is that it has become more and more popular with people of all ages. That's why all kinds of people, both the old and the young, can be found in the swimming pool during the summer time.

There is no doubt that swimming is the best and most popular sport in summer. People can get entertainment and relaxation while they are in cool water. It makes people stronger, happier and more energetic.

三、听下面两段材料，根据所听内容完成各个小题，并将代表最佳答案的字母填在题前的括号内。

听下面的一段电影片段，完成第 1 ~3 题。

（略）

听下面的原声录音，完成第 4 ~6 题。

（略）

四、听下面一段独白，请把独白中的每一句话完整地记录下来。

Look at the picture. This is a British Family. Jerry is an English boy. He is 11 years old now. He is a student of an international school. He is good at all subjects, and all his teachers like him. This is Jerry's father. He is a computer engineer. He is 40 years old. But he works in Germany now. This is Jerry's mother. She is a teacher. She is 38. Jerry's parents like him very much. They are a happy family.

Unit 15

Section 1

一、听下面关于职业的十个单词，并将它们写在横线上。

1. baker 2. barber 3. butcher 4. dentist 5. engineer
6. lawyer 7. nurse 8. policeman 9. scientist 10. postman

二、听下面的十个句子，根据所听内容选出相应的答语，并将代表该答案的字母填在题前的括号内。

1. Merry Christmas!
2. What time did you get up this morning?
3. How do you usually go to school?
4. Is your father a teacher or a doctor?
5. You are late again.
6. Which subject do you like best?
7. How old is your cousin?
8. Excuse me. May I use your bike?
9. I'm sorry, I have broken your glasses.
10. Whose car is that?

三、听下面的十句话，根据句意选出相应的图片，并将代表该图片的字母填在题前的括号内。

1. The upper line is longer than the other line.
2. The man with the mustache is shorter than the other man.
3. Both the man and the woman are seated at the table.
4. Sally signed her name at the bottom of the check.
5. The man wearing a cap is in the third row.
6. Sandy and Sue like watching the others dance.
7. A group of children are playing in the park.
8. Kelly is locking the door.

9. The full moon looks lovely in the starry night sky.
10. Half of the circles are black.

四、听下面三段独白，根据独白内容回答问题。

听第一段独白，回答1～2题。

Mr. White likes coffee. He drinks a lot of it. He has one cup for breakfast, another at ten, and another at eleven. He drinks two cups for lunch. His wife tells him, "You drink too much coffee."

听第二段独白，回答3～4题。

Hebie likes collecting stamps. She has 5 American stamps. After that, her father gives her 3 Italian stamps. Her mother gives her 4 Chinese stamps. And her brother gives her 2 French stamps. So she has many stamps now.

听第三段独白，回答5～6题。

Kathy doesn't like coffee or stamps. She likes candy. She eats a lot of it. She has two pieces after breakfast, another after lunch, another after class, and three for dessert at dinner. Her mother tells her, "You eat too much candy."

Section 2

一、听下面一首歌，根据歌词填空。

Lemon Tree
I'm sitting here in the boring room
It's just another rainy Sunday afternoon
I'm wasting my time, I got nothing to do
I'm hanging around, I'm waiting for you
But nothing ever happens, and I wonder
I'm driving around in my car
I'm driving too fast, I'm driving too far
I'd like to change my point of view
I feel so lonely, I'm waiting for you
But nothing ever happens, and I wonder
I wonder how, I wonder why
Yesterday you told me about the blue-blue sky
And all that I can see is just the yellow lemon tree
I'm turning my head up and down

I'm turning, turning, turning, turning, turning around
And all that I can see is just another lemon tree

二、听下面七段独白，根据独白内容依次写出七种职业。

1. I spend most of my day in front of the typewriter. We have so many letters to send out every day.

2. Well, the first thing I have to do every morning is to go round and give everyone their post.

3. Yes, it's a wonderful job. I like teaching. I also like the long holidays. The students are very nice, too.

4. I love my work. I see so many new books. I like reading. When no people come to borrow books, I just stand there and read.

5. It's an interesting job, but I often have to work long hours at the hospital. I'm good to my patients.

6. I've always wanted to do this kind of job. I love cars and engines. When I'm running on the road, I feel so good, and I have so many people with me in the bus.

7. It's all right. I like working in the fields. It's hard sometimes, but I enjoy the life in the country.

三、听下面五段小对话，根据对话内容回答相应的问题，并将代表该答案的字母填在题前的括号内。

1. M: Can you tell me when I can come to see the dentist, nurse?
W: Let me see. Today is Wednesday. Maybe it is OK two days later from now. Oh, no, three days, I think.

2. M: I must catch the 9:15 flight to Japan. It's nearly 8 o'clock now. Can you drive me there?
W: No hurry. I'll try to drive you there in 10 minutes.

3. M: Which box is the better of the two?
W: Er... I prefer the smaller one to the bigger one.
M: So do I.

4. M: What does your sister do?
W: She was a teacher 3 years ago, but now she is a reporter, and she wants to be a doctor.

5. M: How's the weather in Wuhan today? I'm going to visit my aunt there.
W: It's windy and cloudy.
M: That's too bad. Here in Tianjin there's no cloud at all.

四、听下面一段独白，在图片人物上方标出其名字所属序号。

At my grandfather's birthday party last night, everybody listened to American music and danced. My sister Sophie wearing a pair of glasses sang my grandfather's favourite songs all evening, and my brother Jack played the guitar. His best friend Tim ate a lot of delicious food. My grandmother and grandfather sat in the living room and looked at old photographs. We laughed all the time. What did I do at my grandfather's birthday party? I danced to the music in the middle of the living room all the time.

Section 3

一、听下面一篇文章，根据文章内容填空。

Early Monday morning is usually a very busy time in Cambridge. Men and women usually rush to their jobs. Some people walk to work, some people drive, and others take the bus. Children usually go to school. Some children walk to school, some children take the school bus, and others ride their bicycles. The city is usually very busy. Trucks deliver food to supermarkets, mail carriers deliver mail to homes and businesses, and police officers direct traffic at every corner.

二、听下面六段独白，根据独白内容选择相应的图片，并将独白序号与图片连线。

1. It is a ball game between two teams which try to kick the ball.
2. It is a game played by two teams of five people who score points by throwing a large ball through an open net hanging from a metal ring.
3. It is a game in which two teams use their hands to hit a large white ball backwards and forwards over a high net without allowing the ball to touch the ground.
4. It is a game played between two or four people in a court which tries to hit a small green ball across a central net with rackets.
5. It is a game played between two or four people on a specially prepared table and the players strike a small ball across a central net.
6. It is an indoor game in which a large heavy ball is rolled along a wooden track to knock down bottle-shaped objects.

三、听下面一篇短文，根据短文内容将下列活动排序。

Mary works hard in an office all week. This weekend she will be very busy as usual. On Saturday morning, Mary will get up early. Her friends will drive her to

Boston. They will have lunch at a restaurant there. Then they will visit Harvard University. In the evening, they will go to a concert by the Boston Symphony Orchestra. They will enjoy two symphonies by Beethoven there. On Sunday they will visit other interesting places of the city. Mary will go to the airport and fly home in the afternoon. She will have a good time in Boston.

四、听下面一段短文，根据短文内容判断下列句子的正误，将T（正确）或F（错误）填入题前的括号内。

Bob is studying in a village school. There are two hills not far from his home. There is a valley between the two hills. The school is in the middle of the valley. He walks to school every day. There is a small river next to the school, there is a stone bridge over the river. There is a big playground in front of the teaching building. There are some big trees behind the classroom building and the children often read and play under the trees after school. There are many fields near the school. When autumn comes, all the teachers and students will help farmers with their harvest.

Section 4

一、听下面一篇短文，请把短文中空缺的部分补充完整。

We usually say that people have five senses. Senses are the way that we know what is happening around us. The five main senses are sight, hearing, touch, taste and smell. Each sense usually depends on one organ of the body. This organ receives the information and then the nerves send this information to the brain. For example, eyes control sight, ears control hearing and skin controls touch. Taste depends on the tongue and smell depends on the nose. There are also other important senses. There is the sense of balance, which stops us from falling down. We also have senses of hunger, thirst, heat and cold.

二、听下面三段小对话，回答1 ~6 题。

听第一段对话，回答1 ~2 题。

W：What are you going to do at five?

M：I'm going to make a model airplane.

W：Who is going with you?

M：Tom and Jerry of course. And you?

W：I'm going to the library for some information about my essay.

听第二段对话，回答3 ~4 题。

M：Are you going out，Mum?

W：Yes. I have just received a phone call from a patient. I have to go and give him some treatment.

M：When are you back?

W：I can't tell，maybe in about one or two hours. If he is serious，I shall stay there longer.

M：Shall I do the cooking?

W：Well，if your father comes back as usual，you may do it.

听第三段对话，回答5 ~6 题。

M：Excuse me，I'm a new student，so I don't know how to borrow a book.

W：OK. You may fill in this card and give it to me.

M：How many books can I borrow at a time?

W：Three. And you can renew the books if you haven't finished them.

M：Fine，thanks.

三、听下面一段独白，选出独白内容所涉及活动的图片，并将图片的序号排序。

I'm going to be very busy this weekend. On Friday evening，I'm going to get together with my friends from college. We're going to have dinner，and then we're going to a concert. On Saturday morning，I have to clean my apartment because my parents are going to visit me in the afternoon. In the evening，we're going to go bowling. On Sunday I'm going to teach my Sunday school class in the morning，I'm going to a soccer game in the afternoon，and I'm going to wash my clothes in the evening. How about you? What are you going to do this weekend?

四、听下面一段电影录音，完成下列各题。

（略）

Section 5

一、听下面一段对话，根据对话内容选择最佳答案，并将代表该答案的字母填在题前的括号内。

M：Hello! Alan. I hear you're going on holiday. Where are you going?

W：Oh，I don't know. I'm going overseas for a month. But I don't know where.

M：Well，if you want to have a good time，I think you could go to Paris.

W: Paris?

M: If you want to drink good wine.

W: Yes, but I don't like Paris.

M: Oh, if you want to ski, you could go to Switzerland.

W: But I can't ski very well.

M: What about Hong Kong?

W: Hong Kong? What could I do in Hong Kong? Shopping?

M: Yes. It's a good place for shopping. Hong Kong is called "shoppers' paradise."

W: Mumm. Well, you see. I have a problem.

M: What's your problem?

W: The trip that I'm going on is a prize I won with Italian Airlines. And they only allow me to go to three places—Paris, Beijing and Rome.

M: Well, if you go to Beijing, I'm sure you'll have a good time. And also you can try different delicious Chinese food. And if you go to Rome, you can visit many places of great interests.

W: OK, then. Beijing, it is.

二、听下面十段小独白，分辨是下图中 A，B，C，D 哪个人所说的话，并将独白序号写在下面的横线上。

1. All this hard work is making me thirsty. I want to drink a glass of cold water.
2. I want to make my skin darker. The best way is to lie in the sunshine.
3. This is the life—sitting outside in the shade on a hot day.
4. There is nothing like swimming for exercise. It's good for the body.
5. This story is so interesting. I love reading story books.
6. The grass is so tall now that it's impossible to finish the job.
7. The sunshine is too strong so it's better to have some sunblock.
8. Being in the cool water sure does feel good on a hot day like this.
9. When I finish with this book, I am going to start another one.
10. I am sweating so much. My T-shirt is wet. When I finish this job, I think I will go jump in the pool.

三、听下面两段材料，根据所听内容完成各个小题，并将代表最佳答案的字母填在题前的括号内。

听下面一首歌，回答 1 ~3 题。

(略)

听下面一则录音，回答 4 ~7 题。

(略)

四、听下面一段独白，请把独白中的每一句话完整地记录下来。

I work as a history teacher in a school. At weekends, I go to the cinema a lot. I often go alone, but sometimes my friend comes, too. My husband never comes with me. He is always busy. I buy chocolates to eat during the film. I usually enjoy this night out very much. I hardly want to see the same film twice, but I do if it's really good. I always miss my Saturday night films. It is my favourite way of relaxing.

Unit 16

Section 1

一、听下面一段独白，根据独白内容填上所缺的单词。

I live in a small town near South London. Lots of people in this town do the same thing at the same time every weekday. Every morning, Mr. Brain walks past the town bank at 7 o'clock. He's on his way to his job at the railway station. He must get ready for the first morning train. And just when he walks past the bank, John Smith's fruit shop is open. I can always see them saying hello to each other.

二、听下面五段对话，根据所听到的内容填写下列表格。

1. W: Which bus can I take to get to the Wuhan Zoo, please?
   M: Either a 105 or a 107.
   W: And how often do they leave?
   M: Every five minutes.
2. W: What is the number of the bus to the Summer Palace, please?
   M: That's a Number 332.
   W: Does it go very often?
   M: Oh, yes. Every 4 minutes.
3. W: I want to get a bus to the East Lake, please.
   M: Yes, you can take a Number 320 or a Number 332 bus.
4. W: Is there a bus to the airport here, please?
   M: Yes, Number 938 is a long-distance bus. It goes to the airport.
   W: And when does it leave?
   M: There's one every half an hour.
5. W: Which bus should I take to go to the People's Hospital, please?
   M: The People's Hospital? That would be Number 35 or 44.
   W: And will they be very crowded?
   M: Yes. I suppose so.

三、听下面四段对话，根据对话内容选出最佳图片，并将代表该图片的序号填在题前的括号内。

听第一段对话，回答 1 ~2 题。

W：Can you help me out? I'm trying to find a post office.

M：Go straight and make a right turn. It's near a bank.

W：Should I take a bus?

M：No, it's only a five minutes' walk.

W：Thank you very much.

听第二段对话，回答 3 ~4 题。

W：Would you go to the cinema with me this afternoon?

M：Well, I'm meeting an old friend of mine at 4 pm.

W：Where are you going to meet him?

M：At the airport.

听第三段对话，回答 5 ~6 题。

M：Have you got any plan for the weekend?

W：Yeah, I'm really excited. I'm going to New York for a couple of days.

M：What are you going to do in New York?

W：I'm visiting a friend. Oh, here comes the bus. I have to leave now. Bye.

M：Bye.

听第四段对话，回答 7 ~8 题。

M：Hello. This is Jim speaking.

W：Hello, Jim. This is Linda. Tomorrow a good friend of mine will meet you at the airport and drive you to my flat.

M：What does he look like?

W：He is a young man in his early twenties. He is tall, strong and handsome. And he wears glasses.

M：OK, thank you. See you then.

四、听下面一段材料，根据内容判断下列句子的正误，将 T（正确）或 F（错误）填入题前的括号内。

Joe and Bob are two brothers. They have the same habits and hobbies. They both get up late. They both play the piano well. They both draw pictures beautifully. However, sometimes they are different from each other. Joe does his homework carefully, but Bob doesn't. Joe eats slowly, but Bob eats very fast. Joe helps his mother gladly, but Bob hates housework.

Section 2

一、听下面一首诗，请将诗中所缺内容补充完整。

What is pink? A rose is pink
By the fountain's brink.
What is red? A poppy's red
In its barley bed.
What is blue? The sky is blue
Where the clouds float through.
What is white? A swan is white
Sailing in the light.
What is yellow? Pears are yellow
Rich and ripe and mellow.
What is green? The grass is green
With small flowers between.
What is violet? Clouds are violet
In the summer twilight.
What is orange? Why, an orange,
Just an orange!

二、看下面的图片，你将听见十句描述本图片的句子。根据图片判断句子的正误，将 T（正确）或 F（错误）填在横线上。

1. You can see ten people in the picture.
2. There are two people answering the phone.
3. This is a three-story building.
4. There are three people wearing glasses.
5. All the people are in the building.
6. A boy and a girl are washing the car.
7. There is a door-bell beside the door.
8. There is a boy listening to music.
9. From the picture we can see it is winter.
10. All the people are standing.

三、听下面十段小对话，根据对话内容选择最佳答案，并将代表该答案的字母写在题前的括号内。

1. M：Look at the walls in the restaurant. They are red.
W：So they are! The color red makes people hungry.
2. M：May I see the menu, please?
W：Here you are, sir. I'll be back for your order in just a minute.
3. M：The rain has lasted for three days. Rainy days make me sad.
W：The radio says that it will be sunny in two days.
4. M：Is Linda reading a newspaper?
W：No, she is watching TV.
5. M：Fu Mingxia was born on November 10, 1985 in Shanghai, China.
W：Yes, she started diving in 1991 and joined the national team in 1998.
6. W：David, how do you often go to school?
M：I took a bus before, but now I often go to school on foot.
7. M：Excuse me. Do you mind if I sit here?
W：No, of course not.
8. M：Would you like a cup of coffee?
W：Well, I'd rather have a cup of tea if you don't mind.
9. W：Do you know what time the concert begins?
M：At 9：15.
W：Oh, I got here at nine. It's a little early.
10. M：I hear you are going boating tomorrow?
W：No, I'm going fishing with my friends.

四、听下面一段长对话，根据对话内容填空。

M：Good afternoon.
W：Good afternoon. We'd like to book a room, please.
M：Fine, what kind of room would you like?
W：A single room with a bath and a double bed.
M：Yes, that's OK. Could you tell me your name?
W：Yes, it's Becky Wakeman. That's B-E-C-K-Y and the surname is W-A-K-E-M-A-N.
M：OK. I've got that. And your nationality?
W：Polish.
M：And how long will you be staying?
W：Just 3 nights. Can you tell me the price?
M：Yes, it's 95 dollars per night, breakfast included. And could I take your passport

number?

W：It's EG6662781.

M：Fine, and how will you pay, Mrs. Wakeman?

W：With a Visa Card.

M：Right, here's your key and your room number is 19, on the first floor.

W：Thank you.

Section 3

一、听下面十个句子，把你所听到的句子写在下面的横线上。

1. Wash your hands.
2. Open the packet.
3. Shut the books.
4. Hold my umbrella.
5. Look at that building.
6. Listen to this bell.
7. Show me your new dress.
8. Use the subway.
9. Don't play in the street.
10. Don't cross between two cars.

二、听下面一段长对话，根据对话内容将对话中的地点写在食物下的横线上。

M：Tell us about your trip, Kelly.

W：Well, I want to visit a lot of places. Let's see. First, I want to see San Francisco.

M：San Francisco? Oh, San Francisco is famous for its bread. Try the bread there. It smells and tastes just wonderful.

W：Hmm, OK. Next, I want to go to Seattle.

M：Seattle? Oh, the apples are terrific in Seattle. Try the apples. They are delicious. People also drink a lot of coffee in Seattle. There are many little coffee shops. Go to a coffee shop in Seattle, and have their special coffee.

W：Oh, okay. Eat apples and visit coffee shops in Seattle. Next is Chicago. What's Chicago famous for? Lakes? Tall buildings?

M：Eat pizza in Chicago. The pizza in Chicago is great. Do you want to go to New York?

W：Sure. New York is the next city.

M：New York has delicious cheesecake. Don't miss the cheesecake in New York.

W：Yes, and my last stop is Boston.

M：Boston? Boston is famous for its lobster. Don't miss it.

W：I won't. Thank you.

三、听下面两篇短文，根据短文内容选择最佳答案。

听第一篇短文，完成1~4题。

Last night I went to bed early. As I was sleeping, I was woken up by some noise. I listened and heard the noise come from the living room. I got up and went to have a look. When I went into the living room, I saw something black. Then I saw the window was open. I took out a gun from a drawer. Suddenly the black thing jumped and ran out of the window. I was so afraid that I dropped my gun.

听第二篇短文，完成5~8题。

It was a warm day in September. The White family is sitting in the yard, drinking coffee and talking together. They are very happy because next month is going to be a very good month for the whole family.

Abby White is going to work in New York. Jason White is going to study in Cambridge University. Betty White is going to get married. Jimmy White is going to get his driver's license. He's going to buy a used car. Mr. and Mrs. White are going to take a vacation in Hawaii after their daughter's wedding. They will fly to Hawaii.

The White family is really happy today, for next month is going to be a happy month for all of them.

Section 4

一、听下面一篇短文，填上所缺内容。

20 years ago, Mr. and Mrs. Brown lived in London. Mr. Brown was a dentist. His wife worked in a school. She taught history. Mr. and Mrs. Brown went to work together by car. Mrs. Brown drove because her husband couldn't drive. There were three children in the Brown family. The Browns had two boys and a girl. Peter was 14. Martin was older but he was shorter than his brother. Susan was the oldest. She didn't live with her family. She worked in a hotel.

二、听下面一段采访对话，根据对话内容完成表格。

Reporter：Hello, Mike Li. It's nice to meet you.

Li：Hello. It's nice to meet you, too.

Reporter: You are a very famous gongfu actor, Mike Li. Were you born in Hong Kong?
Li: No. I was born in Beijing. I was born in April, 1965.
Reporter: When did you start to have your wushu training?
Li: In 1971, when I was six years old.
Reporter: Have you won any medals?
Li: Yes. I won three national gold medals in the 1970s.
Reporter: Did you go to a film school to study acting?
Li: No, I didn't. I made my first film in 1985.
Reporter: How many films have you made?
Li: More than twenty.
Reporter: Wow! Did you make all your films in Hong Kong?
Li: I made some films in Hong Kong. I also made some films in Hollywood and other places.
Reporter: I know you made a very popular film in 1998.
Li: Yes, in 1998 I made my first Hollywood film.
Reporter: Yes, it was very successful. Thank you for this interview, Mike Li.
Li: It's my pleasure.

三、听下面一篇短文，根据短文内容选出代表 Sam 和 Lily 周末活动的图片，并填在相应的横线上。图片可以循环使用。

Sam and Lily have a lot to do at weekends. Every Friday afternoon they do their homework. Every Friday night they go to a party. They dance all evening and come home very tired.

On Saturday mornings during the winter, Lily has band practice, and Sam plays on the basketball team. In the summer they go outside to play soccer. Sometimes they go to the beach. There they swim and lie in the sun. On Saturday nights they go to a movie or a disco with their friends.

On Sundays they go to museums, or go skating. In the summer they also spend Sundays in the park or at the beach. They like fresh air. Sometimes they visit their relatives in other parts of the city. On Sunday evenings they do their homework and they get things ready for school the next day. Lily and Sam like the city, and they always enjoy themselves at weekends.

四、听下面两段材料，根据所听内容完成各个小题，并将代表最佳答案的字母填在题前的括号内。

听下面一则录音，回答 1 ~4 题。
(略)

听下面一段电影片段，回答5 ~7 题。

(略)

Section 5

一、听下面一段介绍华盛顿的材料，完成下列各小题。

Good morning, everyone. I'd like to welcome you to Washington, D. C. Our tour is going to take you around the nation's capital this morning. I am Anderson and I'll be your guide. The tour will take two hours, so we will be back about noon.

We are starting at the Capitol Building. The US congress meets here. Next is the Washington Monument. It is such a beautiful tall monument that it has become one of the most popular sights in Washington. And there is the White House. The president and his family live in it. If you have time, you should take a tour of the White House and see the rooms where the American president lives.

Now we are coming to the Lincoln Memorial. This is one of the most loved places in America, because Abraham Lincoln was such a great man. Now the bus is going across the Potomac River to Arlington National Cemetery. Many American heroes are buried there.

If you have any questions about Washington, please ask me. I hope you have enjoyed seeing Washington, D. C. with me.

二、听下面一段长对话，根据对话内容回答下列各题。

W: Hi, Sam, getting ready for a vacation in the USA?

M: Hello. Oh, yes, I'm just checking my baggage.

W: You must be very excited about it. Where are you visiting in the States?

M: Los Angeles.

W: Have you ever been there before?

M: No, never. This is my first time.

W: Are you going to visit New York?

M: Yes, I'll spend a couple of days there, too.

W: Have you gotten your plane tickets yet?

M: Yes, it's right in the envelope over there.

W: You already booked a hotel?

M: Yes, a single room.

W: And your passport and visa?

M：Yes. That's OK. By the way，is there anything you want me to get for you in the States?

W：That's very kind of you. But no，thanks.

M：OK，then can you do me a favor?

W：Yes?

M：Can you water my plants and take care of my cat?

W：Sure，I'll even talk to them every morning like you do.

三、听下面两段材料，根据所听内容完成各个小题，并将代表最佳答案的字母填在题前的括号内。

听下面一段电影片段，回答1～3题。

（略）

听下面一则录音，回答4～6题。

（略）

四、听下面一段独白，请把独白中的每一句话完整地记录下来。

There are about 23 million homes in Britain. Most British people live in small families. A British family usually has got two to four people. But in a quarter of houses there is only one person. Some of these are old people and some are young people living alone. Many British families have one child. When children are about eighteen or nineteen，they leave their parents' home and go to another place. Some of the children don't come back to visit their parents very often.

Test 1

一、听下面几段录音片断，根据所听内容完成各个小题，并将代表最佳答案的字母填在题前的括号内。每段片断仅播放一遍。

听下面一段录音，完成1~4题。

(略)

听下面的录音，回答5~7题。

It is twenty-three hours thirty, universal time. And here is the news in Special English.

President Barack Obama has called for a new beginning in relations between the United States and Muslims around the world. Mr. Obama spoke at Cairo University in Egypt earlier Thursday. He said violent extremists have used tensions between Muslims and western nations for their own purposes. He said the United States and the Muslim world must work together to stop extremism in all its forms.

The President is now left Egypt and is in Germany. Later he plans to travel to France. He is to meet with European leaders and attend ceremonies honoring the 65th anniversary of D-Day.

听下面的录音，回答8~11题。

(略)

二、听下面五个问句，根据所听内容选出相应的答语，并将代表该答案的字母填在题前的括号内。每个问题仅读一遍。

1. What is Tom's father doing?
2. How much does that book cost?
3. Thank you for such a wonderful night!
4. I really love Christmas.
5. How often do you go to the library?

三、听下面五段对话，根据对话内容选择合适的图片，并将代表该图片的字母填在题前括号内。每段对话读一遍。

1. W: Let's do something crazy! How about riding a motorcycle to California?
   M: Come on! It's too tiring! We are having a rest! Just get on the train.
2. M: I'm going to have a date with Jennifer.

W: Congratulations! If you need any help, just tell me.

M: That's what I really expect to hear. I've got everything I need except a car!

3. W: So what do you want to have?

M: I don't want sweet things, and the seafood in this restaurant is terrible! How about some fruit salad?

W: Fine by me.

4. W: What is your best stuff?

M: How about some fruit? These are the best.

5. M: Football is the No. 1 game in America. No bones about it.

W: To you boys, maybe. In my opinion, roller-skating is far more popular than football. It suits everybody.

四、听下面几段对话，每段对话后有一个小题，从题中所给的选项中选出正确答案填在题前括号内。每段对话仅读一遍。

1. W: Look! The sun is covered by thick clouds! It's going to rain I'm afraid.

M: Yeah! Let's go home quickly!

2. M: Look at the words and picture on this stamp. It's beautiful!

W: Sure it is! It looks just like the shape of England.

3. M: Did you go to Ann's birthday party last Sunday?

W: I was going to go there though I really didn't feel well. But my uncle came to see me from Alaska that afternoon.

4. W: Did you go to Langlang's piano concert?

M: Yes. But I was late. When I got to the theatre at 7:50, it had been on for 15 minutes.

5. M: Can you help me with my English now, Mary?

W: Not until this evening. I'm rather busy now.

五、听下面一段独白，根据所听内容选择合适的答案填在题前的括号内。短文读一遍。

A new day begins in the morning, so I should be fresh, too. And the first thing I do in the morning is to take a shower. After a quick breakfast, I go to school by bike. It's also a good way to exercise. Mornings are always busy. I have four classes in the morning, but only two in the afternoon. So that gives me lots of time to read books. After classes, I usually go to the library to do some reading before dinner. And in the evening, I can sit by the fireplace and enjoy my favorite cartoon—*Sponge Babe*. Oh, what a wonderful day!

Test 2

一、听下面几段录音片断，根据所听内容完成各个小题，并将代表最佳答案的字母填在题前的括号内。每段片断仅播放一遍。

听下面一段录音，完成1～3题。

（略）

听下面一段演讲，完成4～6题。

Bush's Statement On Reagan's Passing Away

This is a sad hour in the life of America. A great American life has come to an end.

I have just spoken to Nancy Reagan. On behalf of our whole nation, Laura and I offered her and the Reagan family, our prayers and our condolences.

Ronald Reagan won America's respect with his greatness, and won its love with his goodness. He had the confidence that comes with conviction, the strength that comes with character, the grace that comes with humility, and the humor that comes with wisdom. He leaves behind a nation he restored and a world he helped save.

During the years of President Reagan, America laid to rest an era of division and self-doubt. And because of his leadership, the world laid to rest an era of fear and tyranny. Now, in laying our leader to rest, we say "thank you."

He always told us that, for America, the best was yet to come. We comfort ourselves in the knowledge that this is true for him, too. His work is done, and now, a shining city awaits him.

May God bless Ronald Reagan.

听下面一首诗歌，完成7～9题。

To Autumn

by John Keats

Season of mists and mellow fruitfulness,
Close bosom-friend of the maturing sun,
Conspiring with him how to load and bless
With fruit the vines that round the thatch-eves run;
To bend with apples the moss'd cottage-trees,
And fill all fruit with ripeness to the core;
To swell the gourd, and plump the hazel shells
With a sweet kernel; to set budding more,

And still more, later flowers for the bees,
Until they think warm days will never cease,
For Summer has o'er-brimm'd their clammy cells.

Where are the songs of Spring? Ay, where are they?
Think not of them, thou hast thy music too,
While barred clouds bloom the soft-dying day,
And touch the stubble-plains with rosy hue;
Then in a wailful choir the small gnats mourn
Among the river sallows, borne aloft
Or sinking as the light wind lives or dies;
And full-grown lambs loud bleat from hilly bourn;
Hedge-crickets sing; and now with treble soft
The red-breast whistles form a garden-croft;
And gathering swallows twitter in the skies.

二、听下面五个句子，并从所给的选项中选出意思相同或相近的一项。每个句子仅读一遍。

1. My car number is 1009.
2. Brad is the English teacher of Class 8.
3. Sandra gives some books to Stanley.
4. Jessie and I are desk-mates.
5. It's time to have breakfast.

三、听下面几段对话，每段对话后有一个小题，从题中所给的选项中选出正确答案填在题前括号内。每段对话仅读一遍。

1. M: Where is David, Amy?
   W: I think he must be in his room because the light in his room is on.
2. W: You are really busy with your patients these days, Paul.
   M: Yes. People catch cold easily on this kind of cold days.
3. M: Sally, why are you in such a hurry?
   W: Oh, my Mum is coming today. I have to get her in the airport.
4. W: Morning exercise is really good for your health. You should keep on doing it.
   M: What about rainy days? I can't exercise in the rain.
   W: You can take a walk in the house.
5. M: The popcorn tastes good! Do you want to have a try?

W：Shhhh！We are here to enjoy the movie but not the popcorn. By the way, there are many other people here.

四、听下面的对话或短文，每段对话或短文后有几个问题。从题中所给的选项中选择最佳答案。每段对话或短文读两遍。

听第一段材料，回答 1 ~2 题。

W：Barry, where did you get that poster?

M：Oh, this one? My father got it for me. He works in a movie theater.

W：It's beautiful.

M：Yes. I like movies about magic. And this *Harry Potter* one is my favorite. How about you?

W：I like it, too. Can your father get one for me?

M：Maybe. Or I can just give this one to you.

W：Really? You are so kind！Thanks a lot！

听第二段材料，回答 3 ~5 题。

W：Hi！May I help you, sir?

M：I'd like something to drink.

W：OK！Juice or tea?

M：Neither. Give me two bottles of pop, please.

W：No problem！Anything else?

M：Yes, a cup of coffee for me and a glass of lemonade for my son.

W：Two bottles of pop, a cup of coffee and a glass of lemonade. OK！Ah, by the way, how many people are there in your group?

M：Just my two daughters, my son and me.

W：All right then, you can sit there. And they are 12 yuan in all.

M：Here you are.

五、听下面一段对话，根据你所听到的内容完成各个小题。对话读两遍。

W：Good evening, sir. Can I help you?

M：Yes, I think I left my digital camera on the train from London earlier today.

W：Did you, sir? Oh, well, in that case we'd better fill in a lost property form. Can you tell me your name?

M：Yes, it's Mark Adams.

W：OK. Your address?

M：You mean in Britain or in the States?

W：How long are you staying?

M：Ah? I've still got a few months in Britain.

W: OK. Then, can you give me your address here?

M: Right. It's 18, Lyndon Drive, Leighton, Essex. Do you want the phone number?

W: Yes. I'd better have that, too.

M: OK. 080945233.

W: Thanks. And you say it was a digital camera. What make and model?

M: It's a Samsung, G302.

W: OK. Got that. Now you say it was the London train. What time did it arrive in Edinburgh?

M: At 4:45 this afternoon.

W: Well. Then if we find it, sir, shall we phone you or write to you?

M: No. I think I'll drop in the day after tomorrow to check out.

W: Right you are, sir! We'll do our best.

Keys

Unit 1

Section 1

一、1. A　2. B　3. B　4. A　5. B
6. A　7. C　8. A　9. A　10. C

二、1. C　2. A　3. A　4. B　5. B

图表一：1 = France，2 = America，3 = Germany，
4 = Japan，5 = Korea

图表二：1 = France，2 = New Zealand，3 = Japan，
4 = Mexico，5 = America

Section 2

一、1. farms　2. harvest　3. body　4. picture　5. thin
6. shapes　7. five　8. twenty-five　9. white

二、1. A　2. B　3. B　4. C　5. C
6. A　7. A　8. C　9. A　10. A

三、(一) 1. A　2. B　3. B　4. C　5. A

(二) 1. dig up the soil, loosen it, turn it over
2. Weather, soil, age
3. its color
4. the winter months
5. cut in thin pieces, other vegetables, they are washed

Section 3

一、1. see　2. voice　3. no　4. head　5. mountain
6. move　7. lose　8. fast

二、1. A　2. C　3. A　4. A　5. B
6. B　7. B　8. B　9. B　10. C

三、(一) 略

(二) Step 1: Add oil
Step 2: Add popcorn
Step 3: Heat popcorn
Step 4: Listen
Step 5: Pay close attention

Step 6：Let the popcorn cool

Step 7：Pour popcorn

Step 8：Add butter

Step 9：Add salt

Step 10：Enjoy

Section 4

一、"I'll show you. There is a man walking down there. Let's see who can make him take off his coat."

The sun agreed, and the north wind went first. He started to blow hard, but the man held his coat more tightly. At last, the north wind gave up.

"Watch me." The sun shone brightly on the man. At first, the man felt warm, so he didn't hold his coat. Then, the sun kept shining, the man finally felt hot and couldn't help taking off his coat.

Now, the sun smiled and said, "Well, what do you think?"

二、1. B	2. A	3. B	4. A	5. B
6. B	7. A	8. C	9. B	10. C

三、(一) 略

(二) Step 1：put them into the water for at least 30 minutes

Step 2：half full of oil and heat to 375 degrees

Step 3：Dry the potatoes

Make sure your potatoes are dry

Step 4：Add potatoes to the pan little by little

Step 5：Fry for about 3 minutes or until golden brown

Step 7：watch them disappear

Section 5

一、1. B	2. A	3. C	4. C	5. A
6. B	7. A	8. C		
二、1. B	2. B	3. A	4. C	5. A
6. C	7. B	8. C	9. B	10. A

三、The secret of success is not so much money as a strong will. A great man is one who has a strong will. In other words, if a man does not have a strong will to win the final victory, he will never succeed in his life. He is no more than a failure.

It is quite obvious that there is no difficult thing in the world, if you make up your mind to do it, you will certainly accomplish it in the not far future.

Unit 2

Section 1

一、1. invention 2. ten 3. sees 4. some 5. Three
6. future 7. smartest 8. next 9. travel 10. people

二、1. B 2. C 3. A 4. B 5. C
6. B 7. A 8. A 9. A 10. C

三、(一) 1. dress 2. MP4 3. shoes 4. camera 5. book
6. winter coats

(二) 略

Section 2

一、1. tigers 2. famous 3. forests 4. scientists 5. 125
6. 1980s 7. 100 8. believed 9. half 10. hunters

二、(一) 1. A 2. B 3. A
(二) 1. B 2. B 3. A 4. A

三、(一) 1. C 2. C 3. C 4. B 5. A
(二) 1. drum 2. fast 3. dance music
4. reducing 5. piano 6. classical music
7. a hard day at work 8. better

Section 3

一、1. Why not
2. judge a book by its cover
3. the early 19th century
4. Why does he want to do that
5. No, that's the problem
6. once he dies
7. I see
8. My teacher didn't tell me that
9. It would take a lot less time
10. I'll get the movie and watch it with you

二、略

三、(一) 1. A 2. C 3. B
(二) 1. 50 2. 8 seconds 3. 3 meters 4. High jump

5. 2 meters 6. 1, 500 meters 7. 5 minutes 8. 10 meters

Section 4

一、1. fills 2. shine 3. open 4. comes 5. covers
6. get 7. like 8. live 9. dream 10. recorded

二、1. A 2. A 3. A 4. C 5. A
6. B 7. C 8. B 9. B 10. B

三、(一) 1. bread 2. 3 packets 3. beer 4. a packet
5. butter 6. 12 bottles 7. milk 8. strawberry
9. tomato 10. 2 bottles

(二) 略

Section 5

一、略

二、1. C 2. B 3. A 4. A 5. B
6. A 7. B 8. A 9. A 10. A

三、Before refrigerators were invented, the next best thing was an ice box. But another way to keep food fresh is to use a cooler. A common design is a tall box with several shelves inside to hold the food. The shelves are pieces of metal with many small holes through them. The sides of the box are covered with pieces of thick cloth.

Bottles of water are placed at the top and bottom of the cooler. The ends of each piece of cloth lie in the water so the cloth stays wet.

The cooler is put outdoors, but not in the sun. Air will pass through the wet cloth. The inside of the box will stay several degrees cooler than the outside. And this may be cool enough to keep foods fresh, at least for a short time.

Unit 3

Section 1

一、1. look at me
2. but you'll never know me
3. I can fool the world
4. who is that girl I see
5. and what I believe in
6. what's inside my heart

7. someone I don't know

二、1. B 2. A 3. B 4. A 5. C
6. A 7. A 8. B 9. C 10. A

三、1. C 2. B 3. C 4. A 5. A
6. A 7. A 8. B 9. A 10. A

Section 2

一、1. He said, "Get out of here with that dog!"
2. The guy says, "But this isn't just any dog... this dog can play the piano!"
3. If he can play that piano, they both can stay... and have a drink.
4. Yes, they did.
5. No, she wanted him to be a doctor.

二、1. A 2. C 3. B 4. C 5. C
6. C 7. B 8. A 9. C 10. B

三、1. C 2. A 3. B 4. D 5. E

四、略

Section 3

一、1. clock 2. himself 3. day 4. again 5. old
6. without 7. life 8. hours 9. know 10. twenty-four

二、略

三、1. A 2. A 3. B 4. A 5. B

四、(一) 1. C 2. A 3. B 4. C 5. A
(二) 1. get up early 2. you can't watch 3. older kids
4. drive a car wherever you want 5. go to bed early

Section 4

一、1. Never lose hope 2. As they always do
3. your dreams will come true 4. So put on a smile
5. Know it will pass

二、1. A 2. B 3. A 4. C

三、1. A 2. C 3. A 4. B 5. C

四、1. B 2. C 3. C 4. C 5. C

五、(一) 1. B 2. C 3. A 4. B 5. C
(二) 1. gift 2. 600 3. 1519 4. 1529
5. make and use

Section 5

一、1. A	2. C	3. C	4. C	5. B
二、1. B	2. A	3. A	4. B	5. A
三、1. B	2. A	3. C	4. B	5. C

四、Millions of people all over the world use the word "OK". In fact, some people say the word is used more often than any other word in the world. "OK" means "all right" or "fine". It is used when people agree with something. You might ask your brother, "Is it okay if I borrow your car?" Or if someone asks you to do something, you might say, "Okay, I will." Still, language experts do not agree about where the word came from.

Some people say it came from the native American Indians. The Indian word "okeh" means the same as the American word "okay". Experts say early explorers in the West spoke the Choctaw language in the nineteenth century. The language spread across the country.

Unit 4

Section 1

一、Dialogue 1:

W: Hi, Herb.

M: How are you?

W: OK.

M: So you've been doing well?

W: Um, yes. I guess you're moving soon.

M: Um, to New York.

W: Oh, I just wanted to say goodbye.

Dialogue 2:

M: Hello, Miss. What will you have?

W: I'll have a glass of milk.

M: Milk? OK. Why are you here alone?

W: I'm waiting for a young girl I met on the net.

M: A 16-year-old who likes computers?

W: How do you know?

M: Heh. Heh. It was just a wild guess. Good luck finding your Internet friend!

二、1. C　2. C　3. A　4. C　5. B

三、1. A　2. C　3. A　4. B　5. C

四、(一) Sugar,　Food processor,　Watermelon,　Dessert bowl,
Ice cream maker,　Lemon juice

(二) 1. small　2. cup　3. taste　4. sweet　5. place
6. cold　7. two　8. ready　9. enjoy

Section 2

一、Do you hear me
I'm talking to you
Across the water across the deep blue ocean
Under the open sky, oh my, baby I'm trying
Boy I hear you in my dreams
I feel your whisper across the sea
I keep you with me in my heart
You make it easier when life gets hard
I'm lucky I'm in love with my best friend
Lucky to have been where I have been
Lucky to be coming home again
Ooohh ooooh oooh oooh ooh ooh ooh ooh

二、1. C　2. A　3. B　4. B　5. A
6. B　7. C　8. C　9. C　10. C

三、A. 1. A photographer　2. A camera

B. Step 1: Choose your clothes.
Step 2: Check your face.
Step 3: Take pictures outside in the morning or before the sunset.
Step 4: Make sure camera is eye level.
Step 5: Lean back.
Step 6: Slightly turn your head.
Step 7: Look at a light source.
Step 8: Keep your eyes open.
Step 9: Smile.

Section 3

一、1. great　2. manager　3. give　4. test　5. thousand
6. easy　7. shop　8. away　9. wrong　10. sold

二、(一) 1. A　2. C　3. A　4. B　5. C

(二) 1. A 2. C 3. B 4. A 5. B

三、(一) 1. Paper 2. A pencil or pen

3. Crayons or colored pencils

(二) G C D E F A

(三) Step 1: Write the word "boy"

Step 2: Draw the eyes

Step 3: Make a jawline

Step 4: Connect the head

Step 5: Draw the hairline

Step 6: Draw the face

Section 4

一、1. Before I came out

2. People don't think of money when they're afraid

3. So I took all the paper money that I could find

4. You don't know my work

5. What is your work

6. I'm a policeman

7. And do you know my work

8. No

9. I'm a writer

10. I'm always telling stories about things that never happened

二、1. C 2. C 3. B 4. C 5. B

6. B 7. C 8. C 9. C 10. C

三、(一) 1. Most of them are fine.

2. He's all right.

3. She thinks that dance music is excellent.

4. Football and basketball.

(二) 1. Mike: Smart.

2. Carol: Fun to be with.

3. Tom: Quiet.

4. Jane: Interesting.

5. Serina: Beautiful and good at math.

6. Dorry: The coolest.

Section 5

一、(一) 1. A 2. B 3. A

(二) 1. 3　　2. they hate school dinners
3. a sandwich bar　　4. healthier food
5. a few sandwiches　　6. cold drinks
7. chips

二、1. C　2. B　3. C　4. B　5. C
6. C　7. A　8. C　9. B　10. C

三、A very special teacher in a high school had a husband who died suddenly of a heart attack. About a week after his death, she shared some of her thoughts with a classroom of students. As the late afternoon sunlight shined through the classroom windows, and when the class was nearly over, she moved a few things aside on her desk and sat down there.

With a gentle look on her face, she stopped and said, "Before class is over, I would like to share with all of you a thought which I feel is very important. Each of us is put here on earth to learn share, love and give... and none of us knows when this wonderful experience will end. It can be taken away at any moment. Perhaps this is why we must make the best of every single day."

Unit 5

Section 1

一、1. finger　2. shoulder　3. neck　4. knee　5. toe
6. arm　7. hair　8. nose　9. head　10. ankle
11. bank　12. hospital　13. office　14. park　15. square
16. restaurant　17. station　18. factory　19. hotel　20. club

二、1. B　2. B　3. C　4. B　5. C
6. A　7. B　8. C　9. A　10. B

三、1. E　2. C　3. A　4. D　5. B

四、1. C　2. A　3. B　4. C　5. A

五、1. C　2. A　3. C　4. C　5. B

Section 2

一、1. police　2. driver　3. barber　4. cook　5. scientist
6. waiter　7. 1,000　8. 8:45　9. 1/5　10. 12
11. 1942.1.8　12. 84695007

二、1. March 7th　2. January 19th　3. November 22nd

4. June 18th　5. September 30th　6. Saturday
7. Thursday, November　8. Wednesday　9. Tuesday
10. Sunday, Monday

三、1. A　2. C　3. A　4. A　5. A

四、1. C　2. B　3. A　4. B　5. A

五、2→5→6→4→1

Section 3

一、1. I hardly eat any fruit and vegetables.
2. Tom is the tallest boy in his class.
3. I didn't finish my homework until 10 o'clock last night.
4. Are you strong enough to lift this box?
5. Mary is good at writing funny stories.
6. The women doctors are from France.
7. Did you enjoy your birthday party yesterday?
8. How long has your brother been on the farm?
9. It is hotter today than yesterday.
10. The Greens usually spend their vacation in some foreign countries.

二、(一) A→C→B→D
(二) B

三、1. A　2. A　3. B　4. B　5. A

四、1. country　2. British　3. American　4. holiday　5. rest
6. postcard

Section 4

一、1. B　2. B　3. C　4. A

二、

way	allowed	new	flower	weak	right	buy	sun
×	√	×	×	√	×	×	√

三、1. take off　2. come in　3. look for　4. get up　5. turn off
6. worry about　7. hurry up　8. look up　9. go over　10. wait for
11. take place　12. laugh at

四、1. B　2. B　3. C　4. A

五、1. B　2. A　3. B　4. A　5. A

六、1. B　2. C　3. B　4. B　5. A

Section 5

一、1. B　2. C　3. A　4. C

二、1. C　2. B　3. A　4. C　5. B

三、1. B　2. C　3. B　4. C　5. B

四、(一) 1. F　2. T　3. T　4. F　5. F

(二) 1. A　2. B　3. A　4. A　5. C

五、Our food is very important. We like eating it, and it makes us strong and healthy. In most countries, people have three or four meals every day. Having a good meal is like filling a car with petrol. It gives us fuel for the work we do. The most important meal is breakfast. Doctors say that if you don't have a good breakfast, you can't work well. Vegetables and fruit are also very important. Our bodies need them to stay healthy. We enjoy sweet food, but we don't need it.

Unit 6

Section 1

一、(A) 1. A. cow　B. chicken　C. beef　D. pork

(A) 2. A. cup　B. knife　C. fork　D. spoon

(D) 3. A. violin　B. piano　C. drum　D. band

(D) 4. A. bus　B. taxi　C. lorry　D. bicycle

(C) 5. A. television　B. refrigerator　C. sofa　D. oven

二、1. C　2. A　3. wider　4. dream　5. heart

6. way

三、W: I had a terrible evening, John! (morning)

M: Oh, Rita. What's happened? (What)

W: Well, I went to the bus stop at once. (as usual)

I waited for twenty seconds but the bus didn't come. (minutes)

M: So, what did you do?

W: I hurried to the station. I decided to take the eight o'clock train. (ran)

But I was too unlucky. I missed the train. (late)

M: Oh, no!

W: So, I went outside and got into a taxi. But the taxi driver went the wrong way. (found)

He got lost! I was late for school again! I got there at nine thirteen!

(thirty)

四、(一) 1. C　2. B　3. A

(二) 1. 6:30, 7:00 am　2. breakfast　3. vegetables　4. C

(三) 1. T　2. T　3. F

Section 2

一、

1. Japan　　A. Washington D. C.
2. Germany　　B. Tokyo
3. France　　C. Berlin
4. America　　D. Paris
5. Russia　　E. Moscow

二、Amy: Hi, Victor. How are you?

Victor: Oh, I'm fine.

Amy: So, are you going to go to class tonight?

Victor: Maybe... But I don't think so.

Amy: Really? What's the matter?

Victor: I don't know. I'm just feeling a little sad.

Amy: Listen. Come with me to class, and after class we can go out for dinner.

Victor: Now that's a good idea. Thanks a lot, Brian. I'm feeling better already.

三、

1. *A Tale of Two Cities*　　A. Mark Twain
2. *The Adventures of Tom Sawyer*　　B. Charles Dickens
3. *A Midsummer Night's Dream*　　C. Jules Verne
4. *Pride and Prejudice*　　D. William Shakespeare
5. *Around the World in 80 Days*　　E. Jane Austen

四、1. C　2. C　3. A　4. C　5. A

五、blackboard, fish bowl, desk, clock

六、1. C　2. B　3. A　4. B　5. B

Section 3

一、1. Can I leave a message?

2. How many pounds of potatoes do you want?

3. I'm going to catch the ten o'clock train.

4. Would you like anything to drink?

5. I'll pick you up around seven thirty.

6. What language did the musician learn to speak?

7. He is one of the most famous singers.

8. Nobody can do it like this.

9. It's easy enough for me to answer the question.

10. How beautiful these flowers are!

二、1. C　2. B　3. B　4. A　5. A

6. B　7. C　8. B　9. A　10. A

三、1. A　2. B　3. A　4. B　5. C

6. A　7. B　8. A

四、1. B　2. C　3. C　4. B　5. A

Section 4

一、1. B　2. B　3. B　4. A　5. C

二、1. B　2. A　3. A　4. C

三、排序: 4-1-5-3-2　连线: 4-E　1-C　5-G　3-F　2-A

四、1. A　2. B　3. C　4. B

五、1. Because he was busy.

2. Because I had got driving license with me.

3. Yes, I did.

4. We should drive on the left side.

5. I go to work by bus every day.

6. It means the woman is very fat.

7. No, she can't.

8. Because she thought the seat was too small.

Section 5

一、1. C　2. B　3. bright　4. smile　5. sunshine

6. side　7. remember

二、1. A　2. C　3. B　4. A　5. B

三、1. C　2. B　3. B　4. C　5. C

6. A　7. B　8. A　9. B

四、Do you know anything about the moon? The moon is smaller than the earth, but the sun is much bigger than the earth. The moon is far from the earth. It's 380, 000 kilometers away. On the earth we see that the moon looks like a cake. There is no air on the moon, so there are no living things there. The side of the moon towards the sun is very hot, while the other side is very cold. People can jump higher on the moon than on the earth and walk more easily there. People can't live on the moon. They have been to the moon. It takes more than three days to get to the moon by spaceship.

Unit 7

Section 1

一、1. pear, watermelon, grapes (fruit)
2. sunflower, bamboo, grass (plants)
3. shoulder, arm, knee (body)
4. coffee, wine, orange juice (drinks)
5. pants, blouse, gloves (clothing)

二、1. A　2. B　3. C　4. B　5. C

三、1. C　2. C

四、1. C　2. G　3. E　4. F　5. D

五、1. B　2. B　3. A　4. C　5. A
6. A　7. C　8. B

Section 2

一、1. look out　2. hurry up　3. have a rest　4. all the time
5. have a cold　6. at the weekend　7. go for a walk　8. on duty
9. by taxi　10. make friends　11. high jump　12. turn off

二、1. A　2. A　3. A　4. B　5. B
6. C　7. B　8. A　9. C　10. C

三、I'm a policeman dressed in blue, here are some things I like to do.
Direct the traffic in your town, help to keep you safe and sound.
It's my job and I like it fine. No one has a better job than mine.
I'm a policeman dressed in blue, I want to be a friend to you.
You can see me every day, I will wave my hand and say.
It's my job and I like it fine. No one has a better job than mine.

四、1—C　2—D　3—E　4—B　5—A

五、7—2—5—1—4—6—3

六、

Self-introduction

Name: David
Place of Birth: New York
Age: eighteen
Major Subject: science
Part Time Job: waiter
Hobbies: hiking, reading and hanging out with friends.

Section 3

一、1. That's why a lot of people are swimming in the river.
2. It's going to be warmer later on.
3. Everyone is here except him.
4. Thousands of people are learning foreign languages in our country.
5. I can see a cat running across the street.
6. Is the museum far from here?
7. Nobody knows what to do next.
8. We will go sailing together next Saturday.
9. There will be more and more deserts in the world.
10. Sometimes young people visit their parents once a year.

二、1. town 2. south 3. dentist 4. history 5. together
6. always 7. nineteen 8. family 9. nurse 10. hospital

三、1. B 2. C 3. B 4. C 5. A
6. C 7. C 8. B 9. C 10. A

四、1. A 2. A 3. C 4. A 5. A

五、1. C 2. A 3. C 4. C 5. B

Section 4

一、1. clean (B) 2. empty (C) 3. heavy (B)
4. wet (A) 5. expensive (B)

二、(一) 排序：3-1-2-4
(二) 1. 1928 2. 1937 3. 1928 4. 1452, 1519
5. 1504 6. 1911 7. 1969

三、1. B 2. B 3. A 4. C 5. B

四、左边从上到下：me—Lucy, my brother—Jim, my grandmother—Susan, my mother—Sally
右边从上到下：my sister—Lily, my grandfather—John, my father—Bill

五、1. F 2. T 3. F 4. T 5. F

Section 5

一、

(1) Green Theater
Name: *Ice Age*
Date: January 12th
Ticket Type: children
Price: £5.5

(2) Blue Theater
Name: *Shrek*
Date: May 23rd
Ticket Type: students
Price: £10

(3) Magic Theater
Name: *Harry Potter*
Date: August 5th
Ticket Type: students
Price: £8. 25

(4) Sky Theater
Name: *Garfield*
Date: July 30th
Ticket Type: kids
Price: £3

(5) Garden Theater
Name: *High School Musical*
Date: October 21st
Ticket Type: adults
Price: £15. 99

二、1. A　2. C　3. C　4. C　5. B

三、1. B　2. A　3. B　4. A　5. A
6. C　7. A　8. B　9. A　10. C

四、Dear Tom,

We're having a wonderful time here. When we arrive in New York, it was rainy, but it's fine now. New York is a beautiful city and people here are very kind. The famous Statue of Liberty is here and we will visit it tomorrow. It was built a hundred years ago and it was really very magnificent. I can't wait to go and see it.

I have bought some souvenirs for you and Bob. I do hope you can come here one day.

Hope to see you soon!

Love,
Sara

Tom Hanks
Oxford Gardens
London
LN34TW
U. K.

Unit 8

Section 1

一、1. ticket　2. gift　3. match　4. forest　5. hotel
6. model　7. postbox　8. lake　9. factory　10. question
11. sugar　12. pork　13. tomato　14. delicious　15. soup

16. beef 17. sandwich 18. vegetable 19. sausage 20. pizza

二、1. B 2. A 3. C 4. B 5. C
6. A 7. C 8. B 9. C 10. B

三、Alice—F Mike—E Lisa—C Roy—A John—D

四、1. B 2. C 3. A 4. A 5. B
6. A 7. B 8. B 9. C 10. C

Section 2

一、1. This is the teachers' reading room.
2. The Summer Palace is one of Beijing's finest parks.
3. It's made from cow's milk.
4. I have just received a present.
5. None of the students knew the answer.
6. You'll leave for Beijing next week, won't you?
7. What is your favourite festival?
8. There is a swimming pool near our house.
9. I was listening to a tape at 9 last night.
10. She invited us to go with her.

二、1. B 2. C 3. A 4. B 5. B
6. B 7. A 8. C 9. C 10. C

三、A. furniture B. cafe C. bookstore /bookshop D. drugstore
E. bank

四、1. baby/child/kid 2. fifth 3. looked after/ took care of
4. big/ large 5. seven/7

五、1. T 2. F 3. F 4. F 5. T

Section 3

一、1. For thousands of years men couldn't fly.
2. I wonder what's wrong with the animal.
3. Let's hurry so that we can get there before supper.
4. He walked such a long way that he felt pretty tired.
5. They made it clear that they didn't agree with you.
6. It's impossible for him to work out this maths problem.
7. It's best for people to wear silk clothes in summer.
8. A third of the land is covered with snow.
9. There is no need to have a further discussion.
10. Thanks to your help, I finished the work on time.

二、1. send　2. truck　3. friend　4. town　5. farm
6. making　7. card　8. nice
三、1. B　2. B　3. B　4. C　5. A
四、1. A　2. C　3. A　4. A　5. C
6. B　7. C　8. C　9. B　10. C
五、5—4—3—1—2—6

Section 4

一、1. B　2. C　3. B
二、1. B　2. B　3. B　4. A　5. C
6. C　7. C　8. C　9. A　10. B
三、1. A　2. B　3. A　4. B　5. A
四、1. fifth/ 5th　2. $115/115 dollars　3. breakfast
4. ID card　5. August 18th
五、1. B　2. C　3. B　4. A　5. B

Section 5

一、M: Mary, have I given you my pictures? (1) shown
W: No, you haven't. Are these your pictures of Canada? (2) New York
M: Yes, they are. I took them last week.
W: Did you take any pictures of the modern buildings there? (3) tall
M: Yes, I took some. Here they are.
W: You took wonderful pictures! Did you enjoy yourselves in New York? (4) have a good time
M: Yes, I did. Have you ever been there?
W: No, I haven't. I've never been there! (5) anywhere
M: Don't you want to go to New York sometime? (6) visit
W: Yes, I do. I'll go there someday.
二、1. B　2. B　3. A　4. C　5. B
三、1. B　2. A　3. A　4. C　5. C
6. B　7. C
四、1. C　2. A　3. C　4. A　5. B

五、We can see walls everywhere in the world. But the Great Wall of China is the longest of all. It is more than 6,000 kilometers long. It was really very difficult to build such a great wall without any modern machines long ago. People had to do all the work by hand. It took many men hundreds of years to build it. The Great Wall has a history of over two thousand years. The men began to build the first part of it about 2,700 years ago. Today it has become a place of interests. Both the Chinese people and foreigners come to visit it.

Unit 9

Section 1

一、1. visit　2. cinema　3. ticket　4. read　5. novel
6. watching　7. holiday　8. beach　9. swimming　10. sunglasses
11. garden　12. plant　13. chatting　14. cooking　15. dish
16. football　17. basketball　18. baseball　19. volleyball　20. golf

二、1. C　2. A　3. A　4. A　5. C
6. B　7. B　8. A　9. C　10. A

三、1. C　2. B　3. C　4. A　5. B
6. C

四、(一) 1. T　2. T　3. F　4. A　5. F
6. F　7. A　8. T　9. A　10. A
11. F　12. T
(二) 1. A　2. B　3. C

Section 2

一、1. end　2. say goodbye　3. fly
4. hands　5. end　6. forever friends

二、1. A　2. B　3. C　4. A　5. A
6. C　7. A　8. B　9. B　10. C

三、1. B　2. C　3. A　4. A　5. B
6. C

四、7—3—2—4—1—6—8—5

五、1. Because he just received a letter from one of his old middle school classmates.
2. Only one or two.
3. Because people move around very much.

Section 3

一、1. go away　2. go over　3. give up　4. give in　5. give away
6. take on　7. take off　8. look after　9. look out　10. look for
11. turn on　12. turn off

二、1. F　2. T　3. F　4. F　5. F
6. T　7. T　8. F

三、Robin—fireman—Canada
Ester—cook—France
Bill—teacher—China
Albert—worker—Australia
Kyo—manager—Japan
Bruce—doctor—America

四、1. C　2. A　3. C　4. C　5. B
6. A

五、

NAME	ADDRESS	TELEPHONE
William Abel	6148 Green St.	586-3208
Thomas Eakins	75 Pine Ave.	926-6832
Alice Moore	279 Woodland Dr.	789-5430
Diana Paxon	12-C Lincoln Ln.	287-3952
James Bingham	5213 Rose Rd.	654-8358

Section 4

一、1. Where are you from?
2. What's wrong with Peter?
3. Do you want to have a job there?
4. We'll meet here tomorrow afternoon.
5. How often does his mother water the flowers?
6. How are you doing today?
7. How many days are there in a week?
8. Which country are you from?
9. Thank you very much for helping me.
10. Excuse me. What is this in English?

二、1. B　2. B　3. B　4. B　5. C
6. A

三、1. B　2. C　3. B　4. B　5. A

四、(一) Lee—Picture Two—New York
Sarah—Picture Three—Aspen
Jewel—Picture One—Acapulco

(二) 1. music, art　2. sports, hot weather
3. mountains, big cities　4. too expensive
5. swim, fish　6. New York

Section 5

一、Robert　David　Michael　Billy

Tom　Robin　Steve　Henry

二、1. B　2. A　3. C　4. B　5. C

6. A　7. A　8. B

三、

Event	Wilmette Elementary School	Lincoln High School	Europe	Munich	UCLA	USC Law School	First Job: With Smith and Jones
Year	1960	1968	1972	1973	1975	1979	1982

四、Dear Peter,

How are you? I'm fine. Spring Festival is coming. As you know, it is the most important festival in China. My family are going to get together during the holiday season. My family and I want to invite you to come.

We are going to have a lot of food on Chinese New Year's Eve. And we are going to watch the Festival programs on CCTV. Then as usual we are going to set off fireworks. On the morning of New Year's Day, my classmates and I are going to visit some old people in the nursing home. We are going to sing songs for them. I hope you can play the violin. We're going to have a good time.

Write back soon.

Yours,

May

Unit 10

Section 1

一、1. street　2. road　3. avenue　4. boulevard　5. corner

6. center　7. block　8. village　9. city　10. town

11. English　12. American　13. Germany　14. Swiss　15. French

16. Japanese　17. Korean　18. Indian　19. Mexican　20. Chinese

二、5, 8, 7, 2, 10, 1, 6, 3, 4, 9

三、1. B　2. A　3. B　4. A　5. C

6. C

四、 Kelly's Schedule (January, 2010)

	Time	Event	With
Monday	7:00	Dinner	Jennifer
Tuesday	7:30	Yoga class	/
Wednesday	8:30	Meeting	English teacher and group members
Thursday	8:00	Lecture	/
Friday	8:00	Movie	Edward
Saturday	7:00	Wesley's birthday party	/

五、(一) 1. F　2. T　3. F　4. T　5. F
(二) 1. A　2. C　3. B　4. C

Section 2

一、1. tell; age　2. hungry　3. driver's　4. around, after
5. because, money　6. first　7. walked, came　8. looking after
9. water, himself　10. on their way

二、1. A　2. B　3. C　4. B　5. C
6. A

三、

Place	Post Office	Citibank	Museum of Modern Art	Macy's	Rexall Drugstore
Open	9:00	9:00	11:00	9:00	8:00
Close	5:00	3:00	6:00	6:45	7:30

四、1. B　2. C　3. A　4. C　5. A
6. B　7. C　8. C　9. C　10. B

五、(一) 1. B　2. B　3. A　4. B　5. B
(二) 1. hurt　2. on my back　3. kind　4. helpful　5. myself

Section 3

一、1. who you'll be　2. Don't you worry　3. make them all come true
4. know just what to do　5. Butterfly fly away

二、(一) 11 +4 +12 +5 +31　6 +3 =9
(二) (12 −8 +3) ×6/ 2 =21

三、(一) Monday (Chinese food)　Tuesday (Italian food)
Wednesday (American food)　Thursday (Japanese food)
Friday (French food)　Saturday (Mexican food)
Sunday (Indian food)

(二) 1. C　2. B　3. B　4. C

四、1. March 31st 2. April 4th　3. May 3rd　4. May 11th

Section 4

一、1. Thank you for your present.
2. I want to make friends with you.
3. Could you say something about yourself?
4. He likes sports, so he is healthy and strong.
5. How do you spell the word?
6. Always do as the teacher tells you to do in the lab.
7. Sorry, I can't go to swimming with you this afternoon.
8. How often do you go to the cinema with your parents?
9. Who's on duty today?
10. She's busy reading the book.

二、1. The TV guide. On the table next to the sofa.
2. Reading report. In the file.
3. Aspirin. In the woman's purse.
4. A shirt. On the iron board.
5. The best-selling CDs. On the shelf to the right of the door.

三、1. C　2. A　3. A　4. C　5. A
6. C　7. B　8. B　9. C

四、(一) 3, 9, 1, 4, 2, 6, 5, 7, 8, 10
(二) 1. saved, earned　2. Americans　3. 8, 75%
4. clean　5. don't use it

Section 5

一、

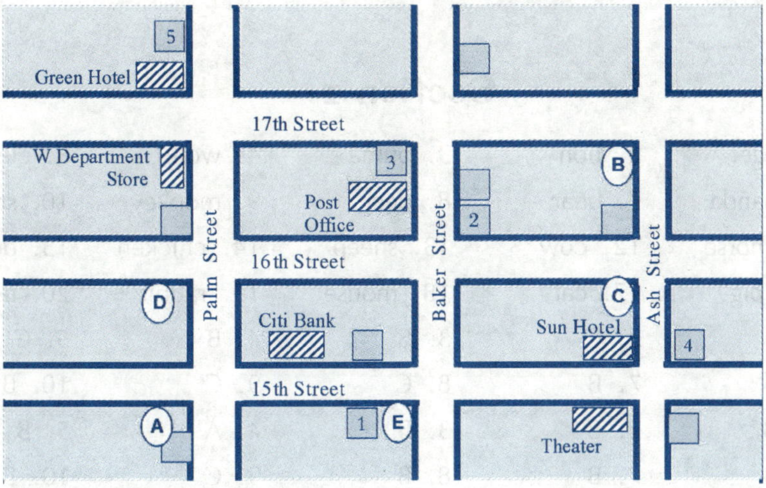

二、1. B　2. C　3. B　4. B　5. C
6. A　7. A　8. B

三、

NAME	JOB	LIKES	WHEN TO MEET	WHAT TO TALK ABOUT
Ronan	Writer	Fishing, playing golf.	When he isn't writing his book.	His new ideas for stories.
Sophie	Singer	Going shopping.	When she isn't having a concert.	Her life as a pop star.
Harry	Scientist	Reading, playing golf.	When he isn't busy in his lab.	His new experiments.
Jennifer	Teacher	Watching movies, taking photos.	When she is on holiday.	Her students.

四、Welcome to our school.

Our school has a long history. Three years ago, there was only a teaching building and a playground. Now we have three teaching buildings, a library, an office building, two dorm buildings and five labs. Last year, we built an indoor gym. There are also many trees and flowers in and around our school.

Our school is one of the key schools in Hubei. The students come from different cities. Both teachers and students are working very hard here.

Now I'd like to show you around the school. Thank you.

Unit 11

Section 1

一、1. tiger　2. lion　3. puma　4. wolf　5. elephant
6. panda　7. bear　8. deer　9. monkey　10. snake
11. horse　12. cow　13. sheep　14. chicken　15. dog
16. pig　17. cat　18. mouse　19. rabbit　20. fish

二、1. A　2. C　3. B　4. B　5. C
6. A　7. B　8. C　9. C　10. B

三、1. B　2. B　3. B　4. A　5. B
6. B　7. B　8. B　9. C　10. B

11. B 12. C

四、

Linton Zoo

Open Time	9:00 am –4:00 pm on weekdays. 8:30 am –5:30 pm on weekends.
Ticket Price	12 dollars for an adult. 6 dollars for children over 1.20 m. Free for children under 1.20 m.
Attention	Do not give food to the animals. Do not get too close to or touch the animals. Keep the zoo clean.

Section 2

一、1. one thing 2. presents 3. make me happy 4. wish come true
5. snow 6. waiting 7. make a list 8. reindeer
9. here 10. Christmas

二、1. B 2. C 3. A 4. B. 5. B 6. A

三、1. X 2. X 3. X 4. X 5. O 6. O
7. X 8. O

四、1. A 2. B 3. B 4. C 5. A 6. B

五、

2010 Summer Camp

Opening time	9:30 am to 11:30 am (July 10th to July 30th)
Members	Children aged 7-14
Fee & Pay time	200 yuan/ person; pay before July 8th
Activities	1. Sports; 2. Hobby groups; 3. English world
Telephone	84857319
E-mail address	labc2010@yahoo. com

Section 3

一、1. bike 2. OK 3. there 4. tree 5. Where
6. shopping 7. need 8. bring 9. key 10. go

二、

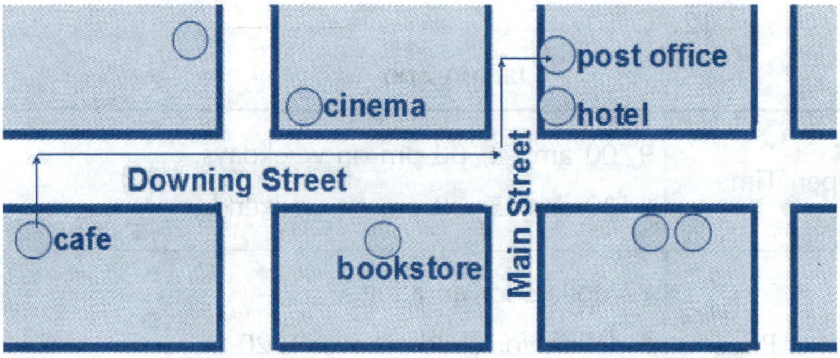

三、1. B　2. A　3. B　4. A　5. A
6. C　7. B　8. A　9. B　10. C

四、1. B　2. A　3. A　4. C　5. B
6. C　7. A　8. C　9. A　10. C

五、(一) 1, 4, 3, 2, 5
(二) 1. Show it off　2. Write, surf, snowboard
3. dead end　4. yourself, iphone, sports car
5. even by us

Section 4

一、1. On Sunday we are going to see Miss Wang.
2. The house is just on the other side of the road.
3. I think people get old because they give up things.
4. My friends and I often sing pop songs together.
5. It's about five minutes' walk from here.
6. How much shall I pay for it?
7. There is a phone call for Alice.
8. What can you see in the picture?
9. He likes reading books about history.
10. Don't be late for class.

二、

Airline	Flight	Destination	Depart	Arrive
Pan Am	PA726	Amsterdam	7:10 pm	10:15 am
Quantas	QU411	Sydney	9:00 pm	6:05 am
Lufthansa	LH634	Frankfurt	8:25 pm	9:50 am
Air France	AF942	Paris	7:30 pm	8:35 pm
Japan Air Lines	JAL27	Tokyo	12:40 pm	5:20 pm

三、1. teach, A　2. sleep, C　3. I, B　4. free, B
5. Sunday, C　6. six, A　7. on, B　8. come, C

四、(一) 1. F　2. T　3. F　4. F　5. F
6. T　7. F　8. T　9. F　10. T
(二) 1. read, no 2. green 3. computers 3. question, English
4. grandma 5. Open

Section 5

一、newspaper—at the end of the hall—magazine shop
letter—next to the coffee shop—mail box
money—next to the elevator—bank
food—opposite the souvenir shop—restaurant
tour—near the entrance—tour desk

二、1. A　2. C　3. A　4. B　5. C
6. B　7. B　8. B

三、

PERSONAL CHART

NAME: Xiao Wei
AGE: 14
GENER: girl
NATIONALITY: Chinese
FAMILY: four people (father, mother, grandmother and I)
CITY: Wuhan
SCHOOL: No. 109 Middle School
FAVOURITE SUBJECT: Chinese
HOBBIES/ INTERESTS: music, computer games

四、Jack Smith is an American boy. He is 15 years old. He lives in New York with his father and mother. His father is a painter and his mother is a nurse. Now, Jack studies at Apple Tree School. Maths and English are his favourite subjects. He loves studying. He likes doing sports in his free time. He usually plays football with friends after school, and he often goes swimming in summer. Jack has a dog. The dog's name is Adam. On Saturdays, Jack helps in the local animal hospital. On Sundays, he stays at home playing with Adam or watching TV.

Unit 12

Section 1

一、1. bottle　2. cup　3. tea-pot　4. glass　5. bowl

6. plate 7. knife 8. fork 9. pan 10. kitchen
11. river 12. sea 13. stream 14. ocean 15. hill
16. mountain 17. grassland 18. travel 19. trip 20. journey

二、1. A 2. A 3. C 4. B 5. C
6. B 7. A 8. B

三、1. B 2. C 3. B 4. A 5. B
6. A

四、1. F 2. T 3. F 4. F 5. T
6. T 7. F 8. T

五、1. 10 kilometers 2. a radio station 3. 250 meters
4. 46, by bike 5. 5:45, 6:10 6. same

Section 2

一、1. boy 2. coins 3. toys
4. long baby hair 5. fat house cat 6. magazine
7. cold and clean

二、1. B 2. A 3. B 4. C 5. C
6. A 7. A 8. C 9. B 10. A

三、1. C 2. B 3. A 4. A 5. C
6. C 7. B 8. A 9. A 10. B

四、1. C 2. A 3. C 4. C 5. B

五、1. American 2. children's hospital
3. children, medicine 4. friendly, helpful
5. speak, read

Section 3

一、1. after 2. flowers 3. classroom
4. Look at 5. 9:00 pm 6. pairs of shoes
7. Wednesday 8. Everyone 9. supper
10. teachers' office

二、1. B 2. B 3. A 4. A 5. C
6. C

三、1. C 2. B 3. C 4. A 5. B
6. A 7. C 8. A

四、(一) 1. F 2. F 3. T 4. F 5. T
6. F

(二) 1. A　2. B　3. C　4. C　5. B

五、2, 7, 3, 6, 4, 5, 1

sunny, fine, cloudy, wet, showery, cloudy, snowy

27℃-33℃, 21℃-27℃, 19℃-24℃, 13℃-18℃, 10℃-15℃, 12℃-18℃, 0℃-2℃

Section 4

一、1. We have seven English classes every week.
2. Let me help you clean the bedroom.
3. We have a walk after supper every Sunday.
4. Is there a computer in your office?
5. How many oranges does the woman want?
6. What color is your coat?
7. School begins at 9 am and ends at 3 pm.
8. They must go home now because it's going to rain.
9. These are his books and those are hers.
10. Where can I get some stamps, please?

二、1. C　2. B　3. H　4. D　5. A
6. G

三、

TOUR BUS 77 SCHEDULE	
Terminal	8:30 am
City Hall	8:45 am
Shopping Center	9:00 am
Swimming Pool	9:20 am
No. 2 Middle School	9:35 am
Sports Stadium	9:40 am
Zhongshan Park	10:30 am
People's Hospital	10:40 am
May's Garden	11:30 am

四、1. A　2. B　3. A　4. B　5. A
6. C　7. B　8. B　9. A　10. B

五、(一) 1. C　2. B　3. B　4. A　5. C
6. B　7. A
(二) 1. 103; 88　2. 5; 11　3. 21　4. 1970　5. 1977

Section 5

一、O　O　X　O　X　XO　O　O
二、1. B　2. B　3. C　4. B　5. B
6. A　7. A　8. B
三、

Time	What does Fiona do?
6:00	Get up, take a shower
7:15	Have breakfast, then ride to school and have four classes
12:10	Have lunch with friends
16:00	Come back home, do homework, play the piano; sometimes help in the kitchen
19:00	Have dinner, then play computer games
21:00	Go to bed

四、Jane likes English very much. She works hard. She reads English in the morning every day. She likes speaking English and she often speaks English with her classmates in school. When Jane is free, she often listens to some English radio programs. She watches TV only on Friday evening. Does she like dancing? No, she doesn't. But she likes drawing and playing the piano. Her parents like her very much. And all the teachers and her friends like her, too.

Unit 13

Section 1

一、1. give up　2. dress up　3. turn up　4. care for　5. call for
6. look for　7. get in　8. break into　9. slow down　10. throw away
二、1. A　2. B　3. C　4. B　5. A
6. B　7. B　8. A　9. C　10. A

三、

1\.    

2\.   

3\.   

四、1. F　2. F　3. T　4. F　5. T
6\. F　7. F　8. F　9. T　10. T

Section 2

一、1. Life　2. Younger　3. Growing　4. take me home
5\. I belong,　6. around　7. blue water　8. on the sky
9\. moon shine　10. in my eyes

二、1. B　2. A　3. C　4. B　5. C
6. A　7. B　8. A　9. B　10. A
11. B　12. C　13. B　14. A　15. C

三、

	City	Weather	Temperature
1.	London	Sunny	6℃ to 15℃
2.	Paris	Rainy	3℃ to 11℃
3.	Washington	Rainy	18℃ to 28℃
4.	New York	Sunny	21℃ to 32℃
5.	Wuhan	Windy	15℃ to 26℃

Section 3

一、1. What's wrong with you?
2. How are you recently?
3. What is your favourite fruit?
4. How can I get there?
5. Which do you prefer?
6. I will go shopping next week.
7. She gets on well with her classmates.
8. My father is an engineer.
9. I like playing the piano.
10. My best friend is a basketball fan.

二、1. D　2. C　3. B　4. E　5. A
6. F　7. I　8. H　9. J　10. G

三、1. A　2. C　3. B　4. C　5. B
6. A　7. B　8. A　9. C　10. A

四、1. I am a teacher, but my sister is a doctor.
2. I live in New York, but she lives in London.
3. I have a large house in the suburbs, but she has a small apartment in the city.
4. I am married, but she is single.
5. I play golf, but she plays tennis.
6. I play the piano, but she doesn't play a musical instrument.
7. On the weekend I usually watch videos, but she never watches videos.
8. On the weekend I rarely go out, but she always goes to parties.

Section 4

一、Sindy：How far is it to the National Park?

Guide：It is about 50 miles.

Sindy：How long will it take to get there?

Guide：About an hour.

Sindy：Look at that high mountain！How high is it?

Guide：It's a volcano. It's about 2,500 meters.

Sindy：How many feet is that?

Guide：It's about 8,200 feet.

Sindy：How deep is the hole?

Guide：It's about 350 feet deep.

Sindy：Oh！There is a temple. How old is this temple?

Guide：It's about 400 years old.

Sindy：Is that the beach? How long is it?

Guide：I'm not sure，but it's probably 10 miles long.

二、

Monday	Tuesday	Wednesday	Thursday	Friday	Saturday	Sunday
Italian food	Greek food	Chinese food	Indian food	Japanese food	Mexican food	American food

三、1. C　2. A　3. C　4. A　5. B

四、(一) 1. E　2. A　3. C　4. B　5. D

(二) 1. 1927　2. expensive　3. dinosaurs　4. 1.6 kilometers

5. Los Angeles

Section 5

一、

1. 

2. 

3. 

4. 

5. 

二、

Monday	Tuesday	Wednesday	Thursday	Friday	Saturday	Sunday
jog	play tennis	do yoga	swim	go to a health club	play basketball	ride a bike

三、1. B　2. A　3. C　4. B　5. C

6. C

四、Peter works in a bank, and he works 40 hours a week. He begins working at half past eight in the morning and stops at half past five in the afternoon. At half past five the bank closed. Everybody goes home. Some people drive home. Some people take the train and other people take the bus.

Unit 14

Section 1

一、1. January the twenty-first　2. February the fourteenth

3. September the nineteenth　4. March the twelfth

5. June the twenty-ninth　6. October the thirty-first

7. May the first　8. December the twenty-fifth

9. November the twenty-fourth　10. April the first

二、1. B　2. C　3. C　4. A　5. A

6. B　7. C　8. B　9. B　10. A

三、

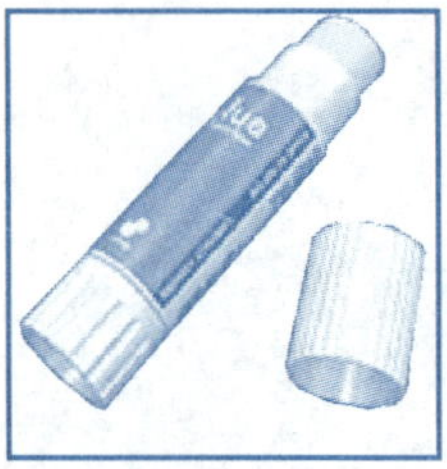

Mary

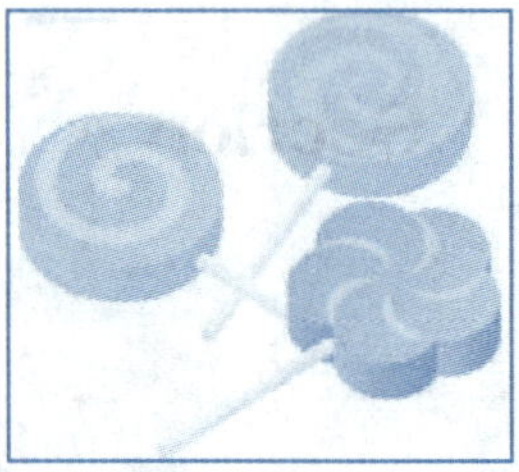

Peter

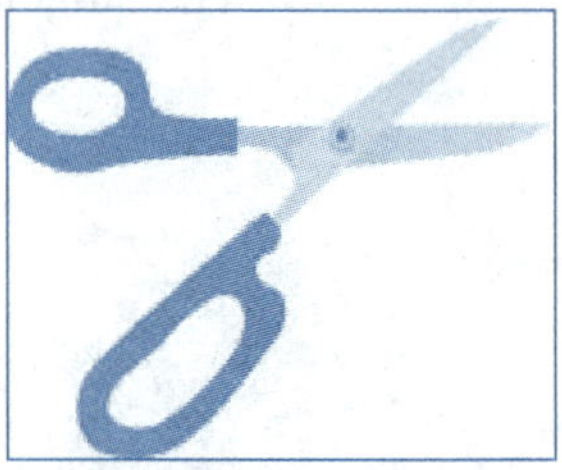

Ben

Helen

Betty

四、(一) **Peter's Time Table**

7:30	Get up
8:00	Have Breakfast
9:30	School Starts
13:00	Have lunch
14:00	Have lessons or sports
15:45	School finishes
18:00	Have supper
19:30	Do homework
22:00	Go to bed

(二) 1. T　2. F　3. F

Section 2

一、1. trees　2. brave　3. patient　4. wind　5. quiet
6. heart　7. mountains　8. honest　9. you're going to do
10. flowers and small plants　11. simple　12. change　13. moon
14. share love　15. understanding　16. earth
17. I give you life　18. around

二、1. C　2. A　3. A　4. C　5. A

三、1. C　2. B　3. A

四、(一)

Spain	Date	Ship (s)	People
Leaving	September 20, 1510	5	240
Returning	December 21, 1512	1	31

(二) 1. F　2. F　3. T　4. T

Section 3

一、(一) 1. by using it
2. to talk in English as much as possible
3. when people will speak too quickly
4. might not understand you
5. laugh at your mistakes

6. much better for people
7. to be angry
8. what you are saying
9. be afraid of making mistakes

(二) 1. angry 2. possible 3. afraid 4. better

二、1. A 2. B 3. C 4. B 5. C

三、(一) a d b g f e c

(二) 1. how to grow pumpkins
2. three weeks
3. a heart

Section 4

一、1. Jack can play basketball very well.
2. Watching TV is my favourite hobby.
3. She plays the piano three times a week.
4. It is relaxing to climb the mountains and ride a horse.
5. How does the mother go to the shop?
6. Jerry is reading under an umbrella on the beach.
7. The girl in a blue dress is my sister.
8. Sandy needs 40 minutes to go to school on foot.
9. Does the woman try the sweater on?
10. The child in England are very lucky for they don't have many classes and much homework.

二、

(1)

(2)

(3)

(4)

(5)

三、1. B 2. A 3. B 4. A 5. C

四、1. A 2. B 3. C

Section 5

一、1. B　2. C　3. B

二、1. A　2. C　3. C　4. A　5. B

三、1. B　2. C　3. B　4. C　5. C
6. A

四、Look at the picture. This is a British Family. Jerry is an English boy. He is 11 years old now. He is a student of an international school. He is good at all subjects, and all his teachers like him. This is Jerry's father. He is a computer engineer. He is 40 years old. But he works in Germany now. This is Jerry's mother. She is a teacher. She is 38. Jerry's parents like him very much. They are a happy family.

Unit 15

Section 1

一、1. baker　2. barber　3. butcher　4. dentist　5. engineer
6. lawyer　7. nurse　8. policeman　9. scientist　10. postman

二、1. B　2. C　3. A　4. B　5. A
6. A　7. C　8. C　9. B　10. B

三、1. C　2. C　3. B　4. A　5. B
6. C　7. A　8. B　9. C　10. A

四、1. No, he doesn't.
2. He drinks 5 cups of coffee every day.
3. No, she doesn't.
4. She has 14 stamps now.
5. Kathy eats 7 pieces of candy every day.
6. She eats 4 times every day.

Section 2

一、1. boring room　2. Sunday afternoon
3. waiting for you　4. around in my car
5. change my point of view　6. lonely
7. nothing ever happens　8. how
9. why　10. just the yellow lemon tree
11. up and down　12. another lemon tree

二、1. typist　2. postman　3. teacher　4. librarian　5. doctor/nurse

6. bus driver 7. farmer

三、1. B 2. A 3. B 4. B 5. C

四、

Section 3

一、1. usually a very busy time 2. rush to their jobs
3. walk to work 4. drive
5. take the bus 6. go to school
7. walk to school 8. take the school bus
9. ride their bicycles 10. supermarkets
11. homes and businesses 12. at every corner

二、1. B 2. F 3. A
4. E 5. C 6. D

三、1. B 2. E 3. C 4. F 5. D
6. G 7. A

四、1. F 2. F 3. T 4. T 5. F
6. F 7. T

Section 4

一、1. we know what is happening around us
2. sight, hearing, touch, taste and smell
3. This organ receives the information
4. send this information to the brain
5. ears control hearing
6. skin controls touch
7. smell depends on the nose
8. which stops us from falling down
9. We also have senses of hunger, thirst, heat and cold.

二、1. He is going to make a model airplane.
2. She is going to the library.
3. His mother is a doctor.
4. He will do the cooking.
5. She is a librarian.
6. He can borrow three books at a time.

三、1. 你所听到的内容涉及的图片：A B C D E H J
2. 图片的顺序：C A D J B E H

四、1. B　2. A　3. B　4. B

Section 5

一、1. B　2. C　3. C　4. B

二、A：3，5，9　B：1，6，10
C：4，8　D：2，7

三、1. C　2. C　3. B　4. A　5. C
6. B　7. B

四、I work as a history teacher in a school. At weekends, I go to the cinema a lot. I often go alone, but sometimes my friend comes, too. My husband never comes with me. He is always busy. I buy chocolates to eat during the film. I usually enjoy this night out very much. I hardly want to see the same film twice, but I do if it's really good. I always miss my Saturday night films. It is my favourite way of relaxing.

Unit 16

Section 1

一、1. town　2. people　3. same　4. weekday　5. walks
6. railway　7. ready　8. fruit　9. saying　10. each.

二、

	Place to go	Bus number
1.	the Wuhan Zoo	105 or 107
2.	the Summer Palace	332
3.	the East Lake	320 or 332
4.	the airport	938
5.	the People's Hospital	35 or 44

三、1. A　2. C　3. B　4. C　5. A
6. B　7. C　8. B

四、1. F　2. T　3. T　4. F　5. F
6. T　7. F

Section 2

一、What is pink? A rose is pink
By the fountain's brink.
What is red? A poppy's red
In its barley bed.
What is blue? The sky is blue
Where the clouds float through.
What is white? A swan is white
Sailing in the light.
What is yellow? Pears are yellow
Rich and ripe and mellow.
What is green? The grass is green
With small flowers between.
What is violet? Clouds are violet
In the summer twilight.
What is orange? Why, an orange,
Just an orange!

二、1. F　2. T　3. T　4. F　5. F
6. T　7. T　8. F　9. F　10. F

三、1. B　2. C　3. A　4. C　5. B
6. A　7. A　8. B　9. B　10. C

四、1. The woman would like to book a single room with a bath and a double bed.
2. Her full name is Becky Wakeman.
3. Her nationality is Polish.
4. The woman will stay 3 nights.
5. She will pay 285 dollars in all.
6. Her passport number is EG6662781.
7. She will pay with a Visa Card.
8. The room number is 19, on the first floor.

Section 3

一、1. Wash your hands.

2. Open the packet.
3. Shut the books.
4. Hold my umbrella.
5. Look at that building.
6. Listen to this bell.
7. Show me your new dress.
8. Use the subway.
9. Don't play in the street.
10. Don't cross between two cars.

二、

A. San Francisco  B. Seattle 

C. Chicago  D. New York 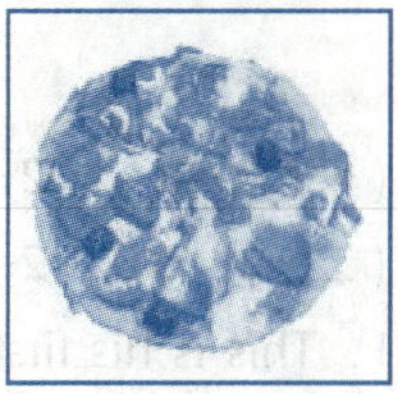

E. Boston 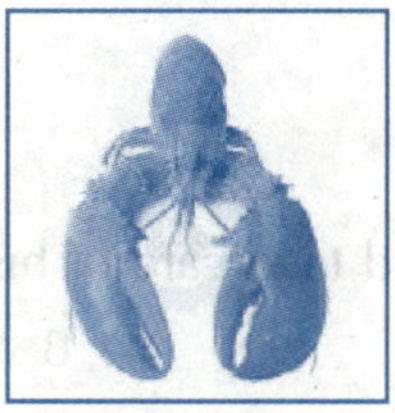

三、1. C　2. A　3. C　4. B　5. C
6. B　7. C　8. A

Section 4

一、20 years ago, Mr. and Mrs. Brown lived in London. Mr Brown was a dentist. His wife worked in a school. She taught history. Mr. and Mrs. Brown went to work together by car. Mrs. Brown drove because her husband couldn't drive. There were three children in the Brown family. The Browns had two boys and a girl. Peter was 14. Martin was older but he was shorter than his brother. Susan was the oldest. She didn't live with her family. She worked in a hotel.

二、

Name: Mike Li
Job: actor
Major events:
1965 Born in Beijing
1971 Started wushu training when he was six years old
1970s Won three national gold medals
1985 Made his first film
1998 Made his first Hollywood film

三、On Fridays: A. D
On Saturdays: C. F. G. J. H. L. B. E.
On Sunday: M. I. N. J. K. A.

四、1. B　2. B　3. C　4. B　5. C
6. A　7. B

Section 5

一、(一) 1. B　2. E　3. D　4. C　5. A
(二) 1. B　2. C　3. A

二、1. This is his first time.
2. New York.
3. In the envelope over there.
4. A single room.
5. He asks lily to water his plants and take care of his cat.

三、1. B　2. B　3. B　4. B　5. C
6. C

四、There are about 23 million homes in Britain. Most British people live in small families. A British family usually has got two to four people. But in a quarter of houses there is only one person. Some of these are old people and some are young people living alone. Many British families have one child. When children are about eighteen or nineteen, they leave their parents' home and go to another place. Some of the children don't come back to visit their parents very often.

Test 1

一、1. B　2. A　3. A　4. B　5. A
6. C　7. B　8. B　9. B　10. A
11. C

二、1. B	2. B	3. B	4. C	5. A
三、1. A	2. C	3. B	4. B	5. C
四、1. B	2. B	3. C	4. C	5. B
五、1. C	2. B	3. B	4. C	

Test 2

一、1. C	2. B	3. C	4. C	5. A
6. C	7. C	8. A	9. B	
二、1. B	2. C	3. C	4. A	5. B
三、1. B	2. A	3. B	4. C	5. B
四、1. A	2. B	3. B	4. C	5. B
五、(一) 1. B	2. C	3. C		

(二)

Lost Property Form

Name: Mark Adams	Nationality: American
Lost Property: (1) a camera (Samsung G302)	
Address: (2) 18, Lyndon Drive, Leighton, Essex.	
Telephone: (3) 080945233	

图书在版编目(CIP)数据

Listen to Us:外语学校初中英语听力等级教程(二级)/武汉实验外国语学校组编;钱晶晶主编.—武汉:武汉大学出版社,2011.3(**2015.3 重印**)
武汉实验外国语学校校本课程/丛书主编:李茵　丛书副主编:王永汉　外语类总主编:徐涛　蔡文静
ISBN 978-7-307-08350-9

Ⅰ.L…　Ⅱ.①武…　②钱…　Ⅲ.英语—听说教学—小学—习题—升学参考资料　Ⅳ.G624.315

中国版本图书馆 CIP 数据核字(2010)第 236585

责任编辑:叶玲利　　责任校对:刘　欣　　版式设计:王　晨

出版发行:**武汉大学出版社**　(430072　武昌　珞珈山)
(电子邮件:cbs22@whu.edu.cn 网址:www.wdp.com.cn)
印刷:湖北恒泰印务有限公司
开本:787×1092　1/16　印张:27　字数:602 千字　插页:1
版次:2011 年 3 月第 1 版　**2015年3月第7次印刷**
ISBN 978-7-307-08350-9/G·1853　定价:120.00 元(含磁带 8 盘)